ACCUSED

ACCUSED

A Heartbreaking Death and the Quest for Justice

BRITTANY DUCKER

New Horizon Press
Far Hills, New Jersey

Requests for permission should be addressed to:
New Horizon Press
P. O. Box 669
Far Hills, NJ 07931

Brittany Ducker
    Accused: A Heartbreaking Death and the Quest for Justice

Cover design: Charley Nasta
Interior design: Scribe Inc.

Library of Congress Control Number: 2014938452

ISBN-13 (paperback): 978-0-88282-484-0
ISBN-13 (eBook): 978-0-88282-485-7

New Horizon Press

Manufactured in the U.S.A.

19   18   17   16   15   1   2   3   4   5

Author's Note

This book is based on the experiences of the author and reflects her perception of the past, present and future. The personalities, events, actions and conversations portrayed within this story have been taken from interviews, research, court documents, letters, personal papers, press accounts and the memories of some participants.

In an effort to safeguard the privacy of certain individuals, some people's names and identifying characteristics have been changed. The events involving the characters happened as described. Only minor details may have been altered.

Table of Contents

Prologue ix

1: The Crime Scene 1

2: Trey 15

3: Big Josh 23

4: Little Josh 41

5: Coming Home 59

6: Dark Reality 91

7: Covering the Bases 107

8: Escape Attempt 117

9: Accused 135

10: Master Manipulator 149

11: The System 175

12: ...And It Begins 187

13: The Prosecution 201

14: Mask on the Monster 223

15: The Defense and the Media   243

16: Closing Arguments   251

17: The Verdict   263

18: The Real Culprit?   269

Epilogue   277

Acknowledgments   293

Endnotes   295

Prologue

"There's a dead body!" a teenaged student shouted as he approached the drainage ditch behind his school shortly after 1:00 P.M.

Responding to the cries of her student, Molly Varner, a teacher at Liberty High School in Louisville, Kentucky, walked briskly toward the creek bed. Her heart sank at what she saw, the unmistakable body of a young male sprawled face down in the shadows of the surrounding trees. She dashed back inside with her students in tow and notified school security. School officials immediately contacted the authorities.[1]

On May 11, 2011, Varner had taken her students for a walk around the grounds. The two-story brick school building was set back from the main road, American flag flying high in front with dogwood trees in full bloom. It was a beautiful, sunny day and she'd felt they would benefit by taking a break from the classroom and enjoying the weather. It was not uncommon for teachers at Liberty High School to allow students the opportunity to walk the grassy grounds of the school, especially when the weather was so lovely. Predictably, the students had opted to walk in the direction of the creek bed, an area known to most of the neighborhood kids as a social gathering place where, outside school hours, teenagers could hang out and talk, free from adult interruption. It was a place with which many of the students were familiar. However, instead of observing the small fish and turtles which were never in short supply, they had observed something different.

The Louisville Metro Police Department responded to the school's 911 call. Officers arrived quickly and began to secure the scene, stretching yards of yellow crime-scene tape around the perimeter of the creek bed. The concrete culvert at the opening of the creek led into a long, dark tunnel formed by the road that ran above it. The tunnel and the slant of the bed partially obscured that particular part of the culvert. Only hours before, another class at Liberty High School had taken a walk around the perimeter of the school but, due to the layout of the creek bed, those students had strolled by without noticing the gruesome scene just feet away. As uniformed police officers secured the area, they too were confronted with the shocking sight of the face-down, decomposing body of a young male on the banks of the creek.

The creek bed was muddy, so as the first responding officer, John Pittenger, inched close enough to confirm that the young male lying on its bank was deceased, his feet squished into the muddy ground below. The victim on the ground was not breathing. Realizing there was nothing he could do to save this person's life, Pittenger did his best to leave the scene undisturbed and waited for the arrival of homicide detectives.

Within minutes of the arrival of the first police officers and their detection of the body, Detective Leigh Maroni of the Louisville Metro Police Homicide Unit arrived at Liberty High School. Careful not to get too close and contaminate the scene, Detective Maroni took mental notes of what she saw. The victim was dressed in dark clothing, wearing a pair of blue jeans, a black t-shirt and all-black sneakers. He appeared to have brown hair, although most of that hair was matted with blood. Upon closer inspection, it looked like someone had struck the person with a hard object in the back of the head: a gaping open wound, long and wide, covered the back of his skull. He appeared young but, without seeing his face, Detective Maroni was unable to determine whether the victim was a teenager or an adult.

The victim remained face down and Detective Maroni took note of the blood pooled around the face, which rested close to the water line. Later, as the body was removed by the coroner, detectives would note that the young male's face was nearly obliterated, eyes blackened, nose broken and countenance caved in, his teeth fractured in pieces. However, as the detective observed the scene at that time, she was unaware of the brokenness of the victim's face, the hate and madness that must have enveloped the murderer as he attacked the victim. Instead, she focused on the head wound and noted the specifics of the person's body she could see as he remained face down in the culvert. She noticed that his left arm was folded beneath his body, while his right arm was outstretched and sprinkled with blood spatter, most likely from his head wound. She also noticed that a set of footprints remained visible in the mud near the body.

The young male lay abandoned and broken in a dreadful resting place. The culvert was littered with trash and debris; cigarette butts and candy wrappers were visible near the body and graffiti covered the concrete tunnel at the mouth of the creek. Officers did their best to catalog each and every piece of trash that they located in the vicinity with the hope that they could link the items to the person responsible for the murder. They collected the neighboring rocks and tree branches which were speckled with blood spatter; they even recovered a lawn mower blade that some thought could be the murder weapon. Detective Maroni interviewed several people in the area in the hopes that they could shed light on the investigation or the identity of the deceased.

As the investigation progressed, Detective Scott Russ, who would become the lead detective on the homicide, arrived and began to supervise the inquiry into the murder. He and Detective Maroni continued to survey the scene and by that time a crowd had gathered in the area, anxious to ascertain what had happened and the identity of the victim. It was not surprising that a mass of people gathered near the creek bed and buzzed with questions about the body found quite literally in their own backyards. The area off Indian Trail near Liberty High School was a close-knit community. Many of the families in the neighborhood had resided there for generations and, in several cases, grandparents, their children and grandchildren resided together in the same home. Most of the neighborhood children played together and many of the adults residing in the neighborhood had grown up there themselves.

Word traveled fast; once one person in the neighborhood noticed the scene at Liberty High School and the arrival of the police cruisers, it was only a matter of time until a crowd of locals gathered. Indian Trail is a well-known street that runs between Preston Highway and Poplar Level Road, two main thoroughfares in Louisville. Although no one would deem the area upper class, the murder of a child was definitely not something that anyone in the neighborhood expected. The majority of the people residing in the area were employed in working-class jobs and worked hard for what they had. Both Preston Highway and Poplar Level Road were littered with fast-food restaurants, car dealerships and gas stations in which many of the area's adults and teens worked.

Nestled between those two main streets was the neighborhood that contained Liberty High School and the surrounding houses. The small yet cozy homes featured petite yards, some unkempt, some meticulously maintained. Older cars were parked in most of the driveways. On school days, students could be observed congregating at the bus stop or riding bikes in the street. It was the type of place where parents felt comfortable allowing a child to play outside or walk to a friend's house. As the crowd assembled outside Liberty High School on that swelteringly hot afternoon, the residents of the neighborhood agonized about whether the person in the creek bed was one of their own. Sadly, their question would be answered in a way no one could have imagined.

Chapter 1

The Crime Scene

Terrence "Terry" Zwicker was just arriving home. An electrician by trade, Zwicker owned his own electric company. He had worked a big job that morning in Trimble County and he came home to an empty house. His wife and their young daughter were absent. His son Trey, fourteen years old at the time, was spending a week with his mother, Amanda McFarland.

Though never married, Terry and Amanda enjoyed an amiable relationship, sharing joint custody of their son. Per a court order established years earlier, Amanda and Terry followed an alternating week-by-week schedule. They generally did their parent swap on Sundays. May 11 fell during Amanda's week.

His cell phone rang and, recognizing the phone number of his friend and neighbor, Terry picked up the call on the second ring.

"Terry, there's a detective here that wants to talk to you," his friend blurted out and then a second voice came through the phone.

"Mr. Zwicker," the officer began. "We've got a problem here at the school. You need to come find your son."

Jumping straight up, Terry started for his truck. Hopping into the vehicle, he called his wife and explained there was a problem with Trey as he drove toward the school. The neighborhood sur-rounding the high school and Amanda's residence consisted of two ditch lines. One of those ditch lines led directly toward the school grounds. Terry had spent his childhood years in that neighborhood. Familiar with the area, he parked his car and followed the ditch line on foot, because he knew it was the quickest way to reach Liberty High School. Recognizing a friend in the crowd gathered near the school, Terry tossed his friend the keys to his pickup truck and dashed toward the barricade. As he ran toward the large assembly of uni-formed police and neighborhood residents, officers inter-cepted him and refused to let him closer to the area roped with yellow crime scene tape.

Terry noticed that his son's mother, Amanda, and her husband, Joshua Gouker, were standing in the crowd, along with Gouker's fifteen-year-old son, Joshua Young. Terry waited nervously until Detective Russ approached him some time later.

Raising the paperwork clutched in his hand, Detective Russ explained that the papers contained a list of all the children who were absent from school that day. The list contained Trey's name and Detective Russ inquired whether Terry had spoken with his son. After leaving his home en route to the school, Terry had called Trey's cell phone repeatedly. He explained to Detective Russ that Trey always responded to his phone calls and texts but that as he rushed to the scene, he had been unable to reach his son. He knew something was desperately wrong. Terry begged the detective to explain what had happened. Those nearby could easily hear his terror and frustration.

"Detective, I'm not ignorant. I know there is something in that ditch that I need to see," he said, gesturing toward the creek bed just yards away from the makeshift waiting area where he and other neighborhood folks stood corralled by police.

The detective regarded Terry for a time and after some consideration, Detective Russ instructed Terry to follow him, explaining that he could not take him to the ditch, but that he would need to view the scene from fifty feet away through a chain link fence. Terry rushed toward the fence with Detective Russ at his heels. From behind that fence on a low hillside, as Terry's eyes focused on the scene below, he recognized his fourteen-year-old son Trey Zwicker face down and lifeless on the muddy banks of the creek bed. Terry would later remark, "It didn't take two seconds to look over and know that was my boy laying there."[1] As his head dropped and he fell to his knees, a wail could be heard in the background. Watching Terry's reaction to viewing the ditch bank, Amanda McFarland, Trey's mother, crumpled to the ground.

Terry and Detective Russ sat in the detective's car, going over every detail and down every avenue they could think of to figure out what had happened to Trey the night before to cause him to end up in the ditch. They'd covered friends, the possibility of Trey skipping school (but Trey was a good kid who didn't skip) and strangers. But there was one person Terry wanted to talk about, one person of whom he was very suspicious.

"Well, here's the thing," Terry spoke up. "I didn't get a phone call at ten-thirty last night...I would've expected a call from him. Me and Amanda, we usually stay pretty close on Trey's experience."[2]

"Right."

Terry looked pointedly at the detective as he continued to speak, "But see, she moved *him* back in. Me and Amanda have a custody agreement that he was never supposed to be back in Trey's life," he emphasized as he referred to Amanda allowing her husband, Joshua Gouker, back into her home. Only seven months prior, Gouker had been released from prison after serving a little over nine years. Within weeks of that release, he had moved in with Trey's mother.

"Really?" Detective Russ asked, his interest piqued. This was a new angle to the case and necessitated further questioning.

"And this is dating back since Trey was three years old. We went through a horrible custody battle. We didn't get along for a long time. You know we pulled it together shortly after her and him got into trouble and he was in the pen for eight years and she was in jail for a little while, due to something they did. Now typically, anything goes on with Trey, she usually calls me or I already know about it. Now, I didn't get no phone call this morning when they seen the backpack and I didn't get no phone call when he didn't come home from school today...Yeah, being as I couldn't get ahold of Amanda and [my friend] couldn't tell me anything, I was going wherever. I went to Trey's mom's house and then I went to [my friend's] house, 'cause I had no clue where to go, and then Amanda said they were up here, 'Hurry, hurry,'" he mumbled as he related Amanda's words once he'd finally reached her via telephone.

"Do you think that Amanda wouldn't call you because she would be scared that you would go off if she told you that he might have skipped school? Do you think it's possible that Amanda or [Joshua Gouker] would have anything to do with it?" the detective asked.

"The way our custody battle went, it went like this. I went down there and I did all the drug testing and stuff through Child Protective Services and they came back with a bunch of findings that she was an unfit parent, especially when she's with him," he related, referring to Gouker. "And, you know, there was a lot of me blowing up at her then, because that wasn't an environment that I wanted Trey into."[3]

Nodding, the detective encouraged Terry to continue. This was a piece of information that could be important to the investigation. "Absolutely, I can understand that."

"Well, when he got outta prison, he showed up on her doorstep and evidently from what I understood, they were still married. He was coming around but last I heard, he was thrown out of her house and was living two doors down..."

"His name, you say, is Josh?" the detective clarified.

"His name is Josh Gouker."

"Now do you, and I'm just gonna ask. Uh, I don't know Josh from anybody." Russ paused and prepared to pose the question that dangled on the tip of his tongue, "Do you think he's capable, do you think Josh could have done anything to your son? Everybody's on the table at this point. I'm not ruling anybody out."

"I'm not saying that he did," Terry began, "but is he capable of it? Oh yeah. He's stupid."

The detective seized on the opportunity and pressed further, "Would there be a reason? I mean, has Trey ever come to you and said that anybody in the household is hurting him, physically abusing him or anything like that?"

"The only thing that stuck in my mind is those don't look like hickeys on [Amanda's] neck."[4]

"I was thinking the exact same thing," the detective said as they both looked in the direction where Amanda and Gouker had previously stood. One of the first things both men had noticed upon seeing Amanda was the trail of purplish-red markings that laced around the front of her neck. Noticing their concern, Amanda had volunteered that the marks were hickeys given to her the evening before by Gouker. They weren't buying it. The markings appeared more akin to strangulation marks or some other type of neck trauma.

"If her and Josh were in a fist fight, well, Trey would intervene. He would try it," his father said, sure that the family-oriented teen would jump into any fracas to defend his mother.

"But it looks like whatever happened, happened right where you saw him today. So if they were fighting in the house and he tried to intervene...I just don't think it was something that happened somewhere else."

"Well, I can tell you that I do believe he is on very strict probation," Terry offered.

"Okay."

"So any police officers involved, he would get in trouble. The thing about it is, he's made it very adamant that, you know, you don't want to get any law involved into any situation down there at Amanda's. I mean, he called me right after they got back together and of course I talked to him," Terry said. He further told the officer that he was cordial with Josh Gouker during any conversations he had with him, but that he tried to keep his distance if at all possible. He didn't like the man and he never wanted him around his child. He knew Amanda loved Trey, but her judgment became cloudy where Gouker was concerned. "I know for a fact that Amanda would not have done anything to Trey," he said.

"Yeah."

"But when I see her neck all bruised up like that, I mean it was like a light bulb that..." he trailed off, thinking of the possible scenarios that set the wheels in motion for his poor son's murder. "What if they were in a fight and Trey tried to do something? What if he tried to get out of there and get to my house like I have told him to? If something like that happened, I've even told him to bring his [half-] sister," he said. "You know, it's been about a month ago that Amanda was walking...right in front of my house.

She had a baseball bat and it was supposedly said that she cracked Josh in the hand with it because he was trying to put his hands on her. Now when they split up many years ago, he almost killed her. This was many years ago, but that's why it was a shock for me to see him even back."[5]

The detective took a few moments to digest the information. Josh Gouker, it seemed, had a violent streak and there were obvious reasons that they should investigate him further. It was best to strike while the iron was hot and he needed to get all of Trey's father's musings on the scenario while he had access to him at the scene of the murder. He ran a thought by him: "I just wanna ask, because I have you here now and I want to find out everything. Would Trey be the kind of kid, if Amanda and Josh were fighting last night and he tried to stop it, would Trey be the type of kid that would try to take Josh on a walk to calm him down? Would Trey leave with him? Would he walk to a place like this with Josh by himself?" he asked, gesturing toward the creek bed. "Do you think? I mean, that's probably a hard question for you to answer."

Terry nodded, "He may trust him enough to do that, yes sir."

As Detective Russ interviewed Terry, Detective Maroni compiled a list of people present at the scene whom she wanted to speak with first. Due to the sweltering heat that day, administrators at Liberty High School allowed Detective Maroni to utilize an empty classroom in the building to conduct interviews. By the time she sat down for her interview with Amanda McFarland, Trey's mother, it was 4:48 in the afternoon. Amanda was noticeably distraught. She retraced her steps for the day, describing for the detective that she and her husband, Josh Gouker, had spent the day running errands, visiting McNeely Lake Park and looking at a potential rental property in that area. She had been unaware that Trey had not arrived at school that day. The school had not called to inform her that he was absent. A high school student, Trey generally woke up before her at around six-thirty in the morning and she had assumed that he left for the bus stop prior to the time when she woke to help her eight-year-old daughter prepare for school. Amanda was inconsolable, so Detective Maroni only interviewed her for fourteen minutes and then turned her attention elsewhere, knowing that she could follow up with Amanda later when she was less agitated.[6]

Immediately following the interview with Trey's mother, Detective Maroni interviewed Josh Gouker, Trey's stepfather. Although she had interviewed Amanda alone as was police protocol, Detective Maroni allowed Amanda to remain in the classroom as she interviewed Gouker. Amanda was understandably distraught and Gouker expressed concern that she should not be left alone. Detective Maroni conceded and Amanda remained in the classroom while the detective spoke with her husband, even though this violated police interview protocol for homicide investigations. It was important to interview potential witnesses separately so that they would not influence each other's accounts of events. However, Detective Maroni deviated from her standard practice under the urging of Gouker.

She felt terrible for the murdered boy's mother and was also concerned for Amanda's well-being. She proceeded with Gouker's interview as Amanda sat quietly to the side.

The interview with Gouker only lasted fifteen or twenty minutes and covered the couple's activities for the previous evening and much of the same information discussed by Amanda. Each revealed that they had held a cookout the prior evening and that Trey had retired to bed at ten o'clock due to the fact that it was a school night. Gouker indicated to the detective that he and Amanda had taken a trip to the gas station later that evening to purchase cigarettes. Police would later collect the surveillance video and noted that the couple was visible on the tape.

At some point during this interview, Gouker indicated that some older boys from a nearby apartment complex had bothered Trey at the bus stop in the month prior to his death. Specifically, he recalled that they had stolen Trey's phone and harassed other kids in the neighborhood. Gouker expressed concern that the boys might have had something to do with the murder. Detective Maroni took note of this suggestion and planned to follow up on it later that evening. She indicated that she might have further questions for the couple as the investigation progressed. However, she allowed them to exit the classroom for the time being.[7]

After speaking with a few of Trey's friends, Detective Maroni had one boy left to interview. At 6:21 P.M., she sat down in the classroom with Josh Young, Trey's fifteen-year-old stepbrother. Although his father, Josh Gouker, escorted him to the room, Detective Maroni interviewed Joshua Young alone. The thin wisp of a boy was dwarfed by his father's husky frame and he seemed very nervous. Gulping deeply, he settled into a seat in the classroom, his voice cracking as he did his best to answer the detective's questions.

When Amanda got word that a body was found at Liberty High School, Josh never could have imagined that it could be Trey. They had just been together the night before and everything had appeared so normal. He told the detective everything he could remember from the previous night but his mind was spinning and everything was a blur. He felt like his thoughts were all jumbled together but he tried his best to recount the night's events.

He indicated that he was present at the cookout at Trey's home the evening before and further stated that when he last saw Trey, he was emerging from the shower dressed in regular clothes, not his pajamas as Josh would have expected. When asked if Trey could have been planning to sneak out of the house, Josh emphatically answered, "He would have told me," but that, "he doesn't really do anything like that."[8]

Josh's voice wavered as he told the detective that the only problem Trey ever had with anyone was the incident at the bus stop when some people from the apartments attempted to take his cell phone the previous month. However, he believed that issue had resolved itself weeks before and they had not spoken of it since. Detective Maroni remained very sweet with Josh; in a sensitive, almost motherly tone of voice, she thanked him for speaking with her as she ended the interview with the young man. She instructed, "If you hear anything, tell your dad." Josh nodded quietly, anxious to get out of the room and rejoin the crowd outside. He wanted to know what had happened to his stepbrother and he hoped he could learn the answer to this question if he located his friends and family outside the school.

As the evening stretched on, detectives were left with little to go on in the investigation. It appeared the most viable lead was the "apartment" boys implicated by Josh Gouker. Gouker had not minced words when he emphatically stressed that a roving band of young males from the nearby apartments could be responsible for Trey's murder.

The apartments were a housing complex located within walking distance of Trey's neighborhood. In the weeks prior, several residents of the apartments had wreaked havoc on the area. Trey's phone was stolen at a bus stop by several teens from the apartments and other children in the neighborhood were victims of similar crimes. One grown man in the neighborhood had been jumped and beaten by a group of young men he recognized as living at the apartments.

Police compiled a list of boys from the apartment complex whom they needed to interview in the coming hours. It was a stretch: the theft and physical scuffles allegedly perpetrated by the apartment's residents were a far cry from the brutal murder of a teenager. However, for the time being, it was a lead that the detectives were compelled to investigate. It did not appear that anyone else had seen anything suspicious, at least nothing that would implicate any specific person in Trey's murder, and the young man was a sweet, intelligent honor student. What motive could there possibly be for anyone to harm him?

Terry Zwicker had conveyed his suspicions about Josh Gouker to Detective Russ as they spoke in the police vehicle, but he was unsure whether the detective would take his concerns seriously. Terry had to leave the investigation in the hands of the detectives—they were the ones skilled and experienced in this type of situation. The investigators expanded their search: could the killer be a violent stranger lurking in the shadows or did they need to concentrate closer to home?

Chapter 2

Trey

Most popularly known as the home of the Kentucky Derby and the University of Louisville men's basketball team, Louisville has more to offer than horses and hoops. People often hear that Louisville, Kentucky is a great place to raise a family and that assertion is true for the most part. Southern hospitality reigns supreme in the city and, although the bustling downtown area houses office buildings, shops and nightlife, it is the suburbs where the majority of people settle.

Nestled on the banks of the Ohio River, Louisville holds no shortage of recreational activities or job opportunities. The cost of living is manageable and homeowners get more "bang for their buck" than in other cities of similar size. Families that thrive in Louisville stay in Louisville for generations. It has a big-city feel with a suburban landscape.

Amanda McFarland's baby, Terrence "Trey" Zwicker, was born in 1997 in Louisville when his mother was sixteen years old and his father was nineteen. He was the first grandchild for his maternal grandparents and he was universally adored from the minute he was born. It was easy to see why. From the start of his life, Trey was a lovable, sweet boy and he enjoyed spending time with both sides of his family. He was likewise adored by Terry's side of the family and no one could quite get enough of the darling little boy.

When Trey was three years old, Terry Zwicker hired an attorney and initiated a custody action. He wanted to pay child support and he wanted to set regular and consistent visitation with his son. He did not want to be a "weekend dad." His attorney was expensive, but Terry worked hard to save up the money. It was clear that he would do anything for his son and he wanted to be a part of his child's life. By the time the case was resolved, he and Amanda had agreed to split their parenting time equally. They would have Trey at their homes on alternating weeks so that each parent could have adequate time to bond with him.[1]

With the agreement in place, Trey's parents got along for the most part, but they did have issues. The main issue Terry had with Amanda was her association with Josh Gouker. Amanda and Josh had an on-again/off-again relationship in their teenage years. Gouker was extremely possessive of Amanda, even when they were teenagers.

It appeared that Terry felt Gouker was a bad influence on Amanda and he did not want to risk that type of influence around Trey.[2] Gouker had divorced his first wife when he began to seek out his old flame, Amanda. By then, Gouker also had a child, Josh Young, from his failed first marriage. Amanda and Gouker began dating and soon got married. Terry Zwicker contacted a family judge because of safety concerns when Gouker was with three-year-old Trey.

The judge in their family court case issued a "no contact" order between Trey and Gouker. Amanda could not have Gouker anywhere near Trey during her parenting time. Most people felt that Gouker was a mean and violent person and, years later, people in the neighborhood still remembered him for his propensity to fight and bully others. Amanda worked at a fast-food restaurant, a job that she had started as a teenager, and Gouker resented this as well. However, his resentment didn't stop him from using her money, despite the fact that he did not maintain employment.

People familiar with both sides of Trey's family often suspected that Gouker resented Trey as well. He was clearly not happy with the fact that Trey had another father. Amanda was very affectionate with her son and this also seemed to make Gouker jealous. He always wanted to be the center of attention and he wanted Amanda's world to revolve around him. When Trey was around, this did not happen; during those times, Amanda's attention was focused on her son.

Although Josh did not appear outwardly mean toward Trey when he was a young child, Amanda grew tired of Gouker's jealousy. Amanda wanted a divorce and she told him so. Apparently that was not what Gouker wanted to hear. They were staying at a hotel at the time and Trey was with his father.

Amanda knew that situations with her husband could often turn volatile. When she asked for a divorce, Amanda attempted to leave the hotel room, but Gouker hollered after her and chased her down the hallway to a public balcony. As she dashed toward the stairwell, he grabbed her from behind and lifted her upward, pushing her against the balcony railing and halfway over it.

Just when it became apparent that he was going to throw her over the balcony several stories down to the asphalt below, a cleaning lady pushing her cart strolled by and stared in horror at the scene unfolding before her. She jerked her cart to a halt.[3]

"Honey, do you need help?" the cleaning lady called out. Gouker froze. For just a second, he loosened his grip on Amanda and looked backward at the maid. Amanda seized her chance and bolted toward the other woman. The cleaning lady was a large woman and Amanda was able to dash behind her, crouching down to the rear of the woman's cart. The woman ushered her away from the area. They slipped quickly into a nearby vacant room and called the police, waiting in the locked room until Gouker was gone.[4]

Amanda was able to stay away from Gouker and although they were still technically married, they lived separate lives. As Trey grew older, he became a big brother twice. His mother entered into a relationship with a man who produced the older of his two baby sisters and his father, Terry, and his new wife had a little girl as well. He was a great big brother and delighted in playing with his sisters. Trey was sweet and kindhearted. He was always willing to help out friends and family and he loved fishing with his dad.

He was a fun-loving kid, but he was also responsible and mature. Trey's sister was scared of the dark and he was a little bit, too. On nights when she was afraid to sleep alone, he would pull a blanket and pillow into her room and make a pallet on the floor, because being near him eased her fears. Ever the responsible boy, Trey would move his alarm clock into her room too. Although he was only fourteen years old, Trey got himself up and ready for school every day and made his way to the bus stop on his own.

Trey's sense of responsibility didn't end with school. While most kids might waste their free time hanging out with friends or goofing off, Trey wanted to make his own money. By the time Trey was fourteen, Amanda had been working at the fast-food restaurant for over fifteen years and she had become a general manager. She helped Trey gain a job at her location and they often worked shifts together. Trey saved his money. It must have given him a sense of accomplishment, as a young teenager, to be capable of buying the things he wanted. Most of the spending money that he earned through his job went toward buying snacks and video games. He also bought a stylish pair of black tennis shoes that he was very proud of and wore almost every day. His parents took turns shuttling Trey back and forth to his job. They were proud of him for displaying such a strong work ethic at such a young age.

In 2011, Trey was a typical high school freshman with a close-knit group of loyal friends. He was a good-looking boy, tall and stocky with close-cropped dark hair and a sweet, shy smile.

His relatives later remarked that Trey was softspoken and shy around people outside his family unit. He was most comfortable at home in the company of his family and a few close childhood friends from the neighborhood. He often sat quietly if he was in the company of new people.

Trey's uncle, his mother's brother, had obtained a degree in culinary arts and Trey spent hours watching him cook and asking questions. His uncle was convinced that Trey would be a great chef and encouraged the boy to consider that career option.

Whenever Trey was around, his uncle would show him how simple ingredients could turn into a delicious culinary masterpiece and Trey seemed very interested. He expressed the desire to possibly follow in his uncle's footsteps several times to relatives on his mother's side of the family.

While he enjoyed cooking with his mother's family, dinnertime was also one of Trey's favorite times at his father's home. Trey's stepmom often cooked dinner for the family and on many occasions Trey, watching her cook, said, "That smells good. What is it?" Their family dinners were especially precious as it was the time of the day when everyone got a chance to chat about the day's events and catch up with each other.[5]

Trey loved both his parents and was comfortable spending time at both of their houses, though the methods by which the houses operated were quite different. Terry's house was stricter and he and his wife were more stringent in the rules they set, enforcing those rules and punishing infractions. They kept a close eye on Trey and were always quick to offer guidance. Amanda's home was more relaxed, especially as Trey grew older and his stepfather, Josh Gouker, reentered his mother's life. Trey was allowed to run around the neighborhood later into the evenings with his friends.

The houses were within walking distance of each other, but several of Trey's friends lived nearby, so it was easier for them to hang out at each other's homes when he stayed at Amanda's house.

However, no matter which house he stayed in, one thing remained constant: Trey Zwicker was a fantastic son and a caring big brother. He was a hard-working boy who balanced his schooling and a part-time job. Most surely he would have gone on to do great things with his life. Unfortunately, his short life was ended by a monster who crept into the life of his family and took their precious boy away from them.

Chapter 3
Big Josh

Joshua Gouker was born on August 5, 1979, to a seventeen-year-old single mother. His mother, Ruby Jessie, was an outspoken woman and Gouker's beginnings were not storybook. The rumor was that Gouker was a product of rape. He later asserted that his maternal uncle raped his mother when she was just a teenager and that her pregnancy with Gouker resulted from that rape. Others have named other men as his father, so there is some ambiguity about Gouker's paternal lineage. Most likely Gouker was not the product of rape. He probably just concocted that story at a time in his life when he told it to garner some type of sympathy. It was this story of his lineage that he revealed to a neuropsychologist who evaluated him for competency in a criminal court case when he reached adulthood.[1]

Garnering sympathy and convincing others to do his bidding was something Gouker was skilled at doing and from an early age he was adept at manipulating his mother into bowing to his every whim, even though life was tough for the young woman. Despite the trying times in her life, no one ever called Ruby Jessie timid and she never shied away from speaking her mind. When Gouker was a baby she still enjoyed spending time with friends. She tried her best to balance all of the responsibilities in her life. She was a petite, attractive brunette but didn't hesitate to cuss like a sailor if someone crossed her. She liked to party and was not perfect but she tried hard.

Ruby loved her son and never hesitated to show it. Her conversations with Gouker, as a boy and later a grown man, always ended with "I love you." She did her best to raise him on her own in those early years. Parenting Gouker was not easy, especially for an ill-equipped young mother who lacked strong role models and a support system. As a child, Gouker was plagued by learning disabilities and displayed a severe reading difficulty. He failed out of two years of school and was required to repeat both the first and sixth grade levels. He alleged that he had been molested by a teenaged relative at a young age.

When Josh Gouker was still a child, Ruby married Gouker's stepfather, who quickly became an important part of the boy's life. Gouker's stepfather was a Pentecostal preacher who tried hard to set a good example for his stepson. Eventually he adopted Gouker and he attempted to provide a home for him. After Ruby married Gouker's stepfather, who was born in Michigan, he thought it would be best to relocate the family from Louisville, Kentucky to the state of his youth. Gouker began to show alarming signs of troubled behavior after the move, at a very early age.

Shortly after the abuse began, Gouker was hospitalized in Michigan. He had begun hurting and killing animals in his neighborhood. When pets went missing, Gouker was often to blame. Ruby and her husband were understandably concerned and sought help for their son via hospitalization for the first time when he was seven years old. The short stint at the hospital appeared to help the boy and he was released to the care of his parents. They hoped that professional help would put Gouker on the right path and keep him from his previous violent behavior. However, young Gouker continued to struggle with criminal issues throughout his childhood. It probably did not help that some of the adults around him used recreational drugs and that the substances were readily available to the young child.

By the age of nine, Gouker was again hospitalized, this time for setting fire to a house. According to some mental health professionals, many sociopaths demonstrate two distinct behaviors and compulsions as children: arson and animal abuse.[2] Gouker admittedly partook in both pastimes from a very early age. As an adult, he would acknowledge homicidal tendencies dating back to his early childhood years. He wanted to know what it would feel like to kill someone and he often fantasized about how he would do it.[3]

When Gouker was a preteen, the family returned to Louisville and he settled back onto his old street. His parents hoped that a change of scenery would help to alleviate his problems. He had begun to act out in Michigan on a larger scale and his behavior was worsening.

By the time Gouker turned fifteen, he was more than his mother could handle. Psychiatrists diagnosed Gouker with schizophrenia and prescribed a host of medications to him. The problem was that Gouker refused to comply with the medication regimen for any extended period of time. He claimed that the medications were like a "kick in the face" and that they prevented him from thinking clearly and feeling like himself. So Gouker continued to act out, defy authority and demonstrate violent outbursts. His mother didn't know what to do with him, so she just let Gouker be Gouker. He started to rage out of control even more so than in the past, so Ruby just let him run the streets. She loved her son, but she could no longer control him.

During these teenage years, Gouker spent a lot of his time with guys in the neighborhood, with Amanda McFarland as they dated "on and off" and with a female cousin his own age.

Gouker had an innate ability to read people and he could be the most charismatic guy in the room if he thought it would benefit him. People who only knew him casually liked him. He was gregarious, humorous and could even be fun to spend time with.

However, once an acquaintance scratched the surface, it was clear that Gouker cared only about himself and he was not above using violence and coercion to get what he wanted. For that reason, after reaching adulthood, Gouker quickly amassed a variety of violent criminal charges and became a frequent visitor to Louisville Metro Corrections, the jail in Jefferson County, Kentucky. It was Gouker's various girlfriends who were most likely to witness his violent streak, especially in the event that they decided to end a relationship with him.

Nancy, a former girlfriend of Gouker, knew this all too well. In July 2001, Gouker was twenty years old and had dated her for a period of time. They ended the relationship and, as always, Gouker was not happy when any of his girlfriends moved on to other relationships. Nancy was talking to another man when Gouker spotted her one day. Gouker went ballistic. He directed Nancy to get into his vehicle and she refused. He asked again and, though scared of what he would do, she still refused.

Immediately, Gouker began to hurl menacing words at her. He threatened to kill her and her family. He screamed that he would murder the man to whom she was speaking. Nancy was terrified. During their short relationship, she saw exactly what Gouker was capable of. He was a bully and would stop at nothing to get what he wanted, never mind that he always had several girls he was seeing at the same time. Even once they were no longer in a relationship, he tried to keep her from moving on. He was completely unpredictable and violent and she couldn't take the chance that her next encounter with him would involve more than words. He was quite capable of carrying out his threats.[4]

She immediately filed a criminal report of his actions and prosecutors filed charges against Gouker. A warrant was issued for his arrest. Police located and arrested him on that warrant and the case proceeded to court. In the end, Gouker pled guilty to one count of terroristic threatening third degree, a Class A misdemeanor that carried a penalty of up to twelve months in jail. By the time Gouker was offered a plea bargain in the case, he had served fifty days in custody. Prosecutors agreed to offer a sentence of three hundred and sixty-five days, of which Gouker would serve one hundred and seventy-five days. The balance of his sentence would be probated for a period of two years and he would receive credit for the fifty days that he had already served.

It was less than a year later that Gouker committed his next serious violation of the criminal code. By that time, Gouker was living in a section of Louisville known as Germantown. The neighborhood was working class and was decorated with countless corner pubs and restaurants that were neighborhood-friendly. Gouker's neighbors were good, hardworking people and there was a sense of community pride in the area. The neighborhood was only minutes from the University of Louisville and in addition to the many families that lived there, college students often rented the smaller houses and apartments that dotted the streets.

One of Gouker's favorite pastimes during this period of his life was kicking back with a beer at a nearby mom-and-pop pub that catered to the local crew. On any given day, several regulars filled the barstools and tables there. Most importantly for Gouker, it was within walking distance of his address. He did not have reliable transportation, so he frequented bars near his home.

It was just after three o'clock in the morning when Gouker, who was settled into his usual spot at the tavern, started getting rowdy. He had recently acquired a cigarette lighter that was designed to look like a pistol and had tucked it into the hip pocket of his jeans. Gouker clearly wanted to portray himself as dangerous. He didn't have an actual gun with him that evening but was acting as though he did as a means to intimidate those around him. Someone at the tavern became nervous at the sight of the tattooed twenty-something seated at the bar with what appeared to be a weapon, so that person contacted police. Just a few minutes later, an officer arrived on scene to investigate. Patrons of the bar were quick to point toward Gouker and the officer calmly approached and advised him that he had received a complaint and needed to further investigate the matter. As he strode up to the bulky man at the bar, the officer began to speak.

"Keep your hands on the tabletop, sir. We received a complaint that you may have a weapon. I just need to detain you for a minute to determine what is going on, okay?" Gouker placed his hands on the top of the bar and leaned forward without a word. The officer reached out toward Gouker's pocket to retrieve what he believed was the butt of a weapon. In an instant, Gouker spun around, liquor heavy on his breath and shoved the officer backward, sending him flying.[5]

Catching himself, the officer reached out, twisting Gouker around in an attempt to place handcuffs on him and Gouker continued to twist and buck him off. Several patrons sprung forward in an attempt to aid the officer in the tussle.

"Stop resisting, sir. You are under arrest!" the officer commanded, winded from the struggle.

Gouker continued to jerk his hands away from the officer and the policeman stuck out his foot, sweeping Gouker's legs out from under him and forcing Gouker to the floor. Even as he lay there, Gouker continued to scream obscenities at the officer as he struck out with his fist again and again, trying to throw the officer off balance.[6]

Finally, with the aid of several bar patrons, the policeman got Gouker under control and slipped handcuffs onto
his wrists. By this point, other officers had arrived at the
melee and Gouker was placed under arrest and transported
to Louisville Metro Corrections. The first responding
officer suffered injuries to his right pinkie finger and his
left ribcage in the altercation and he charged Gouker with
assault in the third degree (assault on a police officer or
other select law enforcement personnel). That crime is
punishable by one to five years in prison in Kentucky and
it is a felony offense. The charge against Gouker was based
on subsection 1(a)(1) of the statute:

1) A person is guilty of assault in the third degree
   when the actor:
   (a) Recklessly, with a deadly weapon or dangerous
       instrument, or intentionally causes or attempts
       to cause physical injury to:
       1. A state, county, city, or federal peace officer.[7]

Authorities also charged Gouker with the misdemeanor offenses of resisting arrest and disorderly conduct.

When a person is charged with a felony offense in
Kentucky, the case generally starts in district court. After
the defendant's arrest, he is brought before a judge and that
judge sets bond which the defendant must post before he is
released. From that point, a defendant is entitled to a preliminary hearing within ten days if he is in custody and within
twenty days if he is out on bond. The purpose of the preliminary hearing is for the judge to hear the Commonwealth's
initial proof in the matter. Specifically, the prosecution must

show that probable cause exists for the charges. The district court has jurisdiction in felony cases only to set bond and hold preliminary hearings.

Probable cause is a low standard. Generally, the Commonwealth needs only to show that it is more likely than not that the crime occurred. After hearing the evidence, the judge makes a finding regarding probable cause. If the judge finds that the Commonwealth has met the probable cause threshold, the case is waived to the Grand Jury. The judge's other alternatives are dismissing the case without prejudice, meaning that the Commonwealth can still proceed with the case at the grand jury level, or the judge can amend the matter to a misdemeanor-level offense if that type of charge is more appropriate in light of the preliminary hearing.

Once a case goes to the grand jury, a person may be held in custody for up to sixty days pending indictment. If the defendant is not indicted within sixty days, he must be released from custody if incarcerated, or his bail must be exonerated if he has been released on bond. Once the grand jury hears the matter, that panel will decide whether to indict. If an indictment is secured, the case proceeds in circuit court.

In a felony case in Kentucky, circuit court is where the action happens. Once a felony case is indicted, the actual casework begins. The Commonwealth must provide its evidence or "discovery" to defense counsel and, after both sides have prepared their cases, the circuit courtroom is where the trial occurs. Josh Gouker's assault third degree case was waived to the grand jury in 2002, shortly after the officer initiated the charges. Gouker was facing up to five years in the penitentiary, but that didn't stop him from committing more acts of violence. He was able to make bond while awaiting trial and continued his crime spree.

During the early morning hours of October 1, 2002, Gouker once again appeared to have a craving for a night of booze and boasting and he decided to visit another local establishment located in the Germantown neighborhood where he had gotten into trouble previously. This time, the night would go far worse for Gouker and the unsuspecting patrons at the bar.

By now, Gouker had moved back to his old childhood street, so the restaurant was beyond walking distance. He managed to gain a ride there but did not have a ride home. Gouker made himself comfortable at the bar and struck up a conversation with an older gentleman, seventy-one-year-old David, who was also drinking alone. After several hours of drinking and engaging in small talk at the bar, Gouker mentioned he did not have a ride back to his house and the man offered to drive Gouker home in his car.

Late in the evening, as the car crept along on its way out of Germantown, the two men began to argue. Gouker had been drinking heavily and was his usual belligerent self. David must have started to realize that he should never have agreed to give the stranger a ride. As he pulled the car to an abrupt stop, David ordered Gouker to exit the vehicle and refused to take him any further.[8]

It happened in an instant. Gouker lunged across the middle of the car and wrapped his hands around the older man's neck, squeezing tighter and tighter as the elderly man frantically dug his fingers into Gouker's hands in a desperate attempt to pry him away. His face reddened as he felt the pressure tighten. He gasped for breath as he felt Gouker loosen his grip. Stunned, David brought his hands to his face and bent over in agony as his chest heaved.

He didn't notice at first that Gouker had slid into the back seat of the vehicle and positioned himself directly behind the driver's seat where David sat gasping for breath. Gouker reached around the seat, placing one arm again around his victim's neck while he used his free hand to undo the man's belt and slide it from its belt loops. He jerked the belt into the back seat and proceeded to loop it around David's neck, pulling it tightly as he braced himself against the back of the front seat.

Again, David clawed at his neck, trying desperately to loosen the belt from his windpipe. He kicked and squirmed, gasping for breath and constrained by the steering wheel. He felt Gouker land blow after blow to the right side of his face from behind and finally sink his teeth into his right ear as they struggled.

At that time, a woman was walking by the vehicle and she noticed the commotion inside. She rushed toward the vehicle just as the driver's door swung open and Gouker pushed David out and onto the concrete. The elderly man's battered body lay sideways next to the car and she bent forward and helped him to his feet just as Gouker clambered into the front seat of the car and sped away with tires squealing.[9]

The woman wasted no time in helping the gentleman out of the street and contacting police. Dispatchers immediately sent officers to the scene and issued a "be on the lookout" alert for the vehicle. Officers arrived quickly and began their search for the thug who had beaten and robbed the elderly gentlemen. As two of the officers drove through the streets of Germantown, they kept their eyes peeled for the car. They eventually noticed it in a driveway on a quiet residential side street just a few miles from the scene of the attack. The driver had backed the car into the driveway in an attempt to hide the license plate and avoid detection.

As their police cruiser slowed in front of the home and came to a stop, Gouker sprang from the front seat of the vehicle and took off through the backyard. The officers dashed after Gouker. However, he was able to elude them, at least initially. Only two streets over from the excitement sat homes worth upward of half a million dollars and a prestigious country club was only a brisk walk from the area. The last thing any of these neighbors would expect to see in the late night or early morning hours was a tattooed convict crouched behind their rose bushes. Yet there he was, hiding in the shadows, desperately hoping that the police would not locate him.

Officers fanned out over the neighborhood. The older gentleman Gouker had attacked was lucky to be alive. Law enforcement knew they were dealing with a dangerous man and they needed to find him as quickly as possible. Movement caught their attention as Gouker, feeling the police were too close for comfort, jumped from his hiding spot and sprinted away again. This time, he was not fast enough and after a short foot pursuit, officers were able to catch him.[10]

Even once apprehended, Gouker refused to go down without a fight and continued to wrestle with the police in an attempt to escape. To the officers' credit, they were able to quickly subdue him and place him in handcuffs. For the second time in just a few months, Gouker was charged with a violent felony offense. He was lodged in Louisville Metro Corrections where he remained as he awaited trial. The violence did not stop there.

Even while incarcerated, Gouker could not let go of his need for brutality and threats. Only a week after he was taken into custody, he made a phone call to Steven, a witness in one of his pending cases. He warned Steven that he would eventually get out of custody and that he knew Steven had spoken to police about the way Gouker had tortured him in the month before his most recent arrest. He told Steven that when he was released from jail, the first thing he planned to do was track him down and kill him.

Gouker and another man had previously lured Steven to a basement and held him throughout the night. Steven was tied to a chair and beaten and assaulted until the early morning hours of the following day. Gouker either believed the man had stolen from him or was a "rat" and had informed the police of Gouker's illegal activities. After enduring a horrific night of torture, the victim was able to escape captivity and had reported the incident to police, revealing that while Gouker was beating him, he'd had no idea whether he would live or die.[11]

After he received the phone call from Gouker, the terrified Steven immediately reported the call to police. Jail telephone calls are recorded, so the allegation was easily verified and Gouker once again found himself charged with a serious felony offense. As he sat in jail in October 2002, Gouker faced a slew of violent felony charges and any hopes that he had of release in the near future were dwindling fast.

Gouker faced the initial charge of assault third degree for his fight with the police officer in the spring of 2002. That charge alone was punishable by up to five years in prison. He also faced a robbery first degree charge stemming from his attack on the elderly man who was nice enough to give him a ride. That charge carried a penalty of ten to twenty years in the penitentiary and another indictment charged Gouker with assault second degree, intimidating a witness in a legal proceeding, resisting arrest and criminal mischief second degree for holding Steven against his will in the basement and torturing him, as well as the subsequent call from prison when he threatened Steven's life. He faced up to fifteen years on that indictment alone.

Gouker's brutal ways had caught up with him and it appeared that even the best legal team available could not dig him out of the violent hole he had dug for himself. In the end, Gouker was ordered to serve one long prison term with the sentence in each of the charges ordered to run consecutively into each other. If Gouker were to serve the entire prison sentence, it would be at least a decade until he was a free man.

In Kentucky, most inmates will not serve their sentences in their entirety. In fact, most offenses are parole eligible after the inmate has served 20 percent of the sentence. However, some crimes are classified as "violent" offenses and any sentence imposed for such charges is not eligible for parole until the defendant has served 85 percent of the sentence.

The robbery first degree charge Gouker obtained was one such offense. In order to be eligible for parole on a robbery first degree charge, Gouker would need to serve no less than 1,551 days in custody. Unfortunately, his charge was amended to robbery second degree, a lesser offense than robbery first degree and, therefore, Gouker would be parole eligible after only 20 percent of his sentence. It was unlikely that the parole board would grant early release to him but it would review his case after he served 20 percent of the sentence. Gouker still received a substantial prison term for his offenses and his victims surely felt that they could rest easy knowing Gouker would spend at least some of his next nine years safety secluded in a Kentucky prison. They had confidence that the parole board would keep him locked away. They probably all hoped they had seen the last of Gouker.

However, Gouker believed they would see him sooner than they expected. He stayed busy in prison compiling a list of people on whom he wanted to exact revenge when he was released. He had nothing but time and a penchant for violence. At age twenty-four, Gouker knew that he had many years left to live, so he spent a great deal of time plotting his movements when his release finally came and he was confident that it would come one day. He enjoyed fantasizing about the people he would kill after the Department of Corrections released him and he spent a lot of time planning how he would kill each one. It kept him busy.[12]

He also stayed busy penning rap song lyrics that predicted the savagery that would underscore his future. In one rap song he wrote, he talked about killing a woman he felt had betrayed him: "Alright you deceiving bitch, you can scream to the top of your lungs/But I'm going to stick one of these nails through your lying tongue." The song went on, "I'm gonna scalp you from your forehead and cut off your titties too/What's that? You're pregnant—again? Do you think it's a son or a daughter?/We'll find out in a minute, cause we're gonna play doctor/Why couldn't you live the life and the lie that you told?!/You've turned my heart from pure to black and cold."[13]

The long, horrifying song concluded, "Back at the house when I killed that kid, it was easy cause he had your eyes/He would have ended up full grown, learning from you telling lies/Your whole body is shaking, it's probably going through shock/Since you ain't feeling no more pain, I guess I'll go ahead and stop."

Gouker drafted these lyrics in 2004 while he was serving his long prison sentence. It seemed that sadistic violence remained on his mind for the duration of that incarceration and his untreated mental illness was likely raging out of control. Even while in custody, he retained the ability to control friends, family members and associates on the outside. Gouker manipulated everyone and did not appear to mind dragging other people into the chaos that was his life.

Gouker's twisted rap lyrics did not surface until years later. When Gouker was eventually released from prison in 2010, he took most of his belongings to his mother's home. Although he did not plan to live with her, he stored several boxes in her basement. This rap song would eventually surface and be important.

During Gouker's incarceration in his early twenties, Ruby was a regular visitor and she appeared to succumb to any request her son made of her. Ruby was no angel. By the time she visited her son at the Green River Correctional Complex in September 2007, she had amassed a criminal history of shoplifting and possession of drug paraphernalia, but those charges were nothing in comparison to what Gouker convinced her to do during that visit in September.

Narcotics are a hot commodity within prison walls. Gouker had the bright idea that he could make some money and amass a stash of drugs for his own use if only he could smuggle some product into the prison. Ruby made regular trips to see her son and by this point was in her forties. He felt the officers responsible for searching visitors would not regard her as suspicious or a threat. He convinced his mother to sneak marijuana and prescription pills into the facility. Things did not go according to plan and she was caught. Officers charged her with promoting contraband in the first degree, a Class D felony. The case eventually worked out as a misdemeanor, with Ruby pleading guilty to promoting contraband in the second degree and serving thirty days in jail.[14] However, the implication was clear. She would do anything for her son, including serving jail time. Gouker, it seemed, could convince anyone to do anything and did not think twice about placing loved ones, even his mother, in a precarious position where she could get in serious trouble.

As Gouker spent years locked up throughout his twenties, outside the prison walls the various players in Trey's short life were going on with their own. Gouker, however, spent his time planning ways he could tear all of their lives apart once he was released.[15]

Chapter 4

Little Josh

Josh Gouker had dated a woman named Angelina Young before he went to jail. Angelina, or "Angie" as she was called, was a beautiful girl, petite and slim. Her golden blonde hair fell lushly down her back. Angie had large, round eyes, fair skin and was quick to break into a gleaming smile. She turned heads everywhere she went and it was easy to see why Gouker was romantically interested in her. Most men who met Angie were immediately attracted to her and she had no shortage of suitors throughout her life.

Angelina was a year older than Josh Gouker. She was sixteen years old when they began dating. Her mother was not happy about the budding relationship, but Angie assured her that there was no harm in dating Gouker. Soon after the pair became a couple, Angie learned that she was pregnant. She and Gouker eventually married after their baby was born. Both were teenagers when Angie gave birth to their son, Joshua Young, on January 6, 1996. Immediately, Joshua became the light of Angie's life. The little blond-haired baby was her spitting image. Everyone who saw them together remarked on how sweet the baby was and how he looked exactly like Angie.

Angie was so proud of him and looked forward to marking all the milestones in his life. She saved her money to take Josh to the mall photographers to take their "family" pictures, just she and him. From the start, they were inseparable, two against the world. She was young but she was determined to be a great mother to her son.

For the first year of little Joshua's life, Angie tried to make things work with Gouker. She got along with his family and she wanted the relationship to work out for the sake of their son. She desperately desired a two-parent family for Joshua. She wanted to give him the best life possible. She tried to keep strong ties between the baby and both sides of his family. She did her best to take little Joshua on regular visits to her own mother and Gouker's mother.

To all who knew him, Josh Gouker appeared to love his son, whom friends and family affectionately called "Little Josh." Naturally, when people began referring to Joshua Junior as "Little Josh," Gouker became known to friends and loved ones as "Big Josh." Angie knew that Gouker could be affectionate with their son and that he was proud of him, deriving a type of self-worth from the knowledge that he had impregnated Angie and produced a son, his namesake. But she couldn't shake the feeling that something wasn't quite right with her husband and his parenting style. He could be aggressive with the baby and he did not seem to have the nurturing capacity necessary to raise a child.

Angie's marriage to Gouker did not last. He was his normal, violent self with her and Angie seemed to know that he was not father figure material. He may have been Joshua's biological father, but that didn't mean Little Josh needed to grow up thinking it was okay for Gouker to act the way he did. If she stayed with him, Angie knew she would be setting a terrible example for her son. Angie realized that she needed to part ways with Gouker and decided to file for divorce. By January 1998, that divorce was final and Angie attempted to move on with her life.

By that point, Angie had taken out an emergency protective order against her ex-husband. She was scared of him and what he was capable of doing and she did not want to expose her baby to his propensity for that kind of behavior. She was thankful they were officially divorced but she was also aware of Gouker's track record of bad conduct after breakups. She did not want to take any chances. Joshua was only a year old at the time. Yet she was hopeful that Gouker's harassment would finally end. She just wanted to focus on her life and raising her sweet baby. She had lived in fear of Gouker for quite a while and finally she could start rebuilding her life.

Gouker did not take the situation well. He continued to harass Angie, especially over the phone. On one such occasion, Angie had had enough. Gouker obviously had no hang-ups about violating the protective order, so she would have to take even more drastic measures. She drove directly to the county attorney's office in downtown Louisville and filed a complaint. Shortly thereafter, a judge entered a

warrant for Gouker's arrest on charges of custodial inter-
ference, violating an emergency protective order and harassing communications. Gouker would eventually serve six
months on the charge.

After the final domestic violence order was entered
against Gouker, Angie was successful in cutting off contact
with him, especially once he went to prison. However, she
did allow Little Josh to maintain contact with his father's
side of the family, especially Gouker's mother. It was Ruby
who took Joshua on the rare visits he had with his father
in prison while Gouker served his nine-year sentence for
his violent crimes. During that nine-year span, Little Josh
visited his father four or five times in the company of his
grandmother. He never quite knew what to think of his
father. The visits were short and supervised and his father
never felt like a true, present father. Josh did not know
what it felt like to have a father who was there for his
day-to-day activities. It was something that he had never
experienced. Instead, he had sporadic visits in a cold penitentiary with a man he barely knew.[1]

When he was ten years old, Josh's grandmother took
him to visit Gouker. It was nerve-wracking for the boy
when he went on these rare visits. He later recalled his
stomach was aching as his grandmother pulled her vehicle
up the winding driveway to the prison. His dad tried to
act nice to him but both Gouker and the stifling walls of
the penitentiary were imposing and intimidating to the
boy. They had to pass through metal detectors before they
could reach the interior of the building where his father
waited for him. It was a place that Little Josh knew he
never wanted to live. It was scary.[2]

As they entered the visiting room, he immediately spotted Gouker. It had been almost a year since the last time he saw his father and the ten-year-old surveyed the scene, noticing that his father, clad in the short-sleeved jumpsuit indicative of his status as an inmate, had shaved his hair into a Mohawk. Joshua noticed the familiar two-word tattoo that adorned his father's right forearm: Bad Ass. He felt his legs shake a little. Gouker strode quickly toward Little Josh and Ruby and quickly enveloped Ruby in a hug. Whipping out her camera, Ruby was permitted to take a picture of her son and grandson. Gouker stood behind Little Josh, wrapping both arms around him, head tilted to the side with his best convict expression on his face. Joshua pressed his lips together tightly, willing himself to smile.

Gouker was his father and Joshua knew his grand-mother expected him to look up to the man and to respect him as his dad. In some ways he did love him, but even at that young age, he realized on some level that his father was different and his interactions with the man were limited. It is understandable that a child, especially the child of an absent parent, would still have love for that parent.

Little Josh's relationship with his mother was a dif-ferent story. Angie loved her little boy, whom she affec-tionately referred to as "Joshy." He was a sweet, fun-loving little boy and he was very smart. She was proud of him and she tried her best to be a good mother. Angie didn't have a lot of money or material things but she lavished what she could on her son. The two were living in an apartment house, where incidentally, Trey Zwicker also lived at the time with his own mother, Amanda. It was just the two of them there in their tiny home. Angie felt a great sense of independence living on her own and taking care of her little boy. She told herself that the public assistance was only temporary. They needed a little help and she was grateful that the state was willing to aid them. She was not getting any form of child support from Little Josh's father due to his incarceration. She was on her own. She was still a very young woman in her early twenties and was trying very hard to make things work. She never wanted Little Josh to realize how she struggled with money, so she put a lot of effort into making sure that he always got everything he needed and special treats.

At the beginning of each month, Angie received her monthly allotment of food stamps. Then she and Little Josh went to the grocery store together to gather the monthly food and drinks for their apartment. Angie always made a big production of apportioning a certain amount of the food budget for Joshua's treats.[3]

It was very exciting for a little boy. He could dash up and down the aisles at the grocery store and pick out the candy and goodies he wanted. He also had to learn to count the dollar amounts of the products to make sure that they fell under the preset amount of money Angie allotted to him. Sometimes, he got to spend up to one hundred dollars on all the foods he loved. This time with his mother was something that he would always remember. He was the number one person in her world and Angie tried to do everything within her means to make sure that Little Josh felt special and that he always felt loved. He always did. Even as a little boy, he knew that despite his mother's faults, she loved him dearly and would do anything within her power for him.

Joshua was a good student. However, it is difficult for a child to excel in his education when he is constantly moving around and changing schools. Joshua attended school in the Kentucky public school systems in both Jefferson County and Bullitt County. Those systems were broken into three different levels. Elementary school was grades one through five, middle school was grades six through eight and high school was comprised of grades nine through twelve.

Looking back years later at the early days of his education, Little Josh would come to the realization that he had attended eight different elementary schools. It was a shocking number. This is almost unheard of for a young child. It is amazing that Joshua was able to do as well as he did in school given his spotty attendance record and lack of stability. In addition to living in different places with his mom, Josh also lived sporadically in homes with relatives when his mother had trouble making ends meet or when she served various prison terms.

As the years wore on, it was said that Angie dabbled in drugs and ultimately developed an addiction. She loved her little boy but people said she also loved to get high. Those around her began to worry. What started initially as a recreational drug habit was slowly beginning to affect Angie's life negatively in many ways.

Later, in the clutches of drug addiction, Angie was caught stealing and passing bad checks. When a neighbor reported her checkbook missing, it didn't take long for the authorities to track it to Angie. She had written checks to several businesses on the account. The total amount of the stolen checks was thousands of dollars. When confronted by the police, Angie admitted her involvement in passing the stolen checks and was charged with several counts of felony forgery. The case wound its way through the legal system and all but one count of forgery were dropped. Due to her limited criminal history, Angie was initially given a diversion. A diversion is a felony case resolution that operates much like probation. The defendant is given a certain amount of prison time but the imposition of that sentence is withheld for a period of years. If the defendant successfully completes the diversion, the charge can be wiped from her record as if it never happened.[4]

The diversion was a good chance for Angie to come out of the charge without a permanent felony conviction and she did well for a few months. However, she eventually violated the terms of her supervision and the judge revoked her diversion. She was sentenced to two years in prison. Learning that she would have to leave her son for years was a shock to Angie's system and she knew that it would be hard for Little Josh.

She had to make arrangements for her little boy, so she turned to her brother and sister-in-law. The couple lived in Bullitt County, Kentucky. They were willing to take Joshua into their home while Angie served her prison sentence and Joshua was familiar with those relatives and loved them.

Angie entered into an agreement with the couple in September 2003 which gave them voluntary, temporary guardianship of Little Josh. While she was incarcerated, they would care for Joshua and he would attend a nearby elementary school. Angie hoped that once she was released from custody, she would get back on her feet and reacquire possession of Joshua. By this point, Gouker was already serving his long prison sentence, so at the age of seven both of Little Josh's parents were serving felony prison terms and he was forced to acclimate to a new life, in a new town, with a new family. This kind of change was something that Joshua became accustomed to over the early years of his life.

His aunt and uncle had two teenage children living in the home, his aunt's children from a previous relationship, and they began to view Josh as a part of the family, affectionately referring to him as their "cousin." However, any amount of familiarity in the household could not substitute for the day-to-day presence of his mother and her absence took a toll on the boy. He became quiet and withdrawn, but he was intent on doing the best he could. He focused on studying hard in the hopes of making his mother proud of him when she did return.

He began to attend his new school and excelled academically. The school placed him in advanced classes and he made friends. He entered the school spelling bee and won, going on to the county and later statewide competition. He didn't cause trouble for anyone and it was a joy for his aunt and uncle that he lived in their household. He could be quiet and introverted but was quick to break into a wide smile when speaking with people he trusted. Unfortunately, those people were few and far between.

When Angelina was eventually released from the penitentiary almost two years later, she attempted to get her life back in order. By that time, Joshua was nine years old and still living with his aunt and uncle outside of Louisville, in Shepherdsville, a small city in Bullitt County. Angie decided that she wanted her son with her and she invited a friend to make an impromptu trip to the household so that she could retrieve Little Josh. They quickly made the twenty minute drive to the home.

As Little Josh played in the backyard that day, he was surprised and excited to see his mother approach. She beckoned him to the side of the yard and motioned him to come with her. Within minutes, she had loaded Josh into her vehicle and they were on the road headed out of Kentucky.

Josh was confused and excited when his mother told him they were going to Florida to live. He didn't have any of his things and he wondered if his aunt and uncle had any idea where he was. Angie had unexpectedly popped back into his world like a tornado and everything was beginning to change again. It turns out that Josh's aunt and uncle did not know that Angie had taken him and very shortly thereafter they realized he was gone. They notified the Shepherdsville Police Department via a frantic 911 call and within minutes officers arrived at the home. Suspecting that Angie was responsible for Little Josh's disappearance, his aunt gave the officers her name and description.

Angie Young and the friend who accompanied her were charged with kidnapping and bench warrants were issued for their arrest. An Amber Alert was broadcast in regard to Joshua. By then the trio were well on their way to Florida, unaware of the craziness that was brewing back home. All Angie wanted was to have her son with her.

Glancing back at him in the back seat of the car, she was happy. She had what she wanted.

Eventually, they noticed the blue lights of a police cruiser behind them and after a short pursuit the police gained control of the two women. Josh was returned to his aunt and uncle and officers arrested his mother and her friend and took them directly to the Bullitt County Detention Center where they both remained incarcerated pending trial. When Angie was booked into the Bullitt County Detention Center, she got into even more trouble. She was carrying some marijuana and tried to hide it at the jail. Officials claimed that she dropped the marijuana in a wastebasket prior to a search of her body. They claimed that they then observed her trying to retrieve it later. Angie was charged with promoting contraband in the second degree. She served two weeks in custody for that offense.[5]

However, the more serious kidnapping charges against Angie and her friend were ultimately dismissed and she was released from custody on that charge. The whole fiasco is just another example of the chaotic world where Joshua lived as a young boy.

After the kidnapping charges were dropped, Angie worked to regain custody of Joshua and she began to get her life together again. When Joshua returned to her care, Angie decided that a move to Florida would be the best for everyone. Her mother had relocated and was living in Florida at the time. Angie likely believed that it would be productive for her to move away from the bad influences that surrounded her in Kentucky. It could be a fresh start for her and Little Josh, so, as Joshua prepared to celebrate his tenth birthday, they traveled to Florida for the second time, this time without police officers trailing them.

Their new life in Florida didn't last long. They moved in with Angie's mother there and Angie enrolled Joshua in school. However, a month later they decided that they did not like living in Florida so far away from family and friends. Within a few days of that decision, they packed up their bags and returned to Kentucky.

As they settled into a home back in Louisville, Josh became used to new a routine and began taking karate classes. He had a great time practicing his karate moves and loved how several members of his extended family attended his karate ceremonies. Angie could not have been prouder as she watched her son excel. It seemed like the hard times were a distant memory and that the Young family of two was moving forward in a positive direction. Things started to settle down and life became a little more stable for Joshua. He was excited to learn that he and his mother were expecting a new addition to the family.[6]

By the time Josh was twelve, Angie had given birth to another child. Like Joshua, the little girl was a spitting image of her mother, with long white-blond hair that fell in soft curls. From the start she became Joshua's absolute favorite person in the world. Once he laid eyes on his sister, he quickly abandoned any notion that a baby brother would be best. He was so happy to have her in his life.

Joshua was very protective of his sister and she became the one constant in his life. Wherever she went, Joshua went and she loved her big brother. Little Josh was in a caretaking role for his sister from the start but by the time she was a year old, his responsibilities became even more heavy. Angelina was diagnosed with hepatitis and she became very ill. Doctors did what they could to prescribe medicine for the young mother, but the medicine made her extremely lethargic.

Joshua noticed that his mother was sleeping most of the time and had difficulty caring for his younger sister. She could sleep throughout the entire day when she was feeling especially sick. He stepped into the "adult" role in the house and practically raised his little sister by himself. He was the one who got up early in the morning to feed the baby and he was the one who changed her diapers when they were dirty. He made sure that his sister had formula to drink and, as she grew older, solid food.[7]

During this time, Joshua rarely attended school. He was supposed to ride the bus but he did not feel comfortable leaving his sister home alone with his mother. She was always so sick and Joshua was afraid she would sleep through his sister's cries or that his sister would get hurt if his mother's medication made it too difficult for her to care for the baby or to stay awake.

As Joshua continued to miss school, the Jefferson County School System finally took notice and he and his sister were temporarily removed from his mother's custody. It was a scary situation. Joshua was no stranger to moving around and over the years he had stayed in many different homes when his mother was unable to care for him. However, this would be the first time Joshua was placed in a foster home that was not a relative's residence.

In the past, when his mother wasn't able to take care of him, Joshua had always stayed with family members, people whom he knew. However, this time when they were removed from Angie, they were placed in the temporary custody of the Cabinet for Health and Family Services (known commonly as Child Protective Services or simply "The Cabinet"), then were placed in a foster home with complete strangers. The saving grace was they were together and Joshua continued to act as the "parent" to his sister. He wanted to minimize the trauma to her and he hoped that she wasn't as scared as he was. They both missed their mother and Joshua worried about her. He knew she wasn't well and he wanted to get home quickly. He was used to taking care of his mom. He knew she needed him.

It was a horrible situation for such a young man. For years, Joshua was the caretaker for his sister and his mother. Especially during his mother's illness, he did not get a lot of time to just be a kid. It was hard and that experience left an imprint on Little Josh. As Angie's health improved, the children were eventually returned to her and she tried to do better. She loved her children and she wanted to be a good mother, so for the next two years she really began to turn things around.

By 2010, Angie was engaged to her fiancé and she had just given birth to a third child, a boy. Joshua finally received the baby brother he'd hoped for years before. He and his sister were excited when they visited their mother in the hospital after their new brother was born and they climbed into the hospital bed to hold the baby. Joshua smiled for the camera as family members took pictures of Angie's three children. He beamed as he held the baby firmly in his arms and wrapped his other arm around his sister.

Angie was doing very well and the kids were happy. In the four months following her youngest son's birth, she had stayed out of trouble and stopped abusing substances. She was taking methadone to help her stay clean. Easter was coming and she had purchased "Easter Bunny" gifts for the kids. She was excited about what the future held.

On the day before Easter, Angie had a great day arranged for her children. She planned to take Josh and his sister to the mall so that her daughter could sit on the Easter Bunny's lap.

As always, Angie ensured that her children looked nice. Josh dressed himself in a red collared polo shirt and Josh's sister, always the diva, was decked out in head-to-toe pink, down to the pink ponytail holders that held her bouncy blonde curls in place. Everyone was having a great time as they settled into the long line of people waiting for the Easter Bunny. By that point, Josh's sister had picked up a pair of pink plastic sunglasses and Angie bought them for her. In love with her new shades, she wore them as she waited in the line to see the Easter Bunny.[8]

Josh made sure that he was there any time his sister needed him. When she decided that she wanted to have her ears pierced that day, it was Little Josh who sat in the chair with her perched atop his lap when the earrings were put in. Comforted by her brother, she did not even cry.

It really was a perfect afternoon and they ended their excursion with a meal at a fast-food restaurant. As they traveled home later in the evening, everything seemed great. Easter was the next morning and it seemed that things were really falling into place.

When Josh woke up the next day, he and his mother's fiancé found Angie dead in their apartment from an apparent methadone overdose. It was Josh who walked into the room and first located his mother, cold and lifeless, and the boy was devastated. The coroner would later rule the death a suicide. It seemed that Angie's demons had finally overtaken her life.

In the wake of her death, Angie's family was left to determine what would happen to the children. Each of Angie's three children had a different father. In the days following Angie's tragic death, the baby went to live with his father. Josh and his little sister went to their aunt and uncle's household for some time and the Cabinet For Health and Family Services eventually intervened. On July 8, 2010, Joshua and his sister were committed to the custody of the Cabinet and taken from their aunt and uncle, a home with which they were familiar and comfortable.

Several relatives stepped forward in an attempt to gain custody of the children, including the aunt and uncle. However, a background check on Josh's uncle revealed a criminal conviction years prior and he was deemed an inappropriate custodian. Joshua's other aunt also sought custody of her niece and nephew, but her request for custody was also denied and she did not understand why. Rather than place the children in the home of a relative, the court felt it was more appropriate to place the kids in the custody of the Cabinet for Health and Family Services.

They were placed together in a foster home in July. Several months later, on September 22, 2010, they were taken to a new foster home, that of George and Debbie Walsh. It was a loving home. Debbie was a middle school teacher and had spent her life caring for children. Joshua and his sister joined the Walsh's other children and settled into a routine at their spacious and comfortable home. It was a relaxed two-parent household and both Walshes encouraged Josh in his studies.

Josh was a high school freshman that year. The school was not far from his new home in Jefferson County with the Walshes. Despite the recent tragedy in his life, Josh did well there. He was the recipient of constant encouragement from his foster parents. Debbie noticed that he had a natural knack for working with computers and they discussed how he could develop that talent into a possible career once he graduated from high school and college.[9]

Josh also thrived in the high school social scene. He met a cheerleader at the school and she became his girlfriend. Josh joined the wrestling team and began training with the squad. He excelled at everything he tried and had no shortage of friends. For probably the first time in his life, Josh was in a completely stable environment where he was allowed to just be a kid. He did not have the pressure of acting as a parent to his sister. He was finally able to function solely as a big brother. He did not have to miss school to care for the adults in his life. Education and extracurricular activities were his focus and he made the most of every opportunity that he had on that front. Josh was still recovering from his mother's recent death and the pain from that traumatic event continued to weigh heavily on his mind. However, he derived comfort from the fact that his mother would have been so proud of the goals he was accomplishing. When he experienced feelings of sadness from the loss of his mother, he buckled down and worked even harder.

The Walshes enjoyed the new additions to their family and made arrangements to adopt Josh's sister, hoping eventually to adopt Josh as well. At that time, Joshua Gouker's custodial rights to his son had not yet been terminated. Josh was in the custody of the Cabinet, but his father still held legal claim to him. Until Gouker's parental rights were terminated by the court, Little Josh was not eligible for adoption. Even if the adoption eventually occurred, Josh was confident the Walshes would continue to foster a relationship between him and his mother's family. They kept the family informed of the children's progress and always treated them with respect, which made the transition much easier for everyone involved.

As Josh settled into life with the Walshes, no one could have imagined what would happen over the next few months. It seemed that the children were adjusting very well to their new foster home, a foster home that could quite possibly turn into a permanent arrangement. While Gouker was in prison, Josh had virtually no contact with him. He did not realize that with his biological father's sentence coming to an end, there was a very real possibility that the parole board would grant parole to Gouker. In October 2010, within months of his foster placement, Little Josh's world would be turned upside down once again.

Chapter 5

Coming Home

After nine years, one month and fifteen days, Joshua Gouker sauntered out of the penitentiary and back onto the streets of Louisville. He was aware that Angie had died the previous Easter and that his son, Josh, had been placed in a foster home. He didn't waste any time. The day after his release, he reported to the Cabinet for Health and Family Services. He knew that a caseworker was assigned to his son's case and he asked to speak with her immediately.

Seated in the caseworker's office, Gouker was the picture of a contrite and caring father. He admitted that he had made mistakes in the past, but his years of incarceration had compelled him to become a changed man. He told her that he loved his son more than anything and he was willing to do whatever it took to get him back.

She couldn't help but feel sorry for the man, although she viewed him with some trepidation. His record spoke for itself and admittedly it had been years since he had held a meaningful relationship with his son, at least a relationship that allowed him to participate in Josh's day-to-day activities. Yet, he appeared honestly to want to raise his child and expressed willingness to take the necessary steps in order for him to do so.

She told Gouker that she was impressed with his sincerity and that, while it would require a lot of work on his part, they could develop a case plan to work toward reuniting Gouker with Little Josh.

"Thank you, thank you," Gouker gushed, clenching his lips together and allowing a single tear to roll down his cheek. "Whatever it takes."

The system is geared toward reunification of children with their biological parents except in the most egregious of circumstances. If a parent adequately works his or her case plan and shows the court that regaining custody is in the best interest of the child, the child is often returned to the custody of that parent. Gouker would have to prove that he was serious and not a danger to his son before he could attain custody of Little Josh.

When he went to prison, Gouker and Amanda McFarland were still married, although they had been living apart for some time. During his years of incarceration, he sent Amanda a "self-help" divorce packet that he completed in prison. When she received those documents in September 2004, Amanda immediately signed them and sent them back to Gouker at the prison. By that point she had moved on with her life; Gouker was just a distant memory. She believed she was divorced. Amanda even remarried in the years that Gouker was incarcerated, unaware of the fact that she and the convict were still legally married. Gouker, on the other hand, had never filed the paperwork with the court and, unbeknownst to Amanda, he ensured that the two remained legally married.

It was the perfect reason for him to reach out to her once he was released from custody. He knew Amanda worked at a fast-food restaurant, the same place of employment she had during their marriage, and he placed a call to her at work. He asked to speak with her and within minutes she was on the line. It would be an uphill climb, he was sure, but Gouker usually got what he wanted.[1]

He hadn't been a good husband, but Amanda was a good woman. He knew she owned her own home. If he could get back with her, that steady relationship would definitely go a long way toward convincing Child Protective Services he was reliable and help him regain custody of Joshua. She worked; she had a regular paycheck.

Amanda hadn't seen or heard from Gouker in years, one of the last occasions being when he assaulted her at the motel before they finally split up.

Gouker told her that he had just gotten out of jail and that their divorce had never been finalized, so they should meet to talk about it. Amanda told him that she would be off work the following day if he wanted to meet then. He agreed.

Early the next day, Gouker and Amanda went to the Jefferson County Judicial Center together. Records confirmed that they were still legally married. The revelation shocked Amanda. They decided to stop at a restaurant to grab lunch and discuss their next steps. At some point during that conversation, a shift in Amanda's thinking occurred and it appeared that the couple might attempt to make their marriage work.

As they enjoyed their impromptu lunch, Gouker apologized to Amanda for the pain that he caused her prior to his stint in prison and promised her that things would be different this time. He once again used his acting abilities and as they chatted in their booth, his eyes welled with tears, reminiscent of the performance he gave at the Cabinet for Health and Family Services. It must have worked, because she let Gouker back into her life.

He started sleeping over at Amanda's home within weeks of his release and everything seemed to be going well.[2] During that time, the dependency, neglect and abuse case was winding its way through the court system. This was the case that initially vested the Cabinet with custody of Joshua after his mother's death. Gouker and Little Josh never really had the opportunity to develop a true father-and-son bond. The court began to foster contact between the two by allowing supervised visits beginning on October 28, 2010, not long after Gouker's initial release from prison. Gouker was ordered to cooperate with Child Protective Services and to attend counseling. Amanda watched as he did both. He seemed sincere to her and the Child Protective Services workers and the courts seemed to buy the act as well.

By Christmas of 2010, Josh Young was allowed an unsupervised visit at Amanda's home after his social worker visited the house and deemed it appropriate. Little Josh seemed interested in seeing his father. He was curious about the man who was biologically tied to him but was a virtual stranger. Gouker was extremely nice to him at first and Joshua watched as Gouker charmed everyone around him. He wasn't really aware of his father's violent tendencies at the time and it felt good to know somebody wanted him to be a part of their family. His father was pulling out all the stops to have a relationship with him. That had to mean that his father loved him, right?[3]

Little Josh's reintegration into his father's life occurred when the boy was already in a fragile state. Not only had he lost his own mother less than a year prior to his father's release from prison, but he was the person who found his beloved mom deceased in their home. The vision of that horrible Easter morning continued to haunt the teen. Little Josh was no stranger to change, but his mom had always come back after their time apart. Her death was final. He would never see his mother again and he grieved intensely for her.

Josh's traumatic childhood caused him to appear distant sometimes. He didn't allow himself to get too comfortable anywhere. He knew that in an instant, anything could be taken away without warning. He was a kind and caring child, but his hard-knock past had taught him that getting emotional didn't solve anything and he was increasingly introverted with his emotions. He was actually sensitive and became emotional about things but, as a defense mechanism, he did so privately.

He didn't know exactly what to think about his father and the time he spent at Amanda's home, but he felt wanted. For a child, it felt good that someone was willing to fight for him. Josh decided to give the visitations with his father a chance and, for a time, everything appeared to be going well.

Amanda was nice to him too during the transition and he enjoyed spending time with Trey. Trey and Josh both loved video games and basketball and they hung around with the same circle of friends. They'd known each other since childhood and it was fun getting to reconnect. As he settled in that Christmas Eve for a short unsupervised visit, perhaps Josh thought things were going to work out well for him. Maybe he thought he'd finally found a family in Amanda's cozy little house.[4]

Amanda had worked really hard for her home and had purchased it herself. It wasn't huge or impressive, but it was hers. It must have felt wonderful to have her own little piece of property in the neighborhood that she had frequented since childhood.

The little beige house sat back a bit from the road. The home was a fixer-upper when she purchased it and there were a few things she had never gotten around to fixing. The front door could not be opened from the outside, only from the inside, so they tried not to use it. Most of the traffic came in and out through the back door.

The largest bedroom was on the first floor near the front door and Amanda used that bedroom for herself. There was one bathroom downstairs that everyone used. She had a small kitchen and a living area in addition to a guest bedroom on the first floor. She used that room to store her workout equipment, although Gouker told Child Protective Services that the room would belong to Little Josh once he regained custody. Both her children had bedrooms upstairs, but it wasn't uncommon for Trey to sleep in his sister's room on the floor if she was scared of the dark.

It was a tight squeeze but they all fit. Even with Gouker's entry into the home, the walls hadn't yet begun to close in that Christmas Eve. Little Josh and Trey laughed and joked as they spent hours in front of the TV playing video games after opening their presents. The visit was a success. It was the first of many unsupervised visits that Josh and his father would have over the next few months. When a visit was scheduled, Gouker would find a ride to the Walsh household to pick up Little Josh and he would then bring him back to Amanda's house. He encouraged Little Josh to reintegrate himself into the neighborhood. Gouker's main focus, however, seemed to be spending his time with Amanda and convincing her that he had changed for the better since the early days of their marriage.

Gouker's favorite female cousin from his childhood, Cassi, with whom it's rumored he may have had a sexual relationship, moved to the neighborhood. Amanda suspected that Gouker was cheating on her, possibly with his cousin, and she confronted Gouker. He threatened Amanda and she locked herself away in her room.[5] Amanda was worried, because she had recently learned she was pregnant. How could she bring another child into this mess? Thank goodness her children weren't home to witness her confrontation with Gouker. She knew that she couldn't have this baby. She had to break free from Gouker and if they had a child together, that would never happen. He would never willingly relinquish that control. She saw the way he was with his own son. As far as Gouker was concerned, Little Josh was an extension of him, his property. There was no way he would ever leave her alone if they were tied together by a baby.

An abortion seemed to be the only way out of the situation.

Only a few weeks later, in mid-January, Amanda underwent the abortion.[6] As she had anticipated, Gouker was not happy when he heard the news several weeks later. In the aftermath of the abortion, Amanda attempted to move on with her life without Joshua Gouker. As hard as she tried, she couldn't get him out of her life. He still attempted to contact her and he still dropped by from time to time. He wouldn't let her go.

As 2011 crept into spring, Amanda was in a tug of war with Gouker. The relationship continued to be "off and on." He found ways to weasel his way back into her life and her home. Then another incident of violence would occur and Amanda desperately tried to get away and leave him once and for all. But he could be exceedingly charming when he wanted and she felt herself repeatedly slipping back into his grasp. It was hard to break the cycle that had begun almost twenty years prior when they were just children.[7]

It was easier to avoid Gouker when the kids were home. Both kids had the same visitation schedule, so every other week they would be with her. During these times, it was easier for her to put Gouker out of her mind and stay busy. But on the weeks when the kids were with their dads, she felt more vulnerable and was probably an easier target for Gouker. Eventually, her daughter's father was sent to prison and, as a result, her daughter began staying with Amanda most days. Even then, Gouker found reasons to call or stop by when the kids were at school or with friends or relatives and by the time the kids came home, he was back in the household.[8]

He usually seemed to be on good behavior when the children were there. Gouker appeared to be aware that neither of their fathers had any patience for Gouker's antics and both kids were close to their dads. Gouker seemed to understand that if he ever mistreated the kids or went too far with Amanda in their presence, the kids would report back to their fathers or their fathers' families, neither of which would hesitate to involve Child Protective Services.

Trey did not confide in his father about the state of affairs at his mother's home. There was still a "no contact" order in effect from Terry and Amanda's previous custody battle that precluded contact between Trey and Gouker. Terry Zwicker had always felt that Gouker was a danger to everyone around him and did not want his son anywhere near him. He knew Amanda and Gouker were seeing each other again, but he was not aware Gouker was residing in the home. Trey didn't tell Terry, probably because he did not want to get his mom into trouble.

Instead, Trey began asking his father if he could go to his mom's after school, even on the days that fell on his father's week of visitation. He framed the request as an excuse that he needed to get his sister off of the school bus and babysit her until his mother arrived home from work. In reality, he likely wanted to ensure that his sister was okay and wanted to act as a buffer between her and Gouker. Trey was a protective big brother and he could likely sense the tension in the home that spring. He did not want the dysfunction in the home to affect his sister.

Another reason Trey likely spent more time at his mother's home in the spring of 2011 is that he used some of his wages from his fast-food job to buy a black mixed-breed puppy and the puppy stayed at his mother's house. From the start, the cute little dog wreaked havoc on Amanda's home and Gouker was not a fan. A condition of Trey acquiring the puppy was that he was supposed to train the dog and clean up after it.

From the start, the puppy had trouble with training and it was not uncommon for Amanda to come home and find urine and feces in her's or the kids' beds. Trey loved the puppy, but Trey was not there all the time to take care of it, so after he had the puppy for a month, Amanda made the decision that the dog could no longer stay at her home.

She informed Trey that the puppy was ruining her carpet and tearing apart the house, but that if he wanted to keep it, his grandma was okay with the puppy staying there. She made Trey responsible for delivering the puppy to its new home, but as the days stretched on, he did not make time to do so. That's why Amanda was so relieved when she came home from a long day of work and realized the dog was no longer there.

Breathing a sigh of relief, she searched the house just to make sure. She was happy that Trey had finally done what he said he would.

Amanda changed out of her work clothes into more comfortable attire and had headed into the kitchen to start planning dinner when Trey entered the house. Amanda knew her son and she could tell from his demeanor that something was troubling him. She asked him what was wrong and commended him for taking the puppy to his grandmother's.

Trey told her that he hadn't taken the dog to his grandmother's house; Gouker had killed it instead.

Amanda asked what Trey meant.

Trey told her how Gouker had described taking the dog into the backyard and killing it with a baseball bat. It was a sickening feeling. Amanda loved animals and was shocked that Gouker could do such a thing. She didn't want to believe it. She reached out to Trey, enveloping him in a hug and became determined to get to the bottom of the situation. Could Trey be mistaken?

Amanda told Trey to go upstairs and then stalked out the back of the house, her eyes immediately falling on Gouker. She asked him if he'd killed the dog.

Gouker shrugged very nonchalantly and looked in her eyes, saying that the dog was a menace that went to the bathroom on everything. He said he'd done them a favor. He also offered a bag of marijuana he had in the house as reparation.

He turned around and walked away. Amanda's heart ached for Trey. She didn't understand how Gouker could be so cruel. Not only did he cause suffering to the puppy but he rubbed the incident in Trey's face.[9]

Gouker also killed a cat that had belonged to Amanda's daughter. Months earlier, Amanda's mother had taken a trip to Tennessee with her sister. While they were there, they discovered a box of abandoned kittens that someone had discarded. She brought the kittens back to Kentucky to find them good homes and she gave one to Amanda's daughter. Amanda allowed her to adopt the little yellow stray cat that she called DJ. It often lurked around her backyard and the kids would leave food out for it. After that, DJ the cat stopped by the house on a regular basis for milk and snacks. He was an outdoor cat, so he came and went from the yard as he pleased, but he was a constant fixture at their home.

Sometime in the Spring, Amanda realized that she had not seen the cat in quite a while. She later learned that Gouker bragged that the cat annoyed him, so he took it to the second story of the garage and dropped it to the concrete, killing it. He excised one of the cat's eyeballs and placed it on a stick, chasing around a neighborhood boy, hissing, "I've got my eye on you," as he laughed.[10]

Once again, Gouker demonstrated sociopathic tendencies in his enjoyment of bringing pain to animals and his inability to empathize with the emotional toll his behavior took on those around him. During this time, he and Amanda once again put an end to their relationship, but later in the Spring of 2011, Gouker and Amanda were "on" again. The drama and abuse resumed. Amanda continued to allow Gouker to stay in her home.

During that spring, Amanda was involved in a car accident that totaled her vehicle and left her without transportation to work. Her mother allowed her to use her car to travel to and from work. Eventually, the battery in the car went dead and it wouldn't start.

Gouker's cousin Cassi allowed Amanda to take the battery from her car and place it in Amanda's mother's vehicle so that she could get to work. When she arrived home one evening, Gouker was waiting. Amanda and her daughter were in the car and she rolled down the window as he swiftly approached. Josh asked to use the car, but Amanda refused, reminding him that it was her mother's car.

Her mother carried the insurance on the vehicle and she was not comfortable with allowing Gouker to take the car anywhere, especially on his own. Her mom was not a fan of Gouker and Amanda knew her mom might withhold the car if she found out Amanda had allowed Gouker to drive it. It was stress that Amanda did not need. The last thing she wanted to deal with that day was an inebriated Gouker. When he drank liquor, which was almost an everyday occurrence, he got meaner. It had been a long day and she did not feel like fooling with him that evening. As she and her daughter sat in the parked vehicle, Gouker grabbed a long iron rod and began tapping on the car, lightly at first and then with more and more force as he looked through the window and directly into Amanda's eyes.[11]

Amanda had already locked the car doors. She knew what was coming and she braced herself for it. He didn't get his way, so now Gouker would make her and her daughter pay for it. As the pounding became louder and louder, Amanda turned to her daughter and squeezed her hand. She told her that she was going to try to calm Gouker down and that the girl should not leave the car. This was not the first time Amanda saw that glint in Gouker's eyes and she started to get nervous. He couldn't be reasoned with when he acted that way and she knew her best bet to prevent an incident of violence was to contact the police to remove Gouker from the premises.[12]

Amanda slid from the driver's seat and took off around the side of the house toward the back door with Gouker in quick pursuit. As she reached the side of the home, she felt Gouker's hands on her hair. Grasping a huge chunk, he jerked her backwards and then pushed her forward into the house. Amanda caught herself as she hit the house's exterior and pulled herself back to an upright position.

She darted away again, intent on getting into the home and calling the police.

She heard the door slam behind her as she made her way inside the house and fled toward her bedroom, but she immediately heard the door reopen as Gouker entered behind her. He grabbed her again, aggressively shoving her forward and then backing her against the wall. She begged him to stop because he was hurting her.

But he just grasped her tighter and pressed up against her, pushing her tightly against the wall. They both heard the back door open again. They looked up to see her daughter standing in the doorway, her eyes round as she saw what Gouker was doing to her mother. Gouker looked back at Amanda. For an instant, Gouker clutched Amanda's shirt a little tighter. Then he loosened and dropped his grip. Turning, he nonchalantly strode out the back door without a word.

Amanda called the police and grasped her daughter's hand tightly, pulling her toward the back door. Sticking her head out slowly, she looked both ways for any sign of Gouker. She didn't see him. She and her daughter silently tiptoed around the corner of the house. There was a long blue rod lying in the driveway. It was the tool used to prop up the hood on the vehicle. She picked it up for protection and she and her daughter dashed quickly across the street and crouched behind their neighbor's home, hiding and waiting for help to arrive.[13]

After that incident, it was a while before Amanda saw Gouker again. The thought of how scared her daughter looked the day Gouker had attacked Amanda seemed to make her feel awful and she probably was aware that none of them deserved to live like this. It wasn't fair to the kids, so she tried to move on.

However, Gouker wouldn't let her. He kept calling, begging to see her, and she was almost afraid to tell him no. It is easy to underestimate the pull of a relationship plagued by domestic violence. Gouker and Amanda's dance was a classic, textbook example of domestic violence and the cycle of brutality that is present in such relationships. Someone who has not lived in that situation may be unable to understand how Amanda could continue to place herself and her children in jeopardy by staying in a relationship with Gouker. However, Amanda seemed to feel like she had no choice in the matter.

Amanda wasn't the only recipient of Gouker's manipulation during this time period. Over the preceding months, Gouker had complied with the demands of Child Protective Services and the family court. On March 24, 2011, the court awarded temporary custody of Little Josh to Gouker and Little Josh moved. However, he wouldn't be residing at Amanda's home as Child Protective Services and the court believed. Instead, he bounced around the neighborhood, staying mostly at Gouker's cousin Cassi's home. There was a dining room area on the first floor that was converted to a bedroom for Josh, with a pallet on the floor where he slept.[14]

Josh was stunned when he learned that his father had gained custody of him. It was something that he never anticipated could happen and his foster parents were similarly shocked. Little Josh had enjoyed some of his early visits with his dad. He was able to see old friends and he tried to get to know his father better, but that was a far cry from actually having to move in with Gouker. He knew there was a court date on March 24th, but it floored him when his foster parents informed him after attending court that day that he would be moving in with his father. He had never lived apart from his sister and he was anxious about leaving her. However, he knew he needed to give it a chance since the court had made its decision, so he packed up his bags and settled in with his father.

Gouker was not the caring father he had pretended to be for the court.

Child Protective Services missed the signs of Gouker's mistreatment of Josh and Trey as did the Division of Probation and Parole. Gouker was not living at the address given to either office and he was continually partaking in alcohol and illegal substances, both of which are prohibited when a person is on parole.

Prior to Gouker regaining custody, Josh had been a good student in Advanced Placement classes who rarely missed a day of high school. Once he moved in with his father, Josh quit the wrestling team. He started missing large blocks of school days and his grades suffered. He fell behind in the Advanced Placement classes that he'd worked so hard to enter. Gouker didn't seem to care. Anyone who paid any attention should have seen that this child was in trouble. But no one came to his aid. He simply fell through the cracks and was left to spiral out of control in the custody of his father.

According to the National Coalition for Child Protection Reform, Child Protective Services is overwhelmed by the amount of cases it encounters: "They often make bad decisions in both directions—leaving some children in dangerous homes, even as more children are taken from homes that are safe or could be made safe with the right kinds of services...So they make even more mistakes in both directions. That is almost always the real explanation for the horror-story cases that make headlines."[15]

Because of how overwhelmed caseworkers become by the number of children in foster care, whether they need to be there or not, CPS often either removes children from homes from which they should not be removed or they leave children in circumstances no child should endure. In Little Josh's case, he was removed from a caring foster family, the Walshes, and placed with a recently released felon who had a history of abuse.

Joshua was forced once again to re-acclimate to life in new surroundings. It was something he had done countless times before, but this time was different. For the first time in his life, he was not under the same roof as his sister and that was hard for him. He knew she was well taken care of, but he still missed seeing the bubbly little girl every day. He spent a lot of nights at his cousin's house. She seemed nice enough but she was basically a stranger to Josh.

As Little Josh tried to make a home for himself, his father came and went as he pleased. Josh was left to his own devices and he spent a lot of time bouncing back and forth between Amanda's home, Cassi's home and the homes of friends in the neighborhood. Gouker was focused on reintegrating himself into Amanda's life and seemed to prioritize spending time with her over spending time with his child. Gouker was happy to let Little Josh fend for himself as long as he knew he could assert control over him when he wanted to.

His father was an intimidating man, so Joshua tried not to say much. He could not express his real feelings to Gouker for fear of angering the man. He couldn't help but notice that his father had a temper, especially when it came to Amanda. He witnessed several altercations between the two and he wanted no part of it. He focused on keeping to himself and staying out of his father's way.[16]

During this time, although he used Amanda's house as his address, Gouker was not faithful to Amanda. Even when he was living in her home, he kept contact with several other women.

Trey worked a shift at the fast-food restaurant on May 8, 2011. After work, Amanda picked him up and Trey realized that he had left some items at his dad's house that he wanted to take to his mother's place for the week. Amanda stopped by Terry Zwicker's home to retrieve those items and Trey ran into the house to do so. Terry and his son spoke briefly about the upcoming fishing trip that was scheduled for the following weekend and Trey hugged his dad and left.

At this time, Gouker was beginning to worm his way back into Amanda's life and after a brief hiatus they had begun working things out in an attempt to reunite. They planned a cookout at Amanda's that evening, throwing some hot dogs and hamburgers on the grill and inviting some of the neighbors over to the home. It was a cookout to celebrate Mother's Day.

Trey sat by Amanda's side for most of the evening even though many of the neighborhood boys, including Josh Young, were roaming the neighborhood together and playing basketball. Amanda encouraged Trey to go with his friends if he wanted to, but he insisted that he wanted to spend time with her since it was Mother's Day.[17] Trey was becoming increasingly independent. He worked hard in school and even made his own money working at only fourteen years old. He had a lot of friends and spent enough time with them. It was nice for him to celebrate with Amanda, especially on a day as special as Mother's Day.

Although Gouker refused to work himself, he began interfering with Amanda's job. Amanda had now worked at the fast-food restaurant for over seventeen years. She began the job as a teenager and was so happy with it that when Trey became old enough, she recommended that he begin working there as well. It was nice to work with her son and a group of coworkers that had been there with her for many years. Over that time, she had worked her way up from cashier to general manager.

All types of people visited the location and it was easy to stay busy there. Through the job, she came into contact with a variety of people and, being the conscientious and dedicated worker that she was, Amanda was always friendly. She was attached to the job and derived a great amount of pride from it. Working at the fast-food place had helped her to save the money to purchase her home. She was grateful to have the job and for the relationships she fostered while working there.

Gouker was not as appreciative. Although he had been living rent-free in her home on and off throughout the preceding months, he was not contributing financially. He was becoming increasingly controlling when it came to Amanda. He did not want her speaking to other people without him and he did not like her working and being away from him for long hours.

On the morning of May 9, 2011, he began to telephone Amanda incessantly as she attempted to perform the duties of her job. Gouker had repeatedly attempted to persuade her to stop working at the restaurant and he made her feel guilty when Amanda did go to work. Her life became a living hell because of his tendency to call both her cell and work phone repeatedly. Amanda was pushed by Gouker to the breaking point that day, so she abruptly quit the job she'd held for so long. It was devastating for Amanda, but she didn't feel like she had a choice.[18]

As she settled into her routine that evening, they decided to have another cookout as a way to lift her spirits. As she began preparing food in the kitchen, Amanda's supervisor called her to check in. It was not like Amanda to make such a hasty decision and her boss was worried. She wanted to set up a meeting for the following day so they could talk about Amanda coming back to work and Amanda agreed, recognizing that her decision to quit was based mostly on trying to yield to Gouker's demands. She hadn't thought the decision through before she made it and she already regretted it.[19]

Gouker overheard the call and it angered him. He stepped up behind Amanda and insisted that she call back and cancel the meeting. Gouker shoved the phone into her hand and watched as she dialed. As her manager answered, she explained that she would not be in for the meeting the following day and that her decision to resign was final. As she hung up the phone, she felt herself begin to cry. How had it come to this? Despite Amanda's pain, a huge

Cheshire grin spread across Gouker's face. Patting her on the back, he was pleased with himself, oblivious and numb to her pain. He'd gotten what he wanted, so he was happy.

When Trey returned home from work that evening, Amanda was hesitant to tell him that she had quit her job. It was a big change and she knew it might affect Trey in a bad way. As she considered how she would tell him, Gouker broke the news to Trey before Amanda had a chance to do so. Gouker seemed to delight in telling Trey about the course of events, knowing that he would be disappointed by the news.

Trey and his mother had always enjoyed working together and he was confused by her resignation. They talked about her decision and about Trey's future at his part-time job. Out of Gouker's hearing, she told Trey that she would likely try to get her job back. She left the decision up to him of whether he wanted to continue. Trey chose to stay.[20] He enjoyed being able to make his own money. He also liked the job but he struggled with Amanda's resignation. It was the only job he could remember her having and it was a big change. Amanda was proud of him for his decision to continue working. It impressed her that he could stand up for himself when she could not.

The evening proceeded and everyone managed to have a nice time at the cookout. Amanda tried to keep her work problems out of her mind. It was just too hard to think about. At some point, Gouker disappeared and Amanda felt the sickness return. That job was such an important part of her life. Not only had Gouker forced her to leave it, but he was not helping around the house or contributing. As the sickness turned to anger, Amanda stalked out the back door and in the direction of Cassi's home where she knew Gouker had gone.

As she beat on the front door, she heard movement inside. She felt for the knob and pushed the door open, sticking her head into the entryway. Gouker, grasping the door, pushed her out onto the front porch. Gouker disappeared back into the home, shutting the front door firmly behind him. Amanda was left to wait. Gouker had a way of making a person feel wrong or humiliated when he was actually the one acting inappropriately.

Amanda was left to stand on the front steps while he re-entered the house and took his sweet time in finishing his business there. After several minutes he reappeared, his demeanor changed. They argued all the way back to her house and Gouker reached out, wrapping his hands around her neck, leaving large, red marks. By the time she entered the house, she was crying.

Trey witnessed his mother's emotional state and looked at Gouker. Trey was getting bigger and stronger every day and Gouker probably felt threatened that he was in the home. Trey would do anything for his mother and he could not stand to see her upset. He had witnessed his fair share of shouting matches between Amanda and Gouker and he did not like the way that Gouker treated her.

He asked his mom if she was okay. She said she was. Trey cast a glance at Gouker, shaking his head. He told Gouker to stop making his mom cry. Gouker shook his head and he and Amanda disappeared into the bedroom. When they emerged, everything seemed fine again.

At the end of the evening, Gouker and Amanda decided to have an even larger cookout the following day. It kept her mind off the drama at work and her personal issues with Gouker. It was good to see her kids having fun and she always enjoyed having their friends over. The more people around, the less chance Gouker would lash out at her.

During the planning stages the following day, she reached out to her brother. It had been awhile since they last saw each other, so she invited him to stop over for the cookout, explaining that they would eat between seven and eight o'clock. Her brother had always been close with her and her children. However, he did not approve of her relationship with Gouker. It was hard to forget the way Gouker had treated his sister in the early days of their relationship and hard to ignore his more recent mistreatment of her. Amanda was a grown woman and he couldn't tell her how to live, so to keep it from upsetting him, he kept his distance. But on the evening of May 10, he decided to let bygones be bygones that evening and stop by.

As her brother pulled into the driveway, he was immediately met by Gouker's cold stare. Gouker adopted a defensive stance and characteristically puffed out his chest, protecting his territory and marking his turf. It wasn't until he saw the man exit the vehicle that Gouker realized he was Amanda's brother so he relaxed. Then, like a switch, fun-loving, friendly Gouker materialized and he quickly led his brother-in-law around back and into the kitchen.

Amanda was thrilled to see her brother and stepped forward to give him a hug. Trey, too, seemed excited and immediately came over and began chatting with his uncle. Everyone appeared to be having a great time. Neighborhood kids congregated near the basketball hoop and played a little as the night progressed. At one point, the kids disappeared over to the creek bed and came back yelling and screaming about a huge turtle they had found. Gouker followed them back to the culvert. The cookout appeared like any other across America, friends and family getting together to eat and hang out. The grill gleamed as the burgers and hot dogs sizzled and before long everyone settled down to eat.

By then, Amanda's brother was gone. He had injured his hand and it required stitches, so he left to go to the hospital. He would testify later that he had cut his hand on the chain basketball net while playing basketball. However, Little Josh later said that there was no net on the hoop. It was broken that day and Amanda's brother actually cut his hand on the grill. Nevertheless, he left without eating and, when he was finished at the hospital, he called Amanda and was told it was too late to return.

As the party wound to a close, Amanda offered Gouker's cousin Cassi the option of bathing her kids at Amanda's house. The water was shut off at Cassi's house, so Amanda knew the kids would be unable to bathe there, but Gouker's cousin said no to the offer.

The majority of the guests had already left. Only Big Josh, Amanda, her kids and Cassi's family remained. Little Josh had already returned to Cassi's house where he planned to stay the night and play video games. Eventually, Cassi's family left as well.

At that point in the evening, Amanda's kids were busy preparing for bed and she told them to begin their showers. Her daughter took hers first and then Trey hopped in the shower after she was finished. Amanda giggled as she watched Trey emerge from the bathroom with a towel wrapped around his waist. As he headed for his room, the towel gaped slightly in the back, exposing a tiny sliver of his buttock. Amused by her son, she shouted at him to cover his "shiny hiney" as Trey dashed for the stairs to his room. He turned quickly to grin and then disappeared up the narrow staircase.

She hollered that she and Gouker were going to go for a walk and Trey should get into bed as she walked toward the back door of the home. The kids were aware of their nightly routine and by that point they were going through their usual motions just like any other school night. They generally took showers at nine and were in bed by ten. It was almost ten o'clock when Amanda and Gouker went out the back door and settled onto the back porch listening to the radio.

Amanda watched as Gouker reached up to unscrew the three motion detection lights. She didn't think much of his actions at the time. They wanted a little privacy and the slightest movement set off the lights, which would then illuminate the entire porch and backyard.

As Gouker unscrewed the last of the lights and settled back into the chair next to Amanda, both were startled by a slight movement at the back door as it was slowly pushed open. Amanda watched as Trey started out the door then, looking to the left, spotted her and Gouker.

Trey had redressed himself in street clothes following his shower. He wore dark jeans and a dark t-shirt with his favorite black tennis shoes on his feet. He froze and locked eyes with his mother before silently slipping back into the house. Amanda raised her eyebrows and rose, following him back inside.

She yelled up from the bottom of the stairs that Trey should get into bed immediately.

Trey responded that he would and told her he loved her.

Amanda turned and headed back out to the porch where Gouker sat waiting. She shared that she thought Trey was trying to be sneaky.

Gouker shrugged his shoulders. The pair stayed on the porch for a little longer. It had been a very hot day but the evening was cooling down into a lovely night. They listened to the radio and relaxed, eventually deciding to retire to Amanda's room around eleven o'clock. Once they climbed into bed, they were intimate. Leaning back on the pillow, Gouker exhaled and said that he needed cigarettes. He asked her to drive to a nearby gas station's convenience store with him.

Amanda threw her clothes back on and they dashed out the door, climbing into her car and leaving the kids sleeping inside the house. They drove to a gas station about a mile away and both strolled inside. Although it was late at night, the area was anything but deserted. That particular part of town housed several late-night establishments. There was a strip club adjacent to the station and, even on a weeknight, cars cluttered the parking lot.

Although he generally smoked anything he could get his hands on, with a little money lining his pocket Gouker chose a more expensive pack and they left the store. At the time, they paid no mind to the surveillance video that was rolling as they made their purchases.

Within minutes of leaving the station, Gouker and Amanda were safely back home, where they entered the house and went back into her bedroom. Gouker was not sated by their earlier romp and he reached across Amanda to the nightstand next to her bed and grabbed her phone. Hitting the record button, he made a quick video of their second tryst of the evening and he then watched it play back, appearing to be impressed by his own prowess. By that time, it was nearly one o'clock in the morning and Gouker rolled over. Within minutes Amanda heard him snoring.

She propped herself up with a pillow and grabbed the remote control. As she flipped through the channels, she tried to ignore Gouker's snoring on the pillow next to her. Finally fed up with the noise, Amanda powered off the television and went to sleep for the night. Since she had quit her job, she did not have to be up as early as usual and she hoped she would have a good night's sleep and get the work stress out of her mind. She must have known she could trust Trey to wake himself up and prepare for school the following morning.

It was not unusual for Trey to get himself off to school in the morning without Amanda's help. He normally woke up around 6:30 A.M. and was out the door to his bus stop within minutes. The bus stop was located just a short distance down the street and he was easily able to walk there and catch his bus. Normally, Amanda got up as Trey was walking out the back door. She would then take a quick shower before getting her daughter ready for school. On the morning of the eleventh, she was exhausted from the evening before, between the cookout and Gouker staying over. She had only had a few hours of sleep when she heard some movement in the bathroom early that morning.

Assuming that it was Trey getting ready for school, Amanda didn't bother to get up and check. The bathroom was adjacent to her bedroom and she often heard Trey banging around in there in the mornings before he left for school. She concluded that the sound was Trey and she rolled over and fell back to sleep. When her alarm went off shortly afterward, Amanda started to stir and pulled back the covers from the bed.

Gouker patted her as he rose from bed and headed out into the entryway, assuring her that he would get her daughter ready for school. Amanda's daughter's bus always came at 8:15 A.M. and it picked her up in front of the house. A few minutes after eight o'clock, she dashed into the room and planted a quick peck on Amanda's cheek.

Within minutes Gouker was back in the bedroom and Amanda was busy taking a quick shower to get ready for the day ahead. It was set to be another nice Spring day and Gouker suggested that they visit McNeely Lake Park. This was something they did often together and Amanda had hinted over the previous few days that a visit to the park was long overdue. Feeding the ducks had always been a relaxing pastime for her and she must have thought that it would put her in a good mood. They were soon en route to the park.

McNeely Lake was about a ten minute drive from their home. It wasn't a huge body of water, but it was large enough that there were always ducks and geese around. When the kids were little, she would often take them there with bread chunks to feed the ducks. It was also a great spot for fishing and for years it had been a place children and families would congregate to swim, fish and play on the jungle gym. It was a popular location for picnics and cookouts. They spent a few hours walking around the area and talking about their future together.

Gouker had brought his football. He told Amanda that he wanted to teach her to throw a perfect spiral with the ball and they spent about an hour tossing it around. Times like this reminded Amanda why she kept going back to Gouker. When things were good, they were really good. They liked doing the same things and when he was in a good mood they could have a great time together and she would put the bad times out of her mind. He talked about wanting to make a home for them together. At that moment, Amanda pictured a future with Gouker and she wanted to make a life with him, a life where they both felt right at home.

As they left the park that afternoon, Gouker noticed a cute little house with a "For Rent" sign in the yard. They walked around the home, which seemed to be vacant, and even peeked in a few windows. Amanda watched as Gouker telephoned the number listed on the sign. He walked away from her as he spoke with the person on the other end of the line. He was able to convince the realtor to come and show them the house.

It had three small bedrooms. As they walked through the cozy little house, Amanda listened as Gouker told the realtor that they had two children who would be living in the home with them. Thinking this was odd, Amanda immediately began questioning him when they left the potential rental home after their walk-through, asking why he had said they only had two children and where would Little Josh be living.

Gouker appeared to catch himself. Was it a slip of the tongue? Until Amanda's question, he didn't seem to realize what he had said. He insisted that it was just a mistake and that the realtor didn't need to know everything about them.[21]

Amanda shrugged it off. She could sense Gouker beginning to puff up and it just wasn't worth the argument. They got into the car and headed back to the house. The day had flown by and Amanda knew the kids should be home soon.

After Gouker and Amanda arrived home, she was bending over near the couch and was shocked to notice Trey's school bag lying next to the sofa on the floor. Glancing quickly at the clock, she realized that it was almost three o'clock. The school day was over, but it was too early for Trey to have arrived home on the bus and to have left his book bag. He shouldn't have been home for at least another hour. She felt her heart beat a little faster. Something wasn't right. She grabbed her phone and dialed Trey, listening anxiously as the phone rang several times before going to voicemail.

She expressed her worry to Gouker, who suggested that maybe Trey had cut school. But Amanda knew that wasn't something a good student like Trey would do.

She picked up the phone again and called him several times in a row. There was still no answer. Every minute was like agony and by the time her daughter arrived home, Amanda was truly worried. She started calling Trey's friends to see if anyone had seen him or if he had been on the bus that day. She started walking around the neighborhood looking for Trey.

By that point, Amanda appeared to be in a full-blown panic. Trey had never done anything like this. It was so uncharacteristic of him not to answer his cell phone. He was always prompt in answering it, especially because he must have known how Amanda could worry. With each house that she visited, her heart pounded more. No one had seen Trey.

As she dashed around frantically, her phone buzzed. Thinking it could be her son, she quickly looked down as her heart skipped a beat. It wasn't Trey. It was Amanda's cousin, wanting to let her know that a body had been found at the high school and he was heading that way.

Amanda reached down and grabbed her daughter by the hand. She dashed two doors down to Gouker's cousin's house, leaving her daughter in Cassi's care. Little Josh rushed up to Amanda and his father, wondering what was happening. He had not seen Trey either but he could tell by the look on Amanda's face that something was desperately wrong. With Gouker and Little Josh in tow, Amanda sprinted down the street toward the high school. A crowd had already gathered and almost immediately she spotted Trey's dad, Terry, approaching.

They stood in the midst of the crowd and waited. No one was giving any answers but Amanda saw that the area where the body had been found was cordoned off with yellow tape. Amanda stared as one of the detectives strode purposefully toward Terry. They spoke for a few moments.

Trey's father was getting even more upset. Amanda strained to watch as Terry walked toward the hilltop with the detective at his side. She focused on Trey's father's agonized face for what seemed like an eternity and gasped for breath at what happened next. Terry's face tightened and he fell to his knees.

Suddenly, Amanda heard a scream. It was her own.

Chapter 6

Dark Reality

T he next few hours were an absolute blur for Trey's family and friends. Homicide detectives secured a warrant to search Amanda's residence. Some of the injuries to Trey appeared to have come from a blunt object, while the head wound could have been caused by a sharp object. The type of murder weapon that was used was unclear.

The warrant allowed officers to search the house, the garage and surrounding grounds for any type of weapon that could have caused Trey's injuries. During this time, officers spoke with Amanda and other members of the household. All the while, crime scene technicians pored over every square inch of the home, ultimately tagging and collecting three baseball bats from Trey's bedroom, a sword and a knife from the garage.

Both Amanda and Gouker submitted to a DNA swab for comparison to the items seized from the home and the crime scene. The officers were there throughout the evening. It was a parent's worst nightmare. The Louisville Metro Police Department homicide detectives launched an investigation. Louisville was no stranger to violent homicides, but homicides against children were rare. Officers were dedicated to solving this case as quickly as possible.

As the investigation progressed, Amanda stayed inside her house and seemed to want to be left alone. Gouker continued to stay there and as Amanda become more and more withdrawn, Gouker became increasingly controlling and violent toward her. His actions began under the guise of helping her through her grief and quickly morphed into emotional abuse and complete control. Amanda did not realize at the time but Gouker arranged to have all her voicemails and calls forwarded to his phone. When her friends and loved ones attempted to visit her home to offer support, Gouker told them to leave and even went so far as to tell some of the visitors not to return, ever.

As the days passed and Trey's family tried to deal with their grief, the homicide detectives continued to investigate the case. On May 19, Detective Scott Russ pulled into Amanda's driveway around 7:00 P.M. with Detective Roy Stalvey accompanying him. He needed to speak with Amanda again. While Terry was available anytime the police contacted him, they had less contact with Amanda. It was a slight cause of concern for the detectives and Detective Russ wanted to speak with Trey's mother face-to-face. As he knocked on the door, it swung open and Amanda stood in the home's entryway.

She had been expecting them. Detective Russ had called earlier in the day and suggested that he would likely stop by later to ask her more questions. As they entered the home, they watched Gouker walk around the corner and he stood directly before them at Amanda's side.

The detective believed people close to Trey and his family possibly knew more than they were disclosing and he wanted to speak with Amanda further to see if there was anything she could add to their investigation. By this point, several people acquainted with Gouker had informed police that he was controlling Amanda and that he was also mean and abusive. With that in mind, they asked Gouker to leave so they could speak with Amanda alone. Although he was not happy about it, Gouker did what they requested. He told Amanda that he would walk to Cassi's house and would see her later that night. Detective Russ asked Gouker to stay at his cousin's until he saw that their cruiser was gone. Once Gouker strode out the door, the detectives settled into chairs in the living room and prepared to talk privately with Amanda.

Until that point, Amanda probably had not imagined that Gouker could be involved in Trey's murder. When Trey was mistreated at the bus stop, it was Gouker who went there with him and warned those bothering him that he should be left alone. He stood up for her son and he slept nightly with her. She must have had trouble believing that he could be involved in killing one of the people she loved most in the world.

Amanda told the officers about how a group of kids had approached Trey at the bus stop and stole his cell phone a few weeks prior to his death. The following day when he exited the school bus, the group was there again and they were forcibly taking cell phones from kids in the area. She was not sure how he got it back, but he did. She appeared to accept Gouker's assertion that the apartment complex kids were involved.

Detectives had already followed up on that lead and they quickly determined that it was a dead end. Several of the young men from the apartments were incarcerated at the detention center in downtown Louisville. Detectives interviewed several of them at the detention center and it was clear they had alibis at the time of Trey's death and that they knew nothing about the murder.

The detectives instead wanted to know more about the dynamics in the home and they started asking questions about Joshua Gouker and his son.[1]

"...And Josh Junior?" the detective asked.

"[He's] Joshua's son with Angie Young. She committed suicide last year," Amanda answered.

"Where does he normally stay?"

"He normally stays with us. Josh and I went nine years without communication, so the past six months, we are getting to know each other again."

"Right," the detective said.

"So he spends, Little Josh goes pretty much with Cassi for now."

"How long has that been going on?"

Amanda hesitated. She knew that Child Protective Services and the court believed that Little Josh was living at her home and she was reluctant to tell the officer differently, "Um..."

"Since the incident happened or since before that?"

"Um, no, before this," she relented.

Amanda continued to reveal information about the family. Little Josh, she disclosed, had returned to school that morning for the first time since Trey's death. Amanda's daughter was devastated at the loss of her brother and Amanda was allowing her to miss school that day. Her daughter was staying with her paternal grandmother while Amanda dealt with her own feelings of grief. She must have hoped that her daughter would return to school the following day, so that she could try to ease back into normal day-to-day activities.

"What about Trey and [Little] Josh's relationship?" Detective Russ asked, leaning forward in his chair.

She sighed and said, "They were good even when Josh was in prison and I lived in Preston Oaks and so did Little Josh's mom. Our kids grew up together. They always knew each other. They never had a bad relationship. They were good to each other. They were friends. They were good friends regardless of being stepbrothers, because in their minds they didn't realize they were stepbrothers when they were little kids."[2]

Detective Russ nodded, "So what about Trey and [Big] Josh? Was there any kind of discipline stuff there?"

Amanda was quick to respond in the negative, "No, I have never disciplined Josh's son and he has never disciplined my son, ever."

"Well, what about your and [Big] Josh's relationship? I've heard it can get physical sometimes?"

"We have a very passionate relationship. When it's good, it's fantastic."

"Right."

"And when it's bad, it's bad...He's never physically hurt me but he has emotionally and I do the same thing to him. He makes me angry and I go after his heart, stuff to make him hurt."

"But you say he never physically hurt you?"

"No, we've never been in no physical...he's never punched me," she quickly responded, making excuses for her husband.

Detective Russ looked up, astonished, remembering anecdotes others had told him about the relationship between Amanda and Josh Gouker, "But didn't he hang you over a balcony?"

"That was many, many years ago and it wasn't..."

"Well, that's part of never. I mean..." Detective Russ was skeptical.

Amanda was quick to defend Gouker for his behavior at the motel: "That's not, there wasn't, that was more of a show," she insisted.[3]

"That's a pretty serious show."

"Yeah well, back then he was a different person."

"Right, and I'm just asking you. I am not trying to be disrespectful. I'm just trying to find out...you say never, but then we hear that he hung..." His voice trailed off and he shook his head.

"Well we, he never..." She paused, pondering. "I've been in physical altercations before with men in my life in many different relationships." This was true. Amanda had emergency protective orders in more than one previous relationship. It appeared that Amanda had not participated in a relationship during her adult life that was not marred by domestic violence.

"Right."

"I haven't had that issue with Josh. He's been a different person since he got out of jail. He sincerely apologized for anything, any wrongdoings he ever caused."

"Um hmm."

"And I sincerely believe him and I still believe him to this day. He loves me and I love him."

"Right."

"And I truly, honestly, wholeheartedly believe that he's my mate for life. We're a good team. Like I said, we have a lot of passion between us. We think alike. The only thing we don't have alike is we can't stand to watch television shows together. He likes sports and I like soaps and all that."

"And you said there was no discipline with him and Trey?" Russ asked.

"No, he did not discipline my child. The worst he ever did was sometimes Trey might sneak into the bedroom and steal loose change or whatever, so Josh put a lock on the door to keep Trey from stealing change."

"Right."

"We just know that Trey was going in there and I told my son not to go in my room. I have adult toys in there and he ran across them once. So I've had to keep my door locked."

"I understand."

"He's a teenage boy," she said, shrugging her shoulders.

"I understand," Detective Russ nodded. "What about when you and Josh had verbal altercations or fights or anything, how did Trey react to that?"

"It hurt his feelings. Of course it would; any kid is going to take their parent's side. So, when I'm mad at Josh, my kid is going to be mad at Josh."[4]

"Trey's a big boy," the detective observed. "I mean he was one hundred and eighty pounds."

Amanda nodded, "He is a big kid."

"Was there ever a point where he confronted Josh and said 'Look, you're not going to do this to my mom. I'm not gonna take it.'"

Amanda pursed her lips and looked upward. "One time they talked," she said, her eyes beginning to well with tears. "And Trey said, look, just don't make my mom cry. It hurts me," she said, clutching her arms across her stomach. "He said, I don't care if you come back in her life. Just don't make my mom cry."

"How long ago was that?"

"Maybe a few weeks," she replied, shaking her head slowly. She paused slightly and seemed to ponder everything, "We have not had a drama-filled life, other than mine and Josh's spats. What we fight over is just testing each other's patience. Like, I texted a friend looking for another friend's phone number for work, 'cause the number was disconnected, so I texted another friend and said 'miss ya' at the end. So I come home and my phone is sitting there and he's like, 'who's this man you missed?'"

"Yeah."

"You know, so that caused a little argument and that was our last breakup. That's what we broke up over," she said, rolling her eyes. "I told another man I missed him and it was actually just a friend!"

"About how long ago was that?"

"Like about two weeks ago, I am guessing, it's hard to…I mean just one week. It's been a hard week. Or maybe a week before that. I'm guessing maybe two weeks, three weeks. I don't know. We break up often because we are just learning each other."

"None of those injuries you had and I know it's hard to answer these questions, none of those injuries we thought you had on your neck; you say they are hickeys?" Detective Russ raised his eyebrows, gesturing toward Amanda's neck.

"All hickeys," she insisted.

"They're not, umm, some of them look like bruises around your neck."

"No," she said, emphatically shaking her head from side to side.

"The ones on your arms, none of them are bruises or anything like that?"

"Promise you," she replied, looking directly into the detective's eyes and raising her hand.[5]

He tried asking one more time: "Nothing over that 'miss you' text resulted in any kind of big knock-down, drag-out fight?"

"Nothing. I promise to God; those are passionate love," she said, her face pale and serious.

"But he was upset obviously, because you all broke up. Do you think he would ever say, 'Hey, I'll do something to Trey to show her?'"

Amanda shook her head and vigorously protested, "No, never. You ask any kid that's ever met [Big] Josh. Every kid loves him. You ask any kid. I'm telling you. Every kid loves Josh. He protects people that are weaker than him. He takes care of kids. Ask Little Josh's half-sister. She loves Big Josh. He's great with kids. He's got a big heart. He grew up with a great man, but his mom was not a great woman."

"What about the whole bird story that I heard about?" Detective Russ asked.

"You heard that story from my mom," Amanda replied matter-of-factly.

"Well, I heard it from some neighbors too."

"That's because Josh told 'em. Josh walks out back and a bird come flying and he saw it out of his peripheral. He raised his arm up and he hit the bird, just like that. It wasn't nothing murderous. It wasn't nothing violent. He just seen something flying toward his head out of his peripheral," she reiterated.

"Right."

"And he went like that," she said, raising her hand in the air and swinging it back and forth, "And he hit the bird. The bird laid on the ground and he said, 'Ya'll come look at this with me and my mom.'"

"Okay, it was some other people. It wasn't your mom I heard it from."

"There's nothing to hide," she stated, minimizing Gouker's third occasion of harming an animal. The detective sensed that Amanda was beginning to bristle at his questioning regarding Joshua Gouker, so he switched gears and began speaking to her about Trey. He wanted to know the identity of Trey's close friends. He needed to get to the bottom of why Trey was at the creek bed in the late night hours of May 10, 2011, and he wanted to know who might have been with him.

Amanda began speaking about Trey's circle of friends. She had no idea who would hurt her son. He was well liked in the neighborhood. "I have wracked my brain and wracked my brain," Amanda said. "I can't think of who would do him harm or why else he would go there. There's gotta be...he only had this one friend circle that I knew of and every one of his friends are here on a regular basis."

Amanda began naming Trey's close friends.

"And these are all the kids that are always around each other?" asked Stalvey.

"Yeah, always. They attend school together and I attended school with their parents and their parents attended school with my parents. This is a very close-knit community, this one street. From the end to the other end, we all grew up together. We are all related in some way or another or connected in some way or another."

"Have you heard about anybody out here shooting at anybody?"[6]

Amanda shook her head, "Never. I mean, you hear gunshots all the time. You're not far from Newburg. You're not far from the apartments and there's rednecks up and down the street. It's common to hear gunshots. On big holidays, you hear a lot of it around here, but it's not rare to hear it in the middle of the summertime for no reason. Just these redneck men shootin' 'em off in their backyards. But this is not a violent neighborhood," Amanda paused, likely thinking about the events of the past week that had turned her life upside down. "At least, it wasn't a violent neighborhood," she added quietly.

As Detective Russ reentered the conversation, he began to question Amanda regarding the boys that she identified as Trey's closest friends, "Do you think [these individuals are] capable of hurting Trey?"

"No, no."

Amanda quickly interrupted the questioning. She did not believe any of Trey's friends were involved in his murder. "None of these boys. They love each other. They are family...they grew up together. They love each other, from kindergarten up..." she trailed off. "They were in my dad's wedding. I mean we're, everybody's happy people."

The detective could clearly see the pain in Amanda's eyes and it was obvious that it was difficult for her to function. She had mentioned earlier that she felt the detectives had abandoned her and that she believed they were not keeping her aware of how the investigation was going. Detective Russ addressed those concerns: "When I talked to you this morning on the phone, you said something about how you felt like I had abandoned you and that kind of confused me. I wasn't really sure what you were talking about, because I've been in constant contact with you the best I could and Josh and Terry. I kind of felt just the way you felt about me, 'cause you've not called me one time since this happened, so I kind of felt like maybe you abandoned me. I've asked you to come to the office a few times and you wouldn't do that."

Amanda hung her head and closed her eyes, "I don't wanna leave the house and I say y'all can come here. I just don't want to go out. I don't want to go out and for some reason, maybe it was misunderstood, but I was under the impression that you wanted me to take a lie detector test the day after my son was put in the grave."

"I never once told anybody. I never told Josh that. I never told your mother that. I never told Terry. I never once asked you to take a polygraph. Never once did I bring that up...Listen to me, the way you could have confirmed that is you simply could have called me. I've not got one phone call from you and it concerns me a little bit."

She was emphatic, "I have nothing to hide. I need to know what happened to my kid. The school never called me...I just need to know. I need someone to help me find out what happened to my kid."

"We are. I'm gonna do the absolute best I can, to follow every bit of leads and evidence that we can, but I also need your help."

"You've got my help."

"Like I told Josh, in the big scheme of things right now, some of the answers you are wanting, are not..." He paused. "They can't be answered. The only person that does know what happened, is the person that did it. The problem is, if we say anything and it gets out and then gets to the papers and then gets to the media, it gets distorted. We simply can't do anything that is going to compromise the investigation. We'd rather catch a murderer than appease everybody with certain bits of information."

Seeming to understand, Amanda nodded. She appeared to want answers, but one could see she did not want anything to interfere with the investigation. The most important thing to her was learning who killed her son. Gouker had achieved his goal of isolating Amanda and she did not have a lot of people to turn to. She surely felt that her family and people on the street hated her and Gouker. She described this to police as they closed the interview with questions regarding the atmosphere in the area in the aftermath of Trey's death. Detectives were beginning to realize that Gouker was unpopular on the street and they wanted to know why.

It seemed the neighborhood already understood what Amanda had yet to realize. Gouker was a dangerous man and the street was a better place when he was not living on it. Within months of him returning to the neighborhood, a child was dead.

The detectives assured her that they would get her the answers she so desperately needed but it could take time. As they spoke, Amanda became increasingly upset and began to cry. Preparing to end the interview, Detective Russ attempted to calm her. "Sometimes these things don't get resolved, obviously, overnight. We are looking at over a week now. So, I mean, I'm gonna be working it til I retire. I'm hoping we can get something resolved quickly, but sometimes it takes time. Evidence gets processed at a slow pace sometimes and we just gotta make sure we get it right." With that sentiment, they ended the conversation with Amanda and she was left alone in the house to think about her talk with the detectives.

They had asked a lot of questions about her husband and it was unsettling. Prior to her meeting with Detectives Stalvey and Russ, she had not allowed herself to consider the possibility that Gouker would hurt Trey or could be involved. However, after her conversation with the detectives, she must have started to wonder. After all, she was aware that Gouker did have a violent streak. Her memory had to have been jogged. Was it possible that Gouker had left her bed the night of Trey's death? Was it possible that he was involved?

Detective Russ had brought up serious doubts about her husband's involvement in Trey's death. The police asked so many questions about him. Gouker seemed to be their main focus that evening. Amanda began to secretly pack a bag, apparently waiting for a chance to escape. She was scared of Gouker and that fear was due to more than the way he treated her. The questioning must have given her serious reservations about him and she probably believed that she and her daughter were no longer safe in the house with him.

On May 30, she took her chance to get away. She slung her bag into her car and drove to her mother's house in Shepherdsville, a city in Bullitt County about twenty minutes outside of Louisville. The calls from Gouker started almost immediately. He threatened her mother that she needed to disclose Amanda's whereabouts. He attempted to intimidate her mom, stating that he wanted to kill Amanda and himself. Amanda's mother would not answer his questions and tried to avoid Gouker as well. He was acting crazy and was quickly spiraling out of control.

Amanda was terrified and had to have become even more convinced that Gouker was capable of anything. One day she rushed to the courthouse to take out an emergency protective order against him. She feared for her life and her daughter's safety. She was so terrified that she called the Sheriff's Department and deputies escorted her to the court clerk's office to initiate the petition.[7] She also met with the county attorney's office where she was staying and she pressed charges for harassing communications, because Gouker would not leave her alone. A warrant was issued for his arrest.[8] Coupled with her already debilitating grief for her son, Gouker's harassment was overwhelming. Amanda was scared and said she wanted nothing further to do with her husband.

She would do whatever the detectives asked of her. They appeared to suspect that Gouker was involved or knew more than he was telling. She was forced to agree and the guilt was devastating. The question resounded: Had she brought a monster into her home, a monster so vile and horrendous that he had killed her only son?

Chapter 7

Covering the Bases

L ittle Josh was at Cassi's house when he received a phone call from his father. Gouker had spoken with the police and they wanted to talk with Little Josh again regarding the timeline of events on the night Trey died. Detective Russ was on his way to the house, so Little Josh stood near the front door waiting for him to arrive.

It was a little after 4:00 P.M. when Scott Russ's police cruiser slid into the tiny driveway at Cassi's house. Josh was waiting on the porch for him and was speaking on the telephone. As he watched the car turn slowly into the driveway, Little Josh quickly disconnected his call and approached the cruiser.

"Hey, what's up, man?" Detective Russ yelled out. "If you just wanna come out here and have a seat in my car, it will be cool. It won't take but a minute."

Josh jogged around to the passenger side door and opened it gingerly, nodding to the officer as he slid into the vehicle. Josh listened as the detective explained his purpose for visiting the home: "I just talked to your dad on the phone. He said it was cool to just come by and talk to you real quick."

"Yeah," Little Josh nodded as he listened to the detective speak.

"And, like I say, I'm not here to yell at you, scream or to jam you up or anything. I just want to talk to you, because I know the female detective that spoke to you that day over there at the school and there's just some stuff I wanted to ask you about, to kinda clarify." He looked at the skinny boy crouched in his passenger seat. "Try to get comfortable. You want a mint or anything?" The detective held out a package of mints in his right hand, offering one to the boy.

Josh shook his head as he looked at the officer, "Nah, I'm good."

Detective Russ turned toward the boy as much as possible in the tight space of the car and began to verify the background information that he had for Josh. Within minutes, he began to discuss the events of May 10, 2011: "Let's just kind of go back real quick, over to the night, I guess the night they had the cookout."

As he led Josh through the events of that evening, the boy named the people present at the cookout and detailed the evening's timeline. As Josh narrated the events as the cookout came to a close, Detective Russ began to narrow in on when Trey decided to take his nightly shower, "Okay. What about, I guess when everybody leaves. What do you all do then?"

"Well, Trey, he was going in to take a shower, so I came down here," he gestured toward his cousin Cassi's house, "and started watching movies. I ended up falling asleep down here. He said he was going to take a shower and just calm down for the night, so I came down here and watched movies."[1]

"Did, uh, do you know if he made plans to go back down there that night or with anybody?"

"He didn't, he didn't tell me if he did; which is strange. He usually tells me everything; that's my brother."

"Yeah," Detective Russ said. "What's your thoughts on what happened?"

Josh said he could not understand what or who could have lured Trey to his death at the creek bed. He'd spent a lot of time wondering and trying to come to terms with the whole tragedy, but it was impossible to do. He didn't have any answers. "My thoughts are, uh, it's blank. I really have no idea who would do it. He really didn't have any enemies," Little Josh said as he shrugged his shoulders.

"Have you ever known him to walk that way by himself at dark time? I mean by himself at ten, eleven, twelve, one or two in the morning?"

"No," Josh said, dumbfounded.

"That's the big question. I'm trying to figure out how or why he would've went down there. 'Cause he didn't call anybody on his phone. There's no phone calls made on his phone after six o'clock that night when you all were still at the cookout. I mean everybody was still having fun playing basketball."

Josh sat quietly, listening to the detective's words. He had rehashed the night repeatedly in his mind. Trey wasn't the type to go to the dark area near the creek bed alone. He wracked his brain trying to think of reasons Trey might have done so.

"So, he never called anybody to say, 'Hey, meet me down there,'" Russ continued. "That's the big question I'm trying to answer. Who he would have been going down there to meet? Was there a girl? Would he have went down there to smoke weed or a cigarette?"

Shaking his head, Josh said, "He wouldn't go down there by himself. I don't see him going anywhere by himself at night."[2]

Little Josh thought about the area where Trey was found; it could be a scary atmosphere. He didn't know anyone who would travel to that area alone in the middle of the night, let alone his fourteen-year-old stepbrother, and he conveyed these sentiments to the detective, who promptly agreed, "I went down there one night about six or eight days ago at one o'clock in the morning. I mean, the soccer field I think is kinda lit up, but down there where he was at, it's pitch dark. I was even," he paused, shaking his head, "I've got a gun and I'm scared down there. You know what I mean?"

"Yeah," Josh responded. He shuddered thinking about Trey being there alone. It was a frightening thought and everyone in the neighborhood, including Josh, was still on edge weeks later.

"So what I'm trying to figure out is why he would have went down there."

"I don't know."

"As far as Trey trying to leave that night, have you heard anything about that?"

As he thought about the question, Josh remembered the conversation he'd had with both Amanda and his father during the afternoon Trey was missing when they were all desperately searching for him, "They said he, uh, went out to the back porch fully dressed. They said they stayed right there the whole night on the back porch." Josh looked down to his lap, embarrassed, "I'm sure you already know," he said, referring to the intimate activities his father and stepmother had engaged in on the back porch.

Gouker previously told Joshua that he and Amanda had sexual intercourse on the back porch of the home on the evening Trey went missing. He saw nothing wrong with disclosing intimate details of his sex life to his fifteen-year-old son.

Josh was embarrassed to repeat his father's story. "They were out there having their time and unscrewed the spotlights and stuff, so I guess [Trey] thought they weren't out there or something. I don't know. I guess he went to leave and then walked back in."

"I know you don't wanna say weird things about your dad," Detective Russ began tentatively, surely noticing the boy's discomfort in relating the information about his father and Amanda's romp on the back porch, "but I have to ask you, as far as his and Amanda's relationship, did you ever see them argue?"

"I mean, yeah, they argued verbally."

"Now what about Trey? Did he ever try to stop your dad from arguing with his mom?"

"He never really does it around me or Trey," Josh said, referring to his father's outbursts. It seemed that generally, if the kids felt an argument coming on, they would scatter and try to get as far away as possible. Just as often,

Amanda and Gouker would go into the bedroom and shut the door if their fighting words became too intense.

"Did you and Trey ever have any problems?"

"We always, I've known him my whole life," Josh explained.

"Yeah," Russ said, leaning forward.

"Even when my dad was locked up, I saw him. We lived in the apartments and him and his mom lived in the apartments. We played the whole time we grew up."

Watching Josh as he sat thinking, Detective Russ next focused on the night that Trey disappeared. It was puzzling to everyone that Trey was able to sneak out of the house without arousing the suspicions of either adult and any light that Josh could shed on the situation would be greatly appreciated. "Tell me about the night, after everybody left and you said something about the shower? Kind of walk through that for me if you could," Russ requested.

"He said he was going to take a shower. We were still on the back porch, in the backyard. The cookout was just ending and he said he was going to go take a shower or something."[3]

"Now was his sister there then?"

"Uh yeah, she took a shower too."

"Were you in the house when he took the shower?"

"Uh, uh, 'cause I came over here," he said, gesturing toward the tiny stone house in front of the cruiser.

"So on the back porch, he tells you he's going to take a shower and you come down here?"

"He said, 'I'm gonna go in here and take a shower...and so I was gonna come down here and calm down for a little bit and watch movies. I ended up falling asleep." Detective Russ seized on a perceived discrepancy in Josh's story and he wasted no time in bringing the apparent inconsistency to the boy's attention.

"Now I guess my only concern is there's a little difference in your story today than what you told the detective over at the gym. You told her that you were in the house when Trey was taking a shower and then when he got out of the shower you watched him put his clothes back on," the detective said, referring to the conversation Little Josh had at Liberty High School with Detective Maroni.

"No, I came over here when Trey was taking a shower. I *heard* that he walked out of the door fully dressed, head to toe, which would have to be after the shower. 'Cause it was after I came over here and he said he was taking a shower."

"But I meant in the interview you told her. She recorded it. You said that Trey took a shower and you were there when he took a shower and you watched him put his clothes back on. Those were your own words."

"That was false."

"So you weren't there when he took a shower?"

"Correct. I was here."

"And you weren't there when he put his clothes back on?"

"No, but I knew he put his clothes back on, 'cause when he walked on the back porch and..." his voice trailed off as the detective jumped in.

"So you kinda got that from them?

"I kinda put two and two together."

"Okay and I just wanted to ask you because it was a little different from what you said that day, but it makes sense."

"Yeah, I understand."

Josh continued to remain straightforward with the officer for the duration of the interview and several times during the conversation both questioned why Trey would have visited the creek bed so late. They wondered who went with him, because neither felt that he would go alone.

As the pair sat in the police vehicle, Detective Russ continued: "I mean, you understand it doesn't make sense, Trey's scared of the dark and he wouldn't go there alone."

"Yeah."

"So it's like who would he have went with? That's the million dollar question, honestly. I mean, I'm sure you ran this through your mind a million times."

"It went through my mind a lot and it comes up blank every time, because I can't picture what he'd be doing."[4]

"Now, he didn't meet you back down there? You all didn't sneak out?"

"No," Josh replied, knowing that he had not left his cousin Cassi's house the entire night after he went to her house to watch movies. He understood that the police had to question everyone and it seemed that popular opinion among the police and neighborhood residents was that his dad was somehow involved.

The detective looked pointedly at Josh, "You know everybody is mad at your dad. They think he had something to do with it. I know people in the neighborhood are probably talking about your dad."

He'd heard rumblings that they were, but Josh tried to stay away from the drama. He'd been through enough in his young life and the last thing he needed was to be involved in neighborhood gossip. However, he knew the detective was right. His dad could be a scary guy, especially to people on his bad side. Josh couldn't fathom that his dad could do something so awful. He couldn't bring himself to say it out loud.

Detective Russ suggested that they run through the circumstances surrounding Trey's relationship with his stepfather, Joshua Gouker. Little Josh sat quietly and listened to the detective: "He's scared of the dark. We don't know who he would've went with. You have no idea who he would have been down there to meet or what would've got him down there. So if I say something wrong, please correct me." He paused, looking at Little Josh. "I'm just trying to run through everything you told me. Um, your dad and Amanda never really argued a lot, maybe verbally a little bit but not a lot. There was never anything physical in front of you all. Was Trey stealing from your dad at all? You know, was he selling any weed or was he stealing any money?

"No!" Josh said, flabbergasted. He knew that Trey wasn't into that type of thing.

"If you had a gut feeling, what does your gut tell you? Who might've done something like this?"

"I can't imagine that anybody would do it to him. Honestly, I have no idea."

"Now is your dad, does he...you don't have to answer this. Or you may not even know this. Does he sell weed or does he use? Does he just smoke it?"

Josh looked at the detective. He knew his father had a penchant for weed. Gouker provided marijuana to his son and encouraged him to smoke it. He knew he was supposed to tell the officer the truth but he was afraid of what his dad might do. He did not want to lie either. Little Josh shrugged his shoulders. "I don't feel comfortable answering that," he said as politely as he could, hoping that Russ wouldn't press the issue further.[5]

"Okay, that's fine. I don't want to put you in a weird spot with your dad or anything like that."

Josh nodded. He was ready for the conversation to end and it seemed like the detective was ready to wrap things up as well. "If I think of any other questions, is it alright if I call you or just come by?" he asked.

"I guess, yeah, that'll be fine."

"Alright, well, I appreciate it. Thanks, man."

Josh nodded and stepped from the vehicle. He hoped that something he said or did would help the detectives. He had no idea that within the next few weeks, they'd be prompted to look in his direction by an unlikely source.

Chapter 8

Escape Attempt

He had to do something. By mid-June 2011, Joshua Gouker had to be well aware that the police were becoming increasingly suspicious that the key to Trey's murder lay somewhere within Gouker's own household. He had spent hours speaking with the detectives regarding the murder of his stepson. During Gouker's last visit to the police station, he appeared to convey astonishment and disbelief when he walked out the front door of the unit rather than through the back, cuffed, with a one-way ticket to Louisville Metro Corrections. It was a close call and he couldn't take that chance again.

Gouker had failed the most recent drug test administered by his parole officer and he had been made aware that Amanda had requested an emergency protective order. The walls were closing in around him and Gouker decided he needed to get out of town fast.

As always, it seemed that Gouker plotted and planned a way to use others to further his own agenda. Over the years, his biggest successes developed from manipulating various women in his life. When he felt the police investigation into Trey's death was coming too close to home, it was to a previous girlfriend that he turned for help when he decided to flee Kentucky with his son.

Despite the sporadic nature of their relationship, his old girlfriend Angelic Burkhead was willing when Gouker contacted her in late June and asked for her help. Concealing his intent to travel across state lines with his son, Gouker borrowed his mom's car. He needed Angelic's help to accomplish his plan and asked her to ride along with him to Mississippi where she would drop him and Little Josh off and then return the car to his mother.[1]

They planned to leave on June 13, a Sunday. Angelic wasn't scheduled to work again until Wednesday, which would give her plenty of time to take a long road trip with Gouker and Little Josh without it interfering with her work schedule.

Although pleased to have several days traveling with Gouker, Angelic apparently didn't want to make the drive back to Kentucky alone, so she invited her friend Jahaira Riddle along for the ride. Friends since they were pre-teens, the two were extremely close and the trip seemed like a great occasion to party with Gouker and then catch up with each other.

Passersby must have regarded this group with suspicion as they blazed down the highway toward the Tennessee/Kentucky border. Gouker, as always, emitted an air of toughness and bravado not easily missed. The two women who accompanied Gouker were examples of the bevy of women Gouker appeared to continually keep at his disposal. Angelic's shoulder-length wavy hair, fair skin and glasses projected a bookish quality and, with her heavyset frame and slight Southern twang, she was the epitome of what one could expect to see at a cookout or country music concert in Louisville, Kentucky. That appearance sharply contrasted with her lifelong friend Jahaira, an attractive woman of Puerto Rican descent who wore her jet black hair in a tight ponytail. Jahaira's blouse revealed the tattoo emblazoned across her left breast and her deep, raspy voice contributed to the image she projected of a hard-lived life.

Josh, skinny at age fifteen, was hunched over in the back seat of the vehicle. He stayed quiet, speaking rarely and even then often failing to raise his eyes. Had he done so, any observer might have guessed his hesitation to accompany his father on this fateful road trip. He was leaving everything that he had ever known behind. As he settled into his car seat for the ride ahead, Josh remained completely dependent on his father, the only person he felt that he had left in the world. With his mother long dead and the controversy swirling at home following Trey's murder, Josh had no other choice but to accompany his father, to do exactly what Gouker told him to do.[2]

As they crossed the Tennessee border, it was smooth sailing for Gouker and his crew. The car had plenty of gas, was stocked with snacks and they were making good time according to Gouker's plan. Gouker surely must have begun to taste the sweetness of freedom and a new life until fate intervened. Shortly after they entered Tennessee, the car broke down in a desolate area. Gouker was able to nurse the car along to the parking lot of a nearby gas station. As they pondered what to do next, Gouker convinced a passerby to give the entire group a ride to a local motel and they abandoned his mother's car.

Despite his impoverished circumstances, Gouker had a steady stream of cigarettes and booze to keep him occupied on the trip, not to mention two women, lifelong friends, who both vied for his attention despite the strain it would ultimately place on their relationship. Throughout the evening, Josh kept primarily to himself, wondering how he had ended up in such a tough situation. He was a teenager trapped in a seedy motel somewhere in Tennessee with his ex-convict father and two female friends who both viewed the unemployed, harsh, violent and unaffectionate felon as a prize to be won and cherished. They were essentially homeless, alone and on the run and there was absolutely nothing Josh could do to change the situation. He was utterly stuck and stranded hundreds of miles from home.

As the hours ticked on, Gouker kept trying to formulate a plan. They needed to get as far away from Louisville as possible and they needed to do so quickly. After two nights at the motel, Angelic knew she was due at work the following day and that weighed on her mind. She did the only thing she could think of and reached out to her grandfather, begging for help to get her back to Louisville. He arranged a bus ticket for her and within hours she found a ride to the depot and headed home, leaving Joshua with his father and a woman who seemed to be Gouker's newest love interest.

Shortly after Angelic's departure, the remaining members of the group learned that a man staying in the room next door to them was planning to drive to Huntsville, Alabama. When he offered to give them a ride, they jumped at the chance. The group was on its way south within minutes and eventually their benefactor dropped them at a motel where they checked into a room with two double beds. Gouker prepared to settle in for the night, one step closer to his Southern escape.

Erin Specth was excited. It was the weekend of her fourteen-year-old son's birthday and she was driving to Huntsville to spend time with him. She had previously separated from her husband and her son was now living with his father. Erin had taken great care planning the entire weekend. She would first visit with her daughter, who currently resided in the area with her grandparents. She would get a good night's rest and then pick up her son first thing in the morning. They would spend the entire day together.

Busy looking forward to the visit and planning the day's activities in her head, Erin paid little attention to what was happening around her at about 10 P.M. as she checked into the room she had rented at a motel in Huntsville. The overhead lights flickered as she hurriedly unloaded several bags from her vehicle and then went to the icemaker to retrieve some ice for her soda. Just as she settled into her room for the evening, a harsh knock at the door caused her to sit upright.[3]

Erin pulled the heavy acrylic curtains slowly to the side and peered out the window. Her eyes rested on a woman with long, dark hair and she hesitantly turned the heavy deadbolt on the door and, against her better judgment, opened it slightly. Running a hand through her hair, the woman introduced herself as "Jennifer" and explained that she and her son were caught in a domestic violence situation. As she ran through the specifics, she nodded toward a teenage boy standing off to her side in the shadows of the stairwell.

Appearing nervous, Erin stared at the teenager who seemed near the age of her own son. He was quiet and kept his eyes downward, only peeking up at her in brief glimpses as the woman spoke to her. She explained that they had bus tickets but no way to reach the local bus station the following morning. Erin must have felt sorry for the woman and her son. How would she feel if her own boy was stranded in a motel, fleeing a desperate situation? She probably hoped that someone would feel sympathetic enough to help him. In that moment, she decided that she would not leave the boy and his mother alone since she could easily take them to the bus station the next day.[4]

She quickly nodded her agreement and instructed Jennifer to meet her at the door in the morning. No sooner had Erin flipped on the television and pulled back the stiff floral comforter on the bed than she heard knocking at the door. Jennifer stood outside once again. Erin opened the door a second time to the woman and her son.

"I am so sorry, but I just realized I gave you the wrong room number for us," Jennifer blurted out quickly. After correcting the information, she gushed her thanks and let Erin know that she really was desperate and that she greatly appreciated her willingness to help. As the two women spoke briefly, Erin noticed the young man again, hovering to the left and staring at his feet. What had she gotten herself into? After they left, Erin retired to her room for the evening.

Before 9 A.M. the next morning, loud rapping on her door woke Erin from a deep sleep. Jennifer stood right outside holding several plastic grocery bags stuffed with various items of clothing and tapping her foot. She was clearly ready to go. Erin explained that she was still tired from traveling the previous day and that she needed more time to get ready before they left. Nevertheless, within the hour, Jennifer reappeared at her door with her belongings stacked next to Erin's vehicle. Erin again informed her that she was not ready and asked that the woman wait another hour before coming back to the room.

Eventually Erin walked out to the car where Jennifer was waiting for her. Jennifer retrieved her son; the teenager climbed into the back seat and Jennifer situated herself in the front, quickly asking if Erin would drive to the motel's office so that she could turn in her key. Thinking nothing of the request, Erin maneuvered her vehicle to the front of the parking lot and parked in front of the rental office as Jennifer dashed inside. She emerged from the lobby almost immediately and jumped back into the car's front seat.

Before Erin could pull away, the back passenger door swung open and a man slid into the back seat. Grinning broadly, he nodded toward Jennifer, "She said you might be able to give me a ride to the bus station as well." It was like he came out of nowhere. Erin had not seen the man as she watched Jennifer walk to and from the motel lobby, yet here he was in her vehicle. Something wasn't right. It was unpleasantly surprising that Jennifer, a total stranger, would volunteer her as a taxi service for this man. It was one thing to help out a single woman and her child; it was quite another to provide a ride to a tattooed man she'd never met.[5]

At that moment, Erin had no indication that her initial passengers knew the man other than through incidental contact by staying in the same motel. She was under the impression that they too had met just like she and Jennifer had, by the chance of staying in neighboring rooms. Although the feeling that something wasn't right continued to creep up her spine, she willed herself to calm down and just drive. She only had to get the passengers a few miles down the road and then she could finally pick up her son.

Although a visitor on this occasion, Erin was actually a former resident of Huntsville and was familiar with the location of the bus station. Downtown Huntsville housed the main bus depot for the city. When the man informed her that they needed a ride to a substation approximately eight miles down the road, she hesitated. As far as she could recall, there was no station in that direction. Her suspicion seemed to intensify when Jennifer pointed out the window as they passed a street sign. "Oh, honey, look," she exclaimed, twisting her body to face the backseat and locking eyes with the man. They had told Erin an untrue story about their relationship and the reason they were in Huntsville. They clearly knew each other. She was in a bad situation, trapped in the car with three strangers, two of whom were adults who had lied to her. Her increased discomfort must have been apparent to her passengers as she pulled the car quickly into a gas station in Madison City and threw the transmission into park.

"Please," she asked, turning to the two adults, "go into this gas station and ask for directions to the bus substation. I don't remember a station in the direction you're asking me to go." She watched as Jennifer and the man exited the vehicle and sauntered toward the automatic doors of the station, Jennifer grabbing snacks and standing briefly at the cash register while the man appeared to retrieve cash from the ATM. The teen remained quietly in the vehicle with his eyes downcast.[6]

As the two reentered the car, Jennifer explained that they needed to turn left on the main road and drive for several minutes to reach the substation. By this point, Erin was frantic. She squeezed the steering wheel, willing herself to stay calm so that the already uncomfortable situation would not intensify. She needed to get these people where they needed to go and out of her car.

"I can't do it. I'm sorry, but I can't go in that direction. I will take you to the downtown station. I know where that one is located. I don't have time to take you where you are asking me to go," she said, steadying herself against the driver's seat.

"That's fine," Jennifer spoke up. "If you could just run me to that store over there?" she asked, gesturing toward the building across the parking lot, "I just need to pick up some toothpaste and then if you can take us downtown to the station that will be fine."[7]

Erin parked the car in front of the store; Jennifer hopped out and went inside. The man too slid from his seat and lit a cigarette as he stood off to the left of the car. As Jennifer emerged from the store, she headed toward the vehicle, speaking briefly with the man before they both reentered Erin's car. This time, Jennifer climbed into the back with the teenager and the man situated himself in the front passenger seat. In one fluid motion he turned to Jennifer and held out his hand. "Pass it up," he barked to Jennifer in the back seat.

With those three words, Erin began to quiver as she watched the woman in the rear of her vehicle slide a shiny pistol out of her purse and into the hands of the man next to her. Her eyes widened and she became pale as he turned to her, a slight smirk playing at the left corner of his lips. He laid the gun in his lap, barrel facing Erin. "Drive," he commanded, his eyes facing forward.[8]

Erin reacted to the command, but she seemed almost frozen in fear. How had she gotten into this situation and, more importantly, was there a way out of it?

She focused on the road ahead as the man began to drone on about his situation. Calling himself "a wanted man," he wove a story that seemed ripped from the script of a movie. He wasn't a bad person, he said. No, he was saving his son, he claimed. The boy's mother had kidnapped his son whom Erin now knew as Joshua. It took the man over eleven months to find them and when he did, he had attempted to take back Joshua. When a man intervened, he accidentally shot the man and it was for that reason that he was on the run with his son. The man reached into his pocket and pulled out a Kentucky State ID, demanding that Erin look at it. She kept her eyes straight ahead, too scared to see who this monster holding her captive truly was. She was too terrified to take her eyes off the road.[9]

The man told Erin the direction she needed to drive and she was quick to follow his orders even though she had to realize that he was taking her away from civilization. At that moment, instinct kicked in and she must have become aware that the only way out of the situation was to convince the man that she was completely sympathetic to his plight. She would play the most empathetic, supportive and caring role that she could muster in the hopes of gaining his trust and saving her life. Nearly twenty years his senior, Erin took on a motherly role, beginning to ply Gouker with advice about his situation, instructing him the way she would her own son.

Willing herself to briefly take her eyes off the road, Erin looked to her right and made eye contact with her captor. She took it all in, forcing her gaze away from the teardrop inked below one eye and concentrating on his eyes, "It's unfortunate that someone was hurt, but as parents we must do what is best to protect our children, so I understand why you did what you did. Look, the way I see it is that you made a mistake. We all do sometimes. The best thing that you can do is stop making mistakes, stop being violent. That's the way people get caught."

Tilting his head slightly, he looked at her, almost as though he was looking through her. Erin watched as he fingered the shiny handgun in his lap, aimlessly running his hand up and down the barrel and around the trigger, seemingly lost in his thoughts.

For the next three hours she followed the man's directions, navigating her car through the highways and streets of Alabama. She was keenly aware that even the slightest movement on her part could set him off. As she drove, Erin must have worried about her fate and more importantly about her own children. Surely by now her son was anxious about where she was. Hours had passed since the designated time she had planned to pick him up. He was probably worried sick. The thought of his disappointment that she was not there with him and his uncertainty regarding her whereabouts was almost too much to bear. She wondered if she would ever see him again; she was terrified that unless she kept her wits about her, the next time they were in the same room would be at her funeral.

She flinched with each movement. Even looking in the rear view mirror caused her captor to lash out at her. If she looked out the window the wrong way, he threatened her and accused her of trying to escape. In the past few weeks, Erin had begun having trouble with her vehicle. Despite having paid a mechanic to fix it, there were still issues. The car was older and occasionally the clutch would slip out of gear. Each time this occurred, she tensed as she felt the man's eyes cut to her. He was evidently suspicious that she was manipulating the car into stalling so that she could attract attention.[10]

It was a maddening tug of war. The man scrutinized every move she made and she was never quite sure which move might be her last. As they sped toward Birmingham, the back seat passengers remained quiet and, despite her intense fear, Erin did her best to keep the man talking. As long as he was speaking with her and engaged with her she felt that she had a chance to escape the situation.

Eventually he directed her into a rest stop off the highway. Erin remembered the prescription that she always kept in her purse. The medication was prescribed to her for anxiety and she knew all too well that in addition to its relaxing effects, it could make the user sleepy. She took a chance and pulled the bottle from her purse and held it out to the man. She offered some of the pills to her captor, hoping he would accept and then fall asleep, giving her a chance to flee the vehicle.[11]

She watched as he took several and downed them. At the very least, she had to be hoping the medication would mellow him and keep him from doing anything more drastic than the earlier events of the day. They sat quietly in the car until he eventually turned to her and instructed her to get back onto the highway. After that short respite, the group continued toward Birmingham and ultimately arrived at a motel where the man wanted to stay.

"Pull the car around to the back of the building," he directed, gesturing toward a parking area far from the front of the lobby. Pulling a wad of bills from his pocket, the man quickly peeled off one hundred dollars and handed them to Erin. "I need you to go get a room for two nights, okay. Don't try anything. I am still deciding what to do with you. Josh!" he barked toward his son who had just exited the back seat, "you go with her."

The boy nodded and moved toward Erin and silently they walked around the building toward the check-in area. As they entered through the front door, they were promptly greeted by the staff. Although it was not a high-end motel chain, it was obvious that this particular location was semi-new construction. The building was clean and smelled of fresh paint. Erin explained to the clerk that she only had one hundred dollars and stated that she needed a room for two nights. The sympathetic employee nodded, explaining that they were new and had plenty of available rooms. The company was willing to adjust the room cost to accommodate them. It likely didn't hurt that the grandmotherly Erin and the young boy appeared nice and normal. This was likely the man's plan in sending Josh along with her to purchase the room. No one would turn away a grandmother and her grandson if they could accommodate them at all, especially with the amount of vacancies the newly-opened motel had.

As the clerk checked them in, when asked, Josh politely requested a smoking room. That was only the second time Erin had heard the boy speak all day.[12]

The clerk assigned the group to a room in the back of the motel that was accessible through a rear door. When Erin explained the location of the room to her captor, this pleased him immensely as the room afforded a great sense of privacy. Before allowing the group to enter the room, he ordered everyone back into the vehicle, only this time he positioned himself in the driver's seat. Erin reluctantly slid into the front passenger seat as he started the vehicle. Without a word, he exited the parking lot and began traveling away from the nearby buildings. After several minutes, the car reached a desolate area and Erin must have known that they were likely miles from any type of civilization. There were no cars or people in sight.

The man eased the car to a stop and off to the right was a grove of leafy trees that surrounded a green, grassy clearing. In any other situation, the natural beauty of the location would have beckoned passersby to a picnic, but Erin was trapped by her kidnapper and other possibilities had to be in Erin's mind. He looked toward her, raising an eyebrow. "That looks like a good place to die," he said, nodding toward the grassy grove.

Erin appeared numb. Although she didn't know the man well, she had seen enough to realize that he thrived on instilling fear in others. She probably felt that the only way to gain this man's respect was to hide her fear. Erin's knees begin to shake. She mustered every bit of courage that she had and looked him straight in the eye. "Now I'm nervous," she said flippantly, giving the impression that she assumed he was making a joke. He tilted his head slightly and cracked a smile. She willed herself to smile back.[13]

The tension was broken. She had passed his test. He started the car and drove back into town.

By then Erin could sense that the man could not decide what to do with her and she felt him evaluating her to see whether he could trust her not to go to the police if he released her. She took every opportunity that she could to get into his good graces and she spoke with him and interacted with him as if she were his mother, giving him advice on how to flee the country successfully with his son. Everyone was beginning to get hungry, so he drove to a restaurant near the motel. He ordered Jennifer and Josh to go inside and order food while he instructed Erin to remain in the vehicle with him. In an attempt to gauge her loyalty to him, the man coached Erin that if he released her, she could not go to the police. For several minutes she assured him that she had no plans to do so.

Eventually he allowed her to walk into the restaurant with him. This was the first real chance that Erin had to escape or alert someone that she was being held against her will. She must have wanted desperately to convey to the employees and patrons that she needed help. However, as she looked around the restaurant, there were several children playing and eating with their families and Erin just could not risk someone else getting hurt. After all, her captor was armed with a gun.

As she tried not to be obvious and her eyes darted around the fast-food joint, the man steered her toward a booth where they sat with Josh and Jennifer. As they ate their meal, the man continued to pressure Erin that he was considering letting her go but that she could not go to the police. He barked at Josh and ordered him to look at Erin. Her captor then turned to Erin and told her to look into Josh's eyes and promise him that she would not go to the police. He emphasized that Josh's life depended on her continued silence. She watched as Josh's face changed. He bit his lip and seemed very disturbed by what his father was doing. It was clear that he wanted no part of the ordeal and yet he was stuck in the situation. He was probably also there against his will.

As they finished their meal, the man again forced Erin to go outside with him alone and he reiterated that she could not go to the police. She could sense the internal struggle in him and she did everything she could to reassure him that she would be loyal to him: she would not alert the authorities. Erin was in survival mode and she could see that her constant reassurance and support were working. The man was beginning to trust her; he was starting to feel confident that he did not need to kill her. He could let her go.

Minutes later, Josh and Jennifer emerged from the restaurant and reentered the car. The man drove to the hotel and everyone filed into their room. The man's unease was apparent. He seemed to be leaning toward releasing her, but she could tell that his mood could change instantly. As a sign of good faith, she reached into her purse and pulled out all of the cash she had, about one hundred dollars. Then she gave him the rest of her anxiety prescription. If he set her free she could call the police; perhaps the medication would cause him to pass out so that no one would be harmed when the police attempted to apprehend him. She did not want anyone to get hurt. What was this man capable of doing? If the events of the day were any indication, he was likely capable of very bad things.

The man instructed her to hug Jennifer and Josh and she did so, promising each one of them that she would not contact the authorities. He then attempted to buy her loyalty. Handing her a watch that he wore on his own wrist, he apologized for taking her away from her son for the day and said the watch was for him. He once again led her outside alone. She watched the man concentrate as crocodile tears sprang to his eyes. In an elaborate show of manufactured emotion, he wiped his eyes and looked into hers. "You know, my son's life depends on you not calling the police," he warned. She took this to mean that he would harm his son if she alerted authorities about her kidnapping.

"I understand and I would never do that to you. I promise that I won't go to the police," she said. Erin held her breath and hoped her words would be enough to calm the man. She watched him stand aside as she opened her car door. She reached out to hug him, praying that it would convince him that she would protect him. In that moment, he allowed her to enter the vehicle, start it and drive away.[14]

Erin held her breath until she made it halfway down the street and then she finally exhaled. She jumped onto the expressway and sped toward Huntsville, immediately calling her son and his father to explain what had happened to her. Her ex-husband notified the police and Erin related her story in detail, praying that police would catch the man and that by the time they did, young Josh would be okay.

Chapter 9

Accused

After Erin reported the abduction, the police quickly descended on the motel room and within a very short period of time they took Gouker, Jahaira and Little Josh into custody. Officers quickly determined that Josh was the subject of an Amber Alert issued in Kentucky and they notified authorities in Louisville and Child Protective Services, informing the agency that they had found Josh and that they could pick the child up at their convenience. Child Protective Services made immediate arrangements for Little Josh's return to Kentucky. Josh's social worker flew to Alabama to retrieve him on June 18, 2011, and the two traveled by plane back to Kentucky. Josh was placed in the Home of the Innocents until further notice from the court.

Home of the Innocents, which first opened its doors in 1888, is a private, nonprofit entity that provides a home and services to children in crisis. Children who have been abused, neglected or abandoned receive both residential and community-based services at the facility. It was a whirlwind for Josh. Within a week, his father had ripped him from his home and school, fled with him to Alabama and forced Josh to watch as he took an innocent woman hostage along the way. Now his father had been arrested in Alabama and Josh had been placed in a home for children in crisis. It was more than any child should have to endure. If he could do anything, it would be to go back to the day the court gave his father temporary custody so that he could step up and beg the judge to allow him to stay with the Walsh family. His last few months had been a nightmare and Josh had no idea that things were about to get even worse than he could have imagined.[1]

Soon after Little Josh's return to Louisville, Detective Russ asked Child Protective Services to bring Josh to the police station so that he could speak with him again regarding Trey's death. Officers were suspicious of Gouker due to the abrupt way he had fled the state with his son. As they walked up the steps to the interview room, Russ informed Josh that he wanted to play several recordings for Josh and that the detective wanted to discuss those recordings with him.

At this point, Little Josh was happy to oblige. Many of Trey's family and friends felt frustrated with the investigation and Josh completely understood that frustration. Nearly a month and a half had passed since Trey's murder and the police weren't giving them many answers. He wanted to help but he had heard rumblings in the neighborhood that people suspected his dad. This made him somewhat defensive. He did not want to believe that the man who fought for custody of him could be capable of hurting his stepbrother. However, after his father's she-nanigans in Alabama, he didn't know what to believe any-more. He hoped his conversation with the officer could answer some of the questions.

"What's on the disc?" Josh asked expectantly as he settled into one of the plastic chairs in the interview room. He was dressed casually in a cotton t-shirt with a red ball cap cocked slightly to the side.

"Oh, just one of the interviews we had with you earlier. You doing all right today?" Detective Russ asked as he also sat down and prepared to question the boy.[2]

Josh spoke briefly about the fact that he had arrived home from the strange adventure in Alabama late the prior evening. He was still exhausted from the flight and his days on the road with his father. Josh strained to listen as the detective started up the recorder, which replayed Josh's conversation with Detective Maroni several hours after Trey's body was found. He immediately replayed his own interview with Josh that had occurred as they sat in his police cruiser in his cousin's driveway a few weeks before.

As the recording came to an end, Detective Russ looked toward Little Josh and purposefully asked, "So you understand my concern with your story, right?" The detec-tive remained confused by what he believed were con-flicting descriptions of Josh's movements on the night of Trey's death.

"Yes, sir," Josh answered.

"I mean, I would think that your first story that you told Detective Maroni at the school is probably the true version of events, because [your cousin Cassi] says she doesn't remember if you stayed there that night or not."

"[My cousin's boyfriend] does," Josh piped up.

"No, [he didn't] either."

Little Josh looked at the detective knowingly. Everyone knew that his cousin's boyfriend was a functioning alcoholic. "'Cause he was passed out on the couch."

"I'm just telling you, so we need to work through what the truth really is, okay. Let's kind of walk through this part first. Tell me the truth about that night."

"We were on the back porch and it was me, him, Dad and Amanda. Dad and Amanda stayed on the porch the whole night evidently, because we were on the back porch and Trey told me that he was going to go take a shower and calm down for the night. I went to Cassi's. I didn't know if I was gonna sleep down there or down at Amanda's, but I got comfortable down at Cassi's and while watching a movie I fell asleep."[3]

The detective seized the opportunity to once again ask about the discrepancy between Little Josh's two most recent statements and his statement made at Liberty High School the day Trey's body was found.

"I guess the first day, it was a bad day," Little Josh explained. "You understand that, right?"

"Okay, but do you see what I am saying? Your stories aren't making sense and I don't want you to get jammed up in this murder case at all."

"Okay," Little Josh replied, nodding, "I don't have nothing to do with it."

"I think you were at the house that night."

"I was not."

"I think you saw him take a shower and put his clothes back on and I think you, him and your dad went back down to where this happened."

"No, sir."

Detective Russ thrust his cell phone onto the table and pointed to its buttons. "And let me just show you this real quick. See on my phone, a lot of people have these nowadays. It's got a voice recorder on it. I can record and I can stop and then I can save it and play it." He quickly recorded himself speaking and played the snippet back for Josh who sat quietly, wondering what the detective was implying. "See how it works?" Russ asked as he demonstrated the recording capabilities on his phone. "You would never know that I was recording a conversation. So if you talked to a few people and they were smart enough to do something similar to this…" he said, looking at Josh. The implication seemed to be that people had secretly recorded Little Josh confessing to Trey's murder. Then the officer took things a step further as he claimed he also had text messages. "You've told your friends a few things, in a little more detail, about maybe what happened to Trey," he said.

"No," Little Josh said.

"Yeah," Russ responded.

"Like what?" Josh asked, disturbed that the officer seemed to be claiming that he had admitted to the murder and that the officer had texts or secret recordings to prove it. Josh knew that he'd said nothing of the sort.

"Why would some of your friends, male or female, come to me and say that you and your dad were talking about how you all have killed people before Trey was murdered? Trey was murdered in a similar fashion and you described how you and your dad would do it."

"I have no idea. I get along with everybody...It's a lie," Little Josh responded. He knew he had never said anything like the horrible things Detective Russ was insinuating and he knew that no one would say he had.[4]

When Josh failed to cave, the detective took things a step further. He told Little Josh that while he, his father and Jahaira were in Alabama, she secretly recorded Josh stating that he kicked Trey in the head. Josh began to get upset.

"That didn't happen. I never said that in my life!" he said, purposefully and forcefully. He could not believe that the detective was so matter-of-factly telling him that others had claimed he hurt Trey in any way. The detective was unrelenting and he immediately switched courses again, trying desperately to trip Josh up and trap him into admitting guilt in the murder.

"Okay, so your friends say you all talked about killing people a couple of weeks before the murder and Trey died similarly. Then there's this girl in Alabama. You're saying that she's lying? Everybody's lying?"

"That's not true at all."

"So they're just all liars," the detective said, tilting his head.

"I don't know what they are. They aren't telling the truth, so that must make them liars."

Josh was conflicted. He could not believe that his father had involvement in Trey's death. He and his father were trying to repair their relationship and after losing his mother, Little Josh had seized on the importance of family. When his father fought for custody of him, it felt good to know that someone cared. Kids love their parents, despite their faults. There wasn't anything wrong with Josh loving his father. He had not known his father long enough to realize the deep-seated issues that plagued Gouker.

"It seems like everybody's telling me stuff and to you everything's like, no, no, no," the detective said, imitating Josh's denial of the allegations.

"I've never said anything like that."

The detective began to question Josh about the events that occurred in Alabama, "So what's the deal with the lady down there?" He was referring to Erin Specth and the ordeal Gouker perpetrated in Alabama when he kidnapped Specth at gunpoint. Josh felt his head spinning. By this point, Josh felt that the officer was just trying to get him to confess. He knew that he didn't do anything wrong, but the repeated questioning and accusations would have made anyone nervous, especially a scared kid with no one to turn to.

"I don't know. I don't want to talk. I ain't in that. I don't feel comfortable talking about that. I had nothing to do with anything about that."[5]

For the next several minutes, Detective Russ questioned Josh extensively about the events of the evening of May 10 and Josh continued to maintain that he left Amanda's home prior to Trey's shower and that he eventually stayed the night at his cousin Cassi's house. The detective pressed him harder, trying to ascertain that Little Josh was at Amanda's during the evening and not where he claimed.

"Well, you weren't at Cassi's," the detective accused after summing up the evidence for the boy he was interrogating.

"I was!" Joshua insisted.

"And you may have been there at some point. You were there maybe after Trey took a shower and got dressed and he tried to leave and put his shoes back on, 'cause you saw all that. If your story is that you didn't see him take a shower; you all weren't getting ready for bed; you didn't see him put his shoes back on or his clothes back on, then how can I believe anything else you are telling me?" He paused and looked at the boy across the table from him and shrugged, offering, "I can play it again if you want to hear it."

Feeling antagonized, Little Josh quickly responded, "I heard everything."

"I can play it again," the detective provoked.

"I heard everything on the CD."

"Well, I can play it again."

Josh looked up at the detective. Becoming upset, he spoke, "You don't have to trust me. I mean, you don't know me." He began to feel desperate, knowing that no matter what he said to the man in front of him, he was not going to believe him. He'd never felt so alone.

Russ answered, "I mean, if you're lying about that, then how do I know you're telling the truth about anything else?"

Josh looked him in the eye, "That's just a chance you have to take."[6]

"I mean, do you see all the information I'm gettin' from lots of different people, from phone records, from autopsy reports?" the detective asked as he gazed at the boy before him.

Josh was indignant. This was not right. He knew he didn't say anything the officer was questioning him about but he didn't know how to convince him. He felt, at that point, any efforts to do so would prove fruitless. "I can tell you I never once talked about killing Trey or kicking Trey in the head. Me, Trey and my Dad were *not* smoking weed together at nine thirty-seven. That's all false," he said, referring to the previous scenario thrown out by the detective that Trey, Josh and Gouker smoked weed together at "The Spot" directly prior to Trey's death. He softened and looked toward the detective, realizing he was getting worked up and that his discomfort was growing. "I would talk to somebody about that if I had your job. I would be doing the same thing and I understand why you are doing it. But I had nothing to do with it."

The detective leaned closer to the boy and asked, "You had time to think about what happened down there that night?"

"I mean, it's just blank in my head. Everybody's talking about it. I don't know what could possibly have happened," Little Josh said, shaking his head slowly and biting his lip.

"My feeling is you know more than you are telling me."

"That's not true."

The detective leaned toward him and calmly asked, "Did you know your dad tried to call me twice yesterday?"

"No, I didn't know. I haven't talked to my dad since the police arrested him in Alabama."

"And you want, you want to find the person responsible for Trey?"

Josh jerked his head up, astonished that the detective would even ask him that question. "Well, of course! What kind of question is that? Yeah, I do!"

"That's not the question I am asking."

"As much as anybody else."

"Your honesty is important in this investigation."

"I understand and I told you, I had nothing to do with it."

Russ continued to repeat the questions, attempting to lead Josh toward the night of Trey's death. "You said ten minutes ago that if you had my job, you would ask the same questions."

"Yeah, but not keep on going and going and saying that you think I know more, which I don't. I think that's harassment. That's calling me a liar."

"Well I think, I think I can play it again if you want to hear your statement, which to me, you're a liar," Detective Russ accused.

"I am sorry if you think that, sir...I was in shock that day along with everybody else," Josh explained as he remembered the heavy feeling weighing on him when they learned Trey was missing and that a body was located at the high school. It had been a terrifying experience that had quite literally torn his world apart. He'd lost another family member barely a year after he found his own mother dead. It was a jarring episode and he had little recollection of any of the events from that day.

"Well, I hope you are telling me the truth. There are certain things I heard on the recording and in your own words. I know it is not the truth." The detective stared at Josh and paused slightly then continued, his words softening, "I just want to give you one last opportunity to tell me the truth."

"I told you the truth," Little Josh offered, frustrated that no matter how many times he told the detective how little he remembered, the man continued to ask the very same questions.[7] Josh had seen enough episodes of procedural police shows to feel the police asked repetitive questions to try and persuade a person to change his story. He had also seen episodes of the very same shows in which police officers got the story wrong and innocent people went to prison for things they hadn't done. He was getting more frightened and felt terribly alone.

"I'd like to go now. I'm starting to feel uncomfortable with this whole thing," Josh said, shutting down. He now understood that the detectives felt that he had something to do with Trey's death and that really scared him. When Little Josh left the police station, he knew that he would have to go back to the Home of the Innocents, where he would remain in foster care away from anyone that he felt he could trust or turn to. Josh had no idea what he was going to do.

The detective asked Josh to sit tight as he went to retrieve the boy's social worker so that she could transport him back to the Home of the Innocents. Russ rose deliberately and strode toward the door. Turning slightly, he regarded the boy in the red hat once again. "I'm just gonna close this door until your worker comes up so that nobody knows your business," he said. "There are a lot of things going on here with other stuff."

Little Josh nodded his understanding and sat alone in the chilly room, wondering how he had gotten to this place in his life. He had always had trouble showing his feelings. He'd learned a long time ago that getting emotional often made things worse but, as he sat there thinking about Trey and his mom and all the bad things that happened in his life, he couldn't hold back his tears.[8]

Shortly after his interview with Little Josh, Detective Russ received an unexpected call from a police officer in Alabama. The Alabama detective advised Russ that after Joshua Gouker's arrest, Gouker had indicated that he had information regarding Trey's death and that he wanted to speak with the Louisville authorities so he could disclose the information. The Alabama detective believed the information could be important to the Louisville police and he placed the call immediately after speaking with Gouker.

It was about four o'clock in the afternoon when Detectives Russ and Stalvey sat down to make a call to Gouker at the Alabama jail that housed him. Russ set up the recorder as Gouker came onto the line. "Can you hear me?" the detective asked when he heard Gouker breathing through the phone.

"Yeah," Gouker spoke into the receiver.

Detective Russ got right to business: "All right, I know you want to talk to me in person; that may probably happen. I may be coming down there."

Both detectives strained to listen to the man on the other end of the line as he sharply exhaled and begin to unload. "Got to 'cause I don't want to do it over the phone, man, and I think you already know what's up," Gouker's voice cracked as he began sobbing through the phone. "This is so hard, man."[9]

The detectives looked at each other, raising their eyebrows. This could be the big break to get the answers

Angelina Young and
her son, Joshua

Angie and Little
Josh outside
karate class

Joshua Gouker and Little Josh, age 11,
during a prison visit

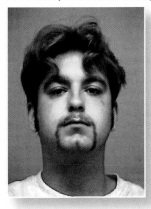

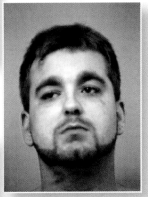

Big Josh Gouker's mug shots
over the years

Students from Liberty High School discovered Trey Zwicker's body in a muddy drainage ditch behind the school building.

The graffiti-covered entrance to the culvert, known locally as "The Spot," near where the body was found

Looking back toward the school from the road where a crowd gathered following the discovery of Trey's body

Gouker spent many years incarcerated in Louisville Metro Corrections for a variety of offenses

Josh Young during a preliminary court proceeding

Photo extracted from trial video

The county courthouse where Big and Little Josh were tried separately for Trey Zwicker's murder

Judge Barry Willett presided over both Joshua Gouker's and Josh Young's cases.

Prosecutor Erin White delivered the opening argument.

Prosecutor Elizabeth Jones Brown established the timeline for the murder and subsequent investigation.

Gouker seemed to relish his appearances on the witness stand.

Amanda McFarland,
the murdered boy's
mother, testified for
the prosecution.

Dr. George Nichols's testimony about the
murder weapon helped the defense.

Josh Young awaited the verdict with his defense team,
from left: co-counsel Pete Schuler, Joshua's social worker,
Josh, co-counsel Leslie Smith.

Josh Young and Leslie Smith listened intently
as Judge Willett read the verdict.

they were waiting for in the Trey Zwicker investigation. Detective Russ began speaking. "I mean, you've got to give me a little something, so I don't drive down there twelve hours for nothing. It's just me and you. There's another detective here with me. Just give me a little bit of something so I know what I am coming down there for. Make sure it's not a wasted drive?"

On the phone, Gouker continued to sob. "I can solve your case; it's about Trey." Gouker's voice trailed off as he waited for the officer to respond.

"So if I drive down there, you are going to give me some information that's going to help me, right?

"But I want to be the one to tell Amanda..."

"Yeah, but I mean you and me, face to face. You're gonna spill it all out and tell me what happened, how things happened and what you know—what you heard—what you saw—everything?"

"I know everything. I've been carrying it with me, man."

"All right. Well, we may not be able to get down there until the morning 'cause it's like a twelve hour drive or some shit," the detective responded.

"It ain't gotta be right now," said Gouker.

"I know you're not going anywhere, but we wanna get this done as quick as we can."

"Uh, look, man, I want to—I'll set and talk to you—just get here."

Detective Russ took a deep breath. After almost two months had passed, Russ was determined to find out what had happened to Trey Zwicker. "Okay. Let me just ask you this real quick, but I want to make sure that I'm coming down there for the right reason."

Gouker burst in, "You know the answers, man. You know who it is." The silence hung in the air. Gouker seemed set on revealing what he wanted the detectives to think.

Detective Russ then took it a step further. "Are we talking about—" he began and then paused, thinking. "Are we talking about your son?" He listened through the receiver as Gouker cried on the other end of the phone line. "Just a quick yes or no. That's all I want to know and then I'll be in my car driving down there."

"Yeah," Gouker sobbed and with that utterance he started a snowball that would ultimately grow and grow.[10]

Chapter 10

Master Manipulator

The two detectives wasted no time advising their superiors that they planned to travel to Alabama to speak with Joshua Gouker in person. They would not be satisfied until he looked them in the eyes as he implicated his own son. They knew they would be better able to gauge his credibility if they could study his body language as he spoke.

The next day, June 22, Detectives Russ and Stalvey sat down with Gouker at the Alabama jail. Gouker immediately set out his agenda. His number one request was that he needed to be the one to tell Amanda about his claim that Josh was responsible for Trey's death. Gouker was by now aware that the emergency protection order sought by Amanda precluded any contact between the two. However, he was desperate to talk to her. His request to speak with his wife was very transparent. He seemed to want to torture her further by finding a way to come face to face with her.

Once assured of that, Gouker got right to the point. He stated that he first became suspicious of his son "by the way he talked to Amanda" after the murder. Gouker did not elaborate on this alleged behavior. Instead, he stated that he later confronted Little Josh and told him that he would be there for him but that Josh needed to tell him everything he knew.[1]

He alleged that Little Josh said that he asked Trey to go "vandalizing" with him and that they first went to "The Spot" to smoke marijuana. He claimed that Trey had an old wooden bat with him. According to Gouker, Little Josh asked Trey for the time and when Trey pulled his phone from his pocket to check, Josh took the bat and hit him with it. After Trey fell, Gouker said Little Josh continued to beat him with the bat and that he couldn't stop. The story rolled off Gouker's tongue as he watched the detectives soak up every word. He claimed that Josh confessed everything to him the Saturday after Trey's death.

Gouker alleged that he convinced his son to confess to him by promising not to tell. He told Little Josh that the police were looking at him and that if Little Josh knew anything that could help him, he needed to say it. He told the officers that he rolled a blunt and sat down with his son to smoke it and the truth came out.

As he watched the detectives, Gouker took a deep breath and continued telling his story, "Yeah, well we done been smoking and shit and I'm freaking out, man, because [the media] is trying to get this whole city thinking I'm a child killer, you know. I'm an easy victim for this, man, 'cause I got a violent past. Everybody on the fucking street hates me anyway. They're just whores that don't want to say nothing."[2]

Gouker placed his head in his hands, portraying the image of a shocked and sickened man, "My son didn't feel nothing. He didn't feel shit, man. Oh my God, when he told me that, man, I just wish I could've taken it outta my head. I knew they was gonna get him, man; they was gonna take him from me, probably forever. This shit is all fucked up, you know, and I can't, I can't, I don't know what the fuck to do."

Gouker continued painting a wild story for the detectives. He claimed that he made the decision to flee Kentucky with his son the Saturday before they left. By that time he was worried, because he claimed that Little Josh had confessed to him and Gouker felt the police were suspicious of his son. He told his mother, Ruby, that Josh was guilty of the murder on that Saturday when she rented a room at a motel near the Watterson Expressway in Louisville. He described a day of lounging at the motel pool, drinking and smoking to settle his frazzled nerves.

Gouker alleged he informed Josh later in the evening that Ruby knew everything and that she asked Little Josh why he would do such a thing. Gouker claimed that Little Josh's response was that he hated Trey and that his demeanor was "just so cold and callous, you know."

The detectives listened closely and, as the interview progressed, they decided it would be fruitful for Gouker to call the people to whom he alleged Little Josh had made a confession. Gouker revealed in his story that his ex-girlfriend, Angelic Burkhead, Jahaira Riddle, his cousin

Cassi, his mother and Cassi's boyfriend all heard his son's confession.

As the detectives stopped for a short break, Gouker alluded to the fact that someone else might be involved in the killing, that he knew the identity of the person who he alleged took his son to dispose of the murder weapon. He dangled that piece of information in front of them like a carrot to a rabbit.

Because Gouker claimed to know a person who had contributed to disposing of evidence in Trey's death, the detectives then called the Assistant Commonwealth Attorney, prior to ascertaining the person's identity or any other information about the person and were able to secure immunity for the person to whom Gouker referred. This meant that as long as that person was completely truthful, he or she could not be charged with a crime or prosecuted.

Detectives were willing to let Gouker call the various witnesses that he alleged heard his son confess. Gouker told the detectives that he needed to phone the people personally. He contended that none of the people he mentioned would speak with the detectives unless Gouker gave them express permission. At first, the detectives seemed skeptical that the alleged witnesses would not cooperate without Gouker's permission. But Gouker was emphatic that these people were so loyal to him that they would not even think about speaking with police without Gouker's explicit authorization.

Gouker attempted to explain his control over these people to the detectives: "You gotta understand, they're not going to tell you nothing unless I tell 'em. I promise you." He was confident in this statement. As it turns out, he was 100 percent correct.

Detective Stalvey stepped in, seemingly disturbed that Gouker expected to play such an integral role in the investigation, "But just understand, we can't just run an investigation based on you doing everything. If I went out there right now without you, there's gotta be something that's gonna make them say 'Oh shit, well, I better go ahead and be straight. What would it be?'"

Gouker leaned back, arms crossed and smug. "Ratting on Josh Gouker's son, it's not an option," he stated matter-of-factly.[3]

"Unless Josh Gouker says talk?" Detective Russ looked assessingly at him.

"I'm not trying to be a hard ass, but I'm telling you, it's not an option. They're not gonna do it." Gouker was nothing if not completely confident and was unrelenting in his assertion that his cohorts would not speak with the detectives unless Gouker called them himself.

Detective Stalvey sighed, "Okay, well, I've heard that before."

"I promise you, that's the truth," Gouker stated. He knew that he controlled all the women in his life through fear and a perverted sense of loyalty.

To prove that he knew more about Trey Zwicker's murder than detectives, he divulged the name of the person he claimed helped to dispose of the murder weapon. He declared that after Trey's murder, Little Josh asked Gouker's cousin Cassi to help him dispose of the bloody clothes and the bloody bat he alleged the killer used to murder Trey. Gouker claimed that when he learned that

Cassi kept that secret from him for four days, he erupted, telling her, "Your loyalty lies with me and not my son!"

He wanted to help, he implored them, and he hoped that they would look past his criminal history to see that. Gouker puffed up, chest out and head high, "You know, my character can't be restored for the shit I did in the past. I'm not gonna be a model citizen to any motherfucker that's known me. What I am is the leader of a gang, a very violent motherfucker. That doesn't argue, you know."

With that sentiment in mind, it was almost two in the morning when the detectives allowed Gouker to call Cassi so that they could hear her version of what happened after Trey's murder. When she didn't answer, they tried Gouker's mother, Ruby. Gouker jumped right in and began speaking with his mother, "Hey, I'm in, I'm up in Madison right now."[4]

"Okay..." Ruby replied slowly. She must have been curious about the reason for her son's late night call.

"Where they got me in that kidnapping case. It's, it's bullshit though. I'm end up beating that."

"Alright, good."

"Hey, listen, umm, Louisville Homicide detectives are here and they know everything," Gouker sobbed through the phone to his mother, his heaving breaths echoing through the receiver.

After a moment of silence she questioned, "What do you mean?"

"About Trey."

"What about him?"

"What happened to him."

Ruby was not taking the bait. She tentatively continued, "Like what?"

"What happened, Mom. The whole thing; they know everything."

Detective Russ interjected and began to speak to Gouker, "Tell her I'm sitting here and just tell her to tell me what she knows and she's not going to be in any trouble."

"Who do they think done it?" Ruby asked, addressing her son.

"They *know* who did it, Mom," Gouker emphasized.

Once again, Detective Russ jumped in. "Let me talk. Can I talk?" he asked, attempting to take control away from Gouker. Only a few minutes into the telephone call, Gouker already seemed to be leading his mother's questioning. It seemed clear that he wanted and needed to control every aspect of the detectives' investigation. He signed heavily as he reluctantly allowed Russ to momentarily take over the conversation.

"Hey, Ruby. This is Detective Russ from Louisville. I'm down here in Alabama with Josh, okay?"

"Yeah."

"So we know everything."

"What is everything?" she asked again, anxious for an answer to the question she had posed several times in the short conversation.

"Well, listen to me for a minute. No matter what you tell me, you're not in any trouble for just having information, okay. But I need you to tell me what Josh Young told you. You're not in trouble; you're not going to be charged. You're not going to jail, none of that stuff. All you are is an informational witness, 'cause you heard somebody tell you something and I need to know what he told you."

Ruby paused, seemingly confused. "Big Josh or Little Josh?" she asked.

"Little Josh," Scott Russ emphatically stated, "about the motel, when you all were there?"

"I didn't believe him."

"Okay, well tell me what he told you," the detective prodded.

"He just told me that he didn't care for Trey."

"Mom!" Gouker exclaimed, apparently upset that his mother was not saying what he wanted her to say.

"What?" she barked back.

"Everybody's told 'em everything. Do you get that?"

"Tell me what Little Josh said," the detective pressed.

Ruby was nonchalant in her response. It was clear that she did not want to commit to Big Josh's revelation. She didn't believe it. "He told me that Trey got him in trouble and stuff all the time and he couldn't stand him. Umm, I know Trey was bigger than Little Josh and he said something about hitting him...That makes me know he didn't do it."

Ruby clearly was not saying what Gouker wanted her to say and he was becoming upset as he listened. "Mom, they're gonna end up trying to get you, man and throw you in prison. Just tell 'em the fucking truth!" he threatened in a raised voice in an attempt to coerce his mother into implicating Little Josh.

"I am telling the truth. That's when you told me that Little Josh had done it!"

Ruby continued to speak with the detective and her son about Gouker's actions in implicating his son in Trey's murder. She continued to vehemently deny that her grandson was involved in Trey's death. Instead, she emphasized that Gouker was in trouble when they were at the motel and spoke about Trey's murder. Prior to fleeing the state, he had received papers regarding the emergency protective order sought by Amanda and he knew it was likely that his parole would be revoked and that he would return to prison. Ruby told the detective that she would never have allowed Gouker to run with the child unless she thought they were in serious trouble. She did not believe that Little Josh was involved in Trey's murder, though she did eventually say that Little Josh told her he hit Trey with a baseball bat. Instead, she felt that her son had convinced Little Josh to go along with his plan of making Ruby believe that they could somehow be involved in the murder so that she would agree with the decision to flee.

It was a convoluted story. It took substantial prodding to convince Ruby to say what she said to police. Gouker had a way of manipulating his mother. In part, she feared him, but she also truly loved her son. As the conversation wound to a close, Gouker gushed at the end of the call, "Mom, I love you."

"I love you too," she echoed. As they said their goodbyes, Gouker once again began to weep loudly.

Afterward, at about two o'clock, Gouker and the detectives attempted to contact Cassi and once again they were unable to connect.

Detective Russ looked toward Detective Stalvey. "Call and have [a patrol car] go by [Cassi's house] and tell Cassi to answer the phone." He wanted to speak with Cassi and he wanted to do so immediately. He further directed Detective Stalvey, "Just say we need to do it ASAP! They gotta get over there like the house is on fucking fire, yeah. Tell them to tell

Cassi to answer the phone 'cause Josh is trying to call 'em. Yeah, they can tell 'em that."

Detective Stalvey immediately contacted the Louisville dispatch center and instructed them to send a police cruiser to Cassi's residence to wake her up so that she could speak with Gouker. As he set those actions into motion, Gouker suggested that they reach out to Angelic Burkhead, his one-time lover and companion as he had fled south just a week earlier. Due to the fact that she worked late hours at a nightclub, he was confident that she would be awake and answer the call.

After just a few rings, Angelic's voice was on the line, "Hello?"[5]

"Angelic?"

"Yeah?" she slowly asked, unsure of the voice on the other end of the phone line.

"Hey, it's me."

"Who's me? I'm at work, baby. I can't even talk right now. I'm at work."

"Hey. This is Josh. I need to talk to you. It's very important. Can you just take a break?"

"How long?"

"Five minutes?"

Obviously nervous because her job could be affected by the call, Angelic acquiesced, "I mean, I'm probably gonna get yelled at real bad for this, but talk."

Gouker wasted no time getting directly to point: "Hey, listen. Louisville Homicide detectives are here and they know everything that happened to Trey."

Silence filled the line and Angelic did not say a word. Gouker continued, "You hear me?"

"Yeah, I hear you," she responded, apparently waiting to see where he was going with the conversation.

Detective Russ quickly joined in. "Hey Angelic, this is Detective Russ with Louisville. I am down here in Alabama. I just need to know what Josh Junior, Josh Young told you about what happened."

"No."

"No, what?"

"No, he didn't tell me what happened," she answered.

Gouker couldn't take it anymore and sighing heavily, he grabbed the reins back and took over the conversation. "Angelic!" he barked.

"Yeah?" Angelic was noncommittal. It appeared that she was unsure what Gouker wanted her to say, so she hesitated. She did not want to say the wrong thing and set him off. Even when he was imprisoned hundreds of miles away, she still feared him and that fear controlled her.

"They know. You're not in any trouble," Gouker coerced.

Detective Russ parroted the sentiment, "You're not in trouble for knowing about what happened. All I need to know is what Josh Junior told you."

"Nothing. I don't know anything about it, except for what has been on the news." As Angelic adamantly denied knowledge of the crime, Detective Russ turned to Gouker for help, "Tell her, tell her what you told me."

Gouker implored Angelic, "Angelic, listen to me. Tell the truth. I need you to tell the truth right now for me. It's okay."

"I don't know what the truth is," Angelic quietly whimpered as she began to cry.

Detective Russ interjected, "Did Josh Junior ever tell you that he did it, that he killed Trey, or did you ever hear him say it in front of you?"

"No," she responded, her voice becoming louder and more forceful.

The detective pushed further, "Angelic, you're not in any trouble for knowing. You didn't participate. You just heard him say it. If you heard him say it, I need you to tell me."

Exasperated, her voice became louder: "No!"

"I can hear you," Scott Russ continued. "I know you're upset and you're crying. You gotta trust Josh and you gotta trust me that you're not in any trouble."

Gouker quickly rejoined the conversation, crying loudly for his former lover's benefit. "Angelic, baby, listen, just tell. Just tell him the truth; it's okay. 'Cause they already know. I just don't want nobody else in trouble. Just tell them, baby."

"I don't know," she whimpered. The "five minute" conversation that Gouker requested with her was spiraling out of control. She was nervous anyway, because her job was at stake. She already suspected that her shift manager would lay into her when she returned from the impromptu break. It was just so hard to say no to Gouker. She loved him but she also feared him. She obviously wasn't comfortable answering the detective's questions, but Gouker was compelling her and she didn't want to disappoint him. She was audibly upset but she couldn't cut Gouker off and get off the phone. She seemed afraid of the ramifications of doing so.

"Did Josh Junior tell you that he did it?" Detective Russ chimed in as she cried softly.

"No!"

When his prompting did not produce the result that he wanted, Gouker appealed to Angelic's love for him by indicating that if she did not say what he wanted her to say, that he would be in trouble. He brought up Jahaira.

"Angelic, how long have I known you?"

"Like ten years…" she trailed off as she remembered their history. She had known Gouker since she was just a teenager.

"How long have I known Jahaira?"

"Uh, not that long. It's only been a couple of months."

"Angelic, remember I didn't want you hanging around her?"

"Yeah."

"I'm not saying how long I've been fucking her. I'm saying how long have I known her?"

"Uh, yeah, a long time, but when we used to date, you didn't fucking like her because she's a bitch," she said, sniffling as she tried to determine where Gouker was going with the conversation. She sounded upset, seeming to still hold a grudge that Gouker momentarily tossed her aside to begin a sexual relationship with her friend whom he previously claimed to dislike.

"Well, that bitch has got this whole thing fucked up. Now just tell the truth for me right now. I need you to do this. Baby, can you hear me? I need you to tell the truth. You know I love *him* more than life. You know that, but I need you to tell the truth right now, okay?" He emphasized "him," seemingly trying to direct Angelic that he wanted her to implicate his son in the murder.

Angelic did not yet take the bait: "Yeah, but I really don't fucking know!"

Gouker turned to the detective, shrugging his shoulders. He explained that Angelic did not believe it was really him on the telephone and that he felt she was afraid to speak up. Russ encouraged him to do something to prove his identity to Angelic so that she would speak more freely. Gouker blurted out of the blue, "I stuck a bottle in your pussy years ago."

Angelic sighed quietly, "Okay, it's you."

Gouker had no reservations in throwing his sexual perversions of days past out for the detectives to hear. In fact, he likely thought that it was amusing that he would speak of such intimate matters in the presence of police officers.

Detective Russ began speaking to the nearly hysterical woman. "This is the right thing to do for Trey. If it was your family member laying down there dead in a ditch, you would want somebody to step up and do the right thing. All I need to know is what Josh Junior told you, what you heard him say. That won't take you ten seconds to tell me what you heard."

Angelic started to cry again and the detective pushed further, "Did Josh Junior tell you that he did it, that he killed Trey?" She continued to cry and did not respond and the detective asked the question two more times. "Tell me what he told you."

"Angelic," Gouker interjected, his voice soothing now, "if you love us, me and Josh at all, just tell the truth, please."

"What did he say to you?" the detective pressed, firmer now.

Once again, Angelic responded, "Tell me? No. Nothing."

By this point Angelic had been asked the same question more than ten times and she continued to deny that Little Josh ever confessed anything to her. However, both Gouker and Detective Russ continued to press her and persuade her to state that Josh somehow confessed to her. Finally the detective pushed one more time and she gave in, "He told you he killed Trey?"

"Yeah."

"Did he say he did it with a baseball bat?

"I don't know."

"Where did he tell you this? Where was you all at?"

"I don't remember."

"Tell me exactly what he told you and I will let you go."

"Yeah, he said he did it, at the hotel room."

"Is there anything else about the conversation that you remember?"

"No."

They had gotten what they wanted. Angelic told the detectives exactly what Gouker wanted her to say, but it took a lot of prodding and coaching. Angelic would later maintain that as they were on the run together in Tennessee, Little Josh had confessed to her that he murdered Trey with "a slugger." At that time, there was no way for her to know that forensics would later show that a wooden bat was not the murder weapon. But at this point in the investigation, the detectives took in every word of the story told by Angelic and Gouker. As the phone call concluded, Detective Russ allowed the two to say their goodbyes to each other, each ending the call with an "I love you," as was characteristic of Gouker when he spoke with any of the women he controlled.

Gouker had successfully coerced two women in his life into implicating his son in Trey's murder. It had taken extended questioning and both women answered in the negative numerous times prior to indicating his son was involved. However, both women finally asserted that Little Josh had confessed to them. The detectives felt that they needed to attempt to reach out to Cassi again. At a quarter after two in the morning, they tried her once more. By that time, the squad car that was sent to her home by the dispatch office had arrived and roused her so that she could take Gouker's call.

"Hello," she answered as she picked up the phone.[6]

"Cassi?" Gouker questioned.

"Yeah."

"What's up?"

"Oh, hi. What are you doing?" she asked nonchalantly.

"Listen, they know everything..." His voice trailing off, Gouker again willed himself to cry for his audience.

"How's that?"

"Everybody was talking when we left." Gouker did not disclose to her that the reason officers "knew everything" was because he had called the officers and given them the story. Instead, he acted as though officers were speaking with him because of some type of tip they received from Louisville. He explained to her that he was sitting with the Louisville detectives and that he needed to speak with her regarding Trey's death. He needed her to tell them everything she knew about the situation.

"Listen to me, okay?" he began.

"I'm listening."

"Your loyalty lies with me," he stated with force.

Without skipping a beat, Cassi replied, "Yes."

"Josh," he said, referring to himself by raising his voice and emphasizing his name.

Sensing that Gouker was beginning an attempt at leading Cassi, Detective Russ stepped in. "Let her tell me," he stated to Gouker.

"Alright. Cassi, who killed Trey?" asked Gouker.

"What?" she seemed taken aback that he would ask the question.

"The truth." He paused. "Who killed Trey?"

Without hesitation, Cassi quickly quipped, "You did, right?"

Gouker was quick to respond, "No, tell the truth. Who did it? This is *Big* Josh, Cassi." He enunciated specifically and deliberately as the word "big" rolled off his tongue.

"What?"

"Do you hear me? This is *Big* Josh." There it was again. He once again emphasized that he was "Big Josh," not so subtly differentiating between himself and his son.

"Tell the truth. Who killed Trey?"

"You did, right?" she asked once more.

Gouker looked over at Detective Russ, sheepishly. His cousin had implicated him twice when asked about the murder. "I told her that I would take it if it ever..." He abruptly stopped speaking to the detective and focused his attention back on his cousin. "Tell the truth. Cassi. You're not in any trouble. They know everything and you're not gonna be in any trouble for helping with that other shit."

Cassi was silent and Detective Russ began to speak to her once again, "Hey, Cassi, this is Detective Russ from Louisville. I've talked to you a few months before. Tell me about the night that Trey was murdered. Who woke you up in your bedroom?

A light bulb went off and it appeared Cassi finally realized what Gouker was alluding to when he addressed himself as *Big Josh*. "Uh," she paused, "uh, well...well, Little Josh?" she asked.

"Look," Detective Russ spoke up, "like he told you, I already talked to the prosecutors. As long as you tell me the truth, on your super, slight, slim involvement, you are not in any trouble."

Gouker obviously wanted to make sure that Cassi said the right thing and he interrupted the conversation and began leading her in the direction that he wanted: "Let me say it like this, Cassi. When Josh woke you up and he asked you..."

Detective Russ likely realized where Gouker's involvement was leading. It didn't take a genius to see that he was trying to put words in Cassi's mouth. "Let her, I want her to tell me that," he interjected. "Cassi, tell me what happened when he woke you up. Tell me the truth and you're not gonna be in any trouble for telling me the truth."

"He got up and uh, he tried to get me up," she fumbled, parroting the words Gouker had said to her just seconds before. "And he said, 'I need your help' or I can't really remember exactly what he said."

Gouker could not let Russ lead the questioning and, after Cassi's initial answers that implicated him, he must have wanted to control exactly what she said to the investigators. He said to the detectives, "Now, let me do it."

"No!" Detective Russ replied, looking at the convict, likely realizing that Gouker was once again jockeying for control of the interview. Things weren't supposed to work that way.

Shooting Gouker a dark look meant to shut him down, the detective continued to extract information from Cassi. In the end, she stated that she was sleeping when Little Josh came into her room and that he attempted to wake her up. She indicated that initially he told her that he had killed Trey and needed her help in discarding the murder weapon. According to her, she did not believe him and rolled over and fell back asleep.

She asserted that it was several minutes later that he came in a second time with the same request. At that point, she climbed out of bed and agreed to drive him to a dumpster. She and Little Josh got into her van and she took him to an apartment complex approximately ten minutes from her home. She claimed that the items they discarded were bloody clothes and an old, wooden baseball bat that belonged to her boyfriend.

She claimed that she saw blood on the baseball bat but that she thought it was likely animal blood and she did not ask any further questions of the boy.

Now, as she spoke with her cousin and the detectives in the early morning hours during that telephone call, she had implicated Joshua Young in the murder of Trey Zwicker and, on Josh Gouker's word alone, the officers had secured immunity for her.

Detective Russ began to question Cassi regarding Gouker's allegation that Little Josh confessed to a room full of people at the motel. Cassi denied having any memory of a confession at that location and she completely contradicted the account that Gouker related to officers during his interview with them prior to the telephone calls. It was likely that Gouker had made up that portion of the interview as he went along.

She admitted that when officers had previously visited her home shortly after the murder, she had lied to them. At that time, she maintained that she had no knowledge regarding Trey's death. She then admitted that her live-in boyfriend also knew that she took the clothing to the dumpster and the detective asked her to wake him up so that they could speak with him on the phone as well. Within minutes, he was on the line. "Hello?"

"What's up, bro?" asked Gouker.

"What's up, man?" Cassi's boyfriend responded, his voice sounding very sleepy.

"Hey, uh, I'm down here in Alabama. I got Louisville Homicide Detectives here. They went and seen Little Josh yesterday. They know everything."

"And just so you know, this is Detective Russ. I've talked to you before. You and your [girlfriend] are not in any trouble for what you know, what you saw, what you heard. All you all are, are informational witnesses, okay. You are not in trouble for anything. I've talked to Josh, Big Josh; I've talked to Ruby; I've talked to Cassi; I've talked to Angelic. I've talked to all these people, okay?"

"Yes, sir."

"So you're not in any trouble. All I need you to tell me is what you know, what you heard and everything will be fine."

Gouker leaned over to the detective, "Let me tell him you're straight." He then began speaking to Cassi's boyfriend, "Hey, it's me, man. Just tell them the truth; you hear me?"

"Okay."

Detective Russ began to ask the man when he first heard that Little Josh was involved in the murder and he indicated that Big Josh told him the day after Trey's body was found. He was emphatic that Big Josh, not Little Josh, told him about the involvement. Once again when Gouker heard something he did not like, he jumped in.

"No, it was Cassi," Gouker corrected Cassi's boyfriend when he stated that it was Big Josh who implicated Little Josh.

Russ shot him a glance, perturbed that Gouker was again interjecting himself in the conversation and trying to influence witness testimony. He looked at Detective Russ and shrugged. "[Cassi's boyfriend] is a drunk," Gouker whispered, implying that the boyfriend was unable to adequately recall the events of the night.

Detective Russ continued, "Did Little Josh talk to you about it?"

"Not really."

Eventually Cassi's boyfriend also stated that Little Josh had told him he'd hit Trey with a baseball bat "numerous times."[7]

Cassi reclaimed the phone and they continued to speak about her version of events the night that Trey was murdered. The officers arranged to visit Cassi's house the following day so that they could check the van in which she allegedly transported the murder weapon for evidence. They also wanted her to drive them on the same route she claimed she took Little Josh to dispose of the items she asserted he had used in Trey's death. As they got off the phone, Gouker was quick to tell Cassi that he loved her and she parroted back the same. She promised that she would soon place money on his "books" at the jail so that he could call her more frequently and buy items from the commissary. Even locked safely behind bars, Gouker still had influence in making his women do his bidding.

The officers prepared to leave Gouker behind in Alabama and they surely felt they were on the precipice of something huge. Trey Zwicker's death was one of the most talked-about crimes in recent history in Louisville and they really wanted to solve it.

Officers arrived at the Home of the Innocents where Little Josh was staying. Ruby Jessie told officers that while at the motel, Big Josh told her that his son murdered Trey and after some prodding by Detective Russ, she stated that Little Josh had indicated that he was involved in the killing. They had a statement from Angelic that Little Josh had confessed to her in a motel room in Tennessee and they also had Cassi's statement that she drove Little Josh to a dumpster to dispose of bloody clothes and a bat she claimed had been used in the crime. They also were suspicious of a perceived inconsistency in previous statements Little Josh had given to law enforcement. In one statement, he said he saw Trey after his shower on the evening of his death. In the other, he told officers that he did not see Trey after his shower, because he was at Cassi's house.

There was no forensic evidence linking Josh Young to the crime scene and he had not given a statement to police admitting guilt. The officers had assertions from four proven liars and an inconsistency between two statements given by a scared and traumatized fifteen-year-old boy as he was questioned by police without the presence of a parent or guardian.

That is probably the reason they allowed Gouker to call several individuals. They wanted to know that he could give them other people who would back up his story. Cassi was the least consistent of the women Gouker phoned. When asked initially who killed Trey, she stated that Big Josh did it. In fact, the first few times officers and Gouker asked her, she claimed that Josh Gouker had killed Trey. It was only after careful prodding and direction by Gouker that she finally, very reluctantly, said that Little Josh was involved. Gouker controlled Cassi and she had a history of doing whatever he asked her to do.

Angelic was also difficult to believe. She was still involved with Gouker and she clearly feared him in many respects. She too refused to tell police that Little Josh was involved until Gouker blatantly led her in that direction. At his direction, she implicated his son.

Lastly, Ruby Jessie also had a vested interest in lying for Gouker. She had a much closer relationship with him than with her grandson. Ruby had a history of doing anything she could for her son. She had served thirty days in jail for trying to smuggle drugs to him while he was incarcerated. She was willing to give up her own freedom for her son; she'd demonstrated that through past behavior. Yet she professed to the detectives time and again that she didn't believe her grandson was involved in Trey's death.

Every witness who spoke out against Little Josh was fiercely loyal to Gouker and feared Gouker's wrath when he did not get his way. They would do anything Gouker told them to do, especially if Gouker's freedom was on the line.

It is difficult for an outsider to comprehend the pull that
Gouker had over people. He preyed on those weaker than
himself and he controlled them through fear and intimida-
tion. Everyone in his inner circle knew that Gouker had no
qualms about lashing out violently at those who crossed
him. It was an incredible amount of control, but it was
tangible and real. At this point in their investigation, the
detectives could not have comprehended the lengths to
which these women would go in order to protect Gouker.

Despite the fact that the only witnesses against him
were women held emotionally captive by Big Josh, the
detectives arrested Little Josh and transported him to
the juvenile detention center. He could not believe the
words he was hearing as officers informed him that he was
under arrest for the death of his stepbrother. He knew in
his heart that he had nothing to do with the brutal murder of Trey Zwicker, a boy he'd considered a friend for the
majority of his life.

When police arrested Little Josh, he was scared
and confused. He just couldn't understand why officers
thought he was involved. It would not be long until he
heard the first rumblings of the evidence police claimed
to have against him. When he learned that his own biological father was the impetus for the charges, he felt
crushingly betrayed. The virtual stranger who called himself Josh's father had apparently sacrificed his child to save
himself.[8]

Only six short weeks before, his father had regained
custody of him and Little Josh, though unfamiliar with
the man, felt good that someone cared enough to fight

for him. It was unbelievable that someone who claimed to care about him could now craft such an amazing lie. As Josh settled into bed that evening, he had no idea of the firestorm that would soon erupt around his case and he waited, hoping that he would go before a juvenile court judge the next day and that everyone would see it was all a mistake.

Chapter 11

The System

In Kentucky, proceedings involving juvenile offenders in juvenile court are confidential. The records are sealed and the courtrooms are closed to the public. Therefore, when Josh was initially taken into custody, his court appearances were not public fodder. He appeared before a juvenile court judge for his initial arraignment on June 24, 2011. His attorneys entered a plea of "not true" on his behalf. A "not true" plea in juvenile court is akin to a "not guilty" plea in adult court.

The case went before the judge again on June 27 for a detention hearing. When a child is "detained," he or she is entitled to a detention hearing within seventy-two hours. Juvenile court must use the "least restrictive alternative" in keeping a young person incarcerated, so the court will decide at that hearing whether the child will be released to a parent, kept in a secure detention facility, placed on house arrest or a variety of other alternatives. The judge ordered that Josh would be remanded to a detention facility pending prosecution of the case.

When a juvenile is charged with a crime, in certain situations the prosecutors can request that the court transfer the case to adult court. In the event that the judge grants that request, the proceedings are open to the public and the case continues in the same manner as any regular adult court case.

The transfer is not automatic and there are specific safeguards in place to protect the rights of the alleged offender. It is not a decision that the court takes lightly. The purpose of juvenile court is to protect the best interest of the child and the goal is rehabilitation. The school of thought is that children are not as mature as adults and may not make adult decisions. The hope is that when a juvenile offender is caught breaking the law, the court can step in and rectify the situation by putting safeguards in place to insure the child has proper support and to rehabilitate the child so that he or she may become a productive member of society upon reaching adulthood. The relevant statute, KRS 600.010, states that the juvenile code which governs the treatment of child offenders "shall be interpreted to promote the best interest of the child through providing treatment and sanctions to reduce recidivism and assist in making the child a productive citizen." It further urges that this goal shall be met by "advancing the principles of professional responsibility, accountability and reformation, while maintaining public safety, seeking restitution and reparation."[1]

This is the reason that juvenile court proceedings in Kentucky are closed to the public: The system does not want to stigmatize a child for his or her entire life for a youthful mistake. Each child whose case is adjudicated in juvenile court will have a "clean slate" upon reaching adulthood. However, in some situations, the circumstances are so egregious that the court must consider allowing the case to proceed in adult court. Such cases are a permanent part of the child's record if a conviction is obtained.

In the case against Joshua Young, the Commonwealth elected to request transfer to adult court. When this occurs, the defendant is entitled to a transfer hearing and certain criteria must be met before the court can consider sending the case to circuit court. If the child offender is charged with a Class A or Class B felony and is fourteen years of age or older, he or she is eligible for transfer to circuit court. When the charge is a Class D Felony or higher and the child is over sixteen, a case is eligible for transfer if the child has at least one previous felony adjudication where he or she was found to have committed the crime.

A Class A felony is punishable by twenty years to life in prison. In Kentucky, Class A felonies are the most heinous of crimes like murder and the rape of a child. A Class B felony is punishable by ten to twenty years in prison. Examples of Class B felonies in Kentucky are crimes like manufacturing methamphetamine and violent robberies or robberies involving weapons. Class C and D felonies carry less jail time. Class C felonies have a penalty range of five to ten years and Class D felonies have a range of one to five years.

Josh was fifteen years old at the time he was charged with Trey's murder. Detective Russ charged him with two crimes: murder and tampering with physical evidence.

Tampering with physical evidence is a Class D felony in
Kentucky that is punishable by one to five years in prison.
The relevant Kentucky Revised Statute, KRS 524.100,
states:

1) A person is guilty of tampering with physical evidence when, believing that an official proceeding is
   pending or may be instituted, he:
   (a) Destroys, mutilates, conceals, removes or alters
       physical evidence which he believes is about to
       be produced or used in the official proceeding
       with intent to impair its verity or availability in
       the official proceeding; or
   (b) Fabricates any physical evidence with intent
       that it be introduced in the official proceeding
       or offers any physical evidence, knowing it to be
       fabricated or altered.
   (2) Tampering with physical evidence is a Class D
       felony.[2]

In order to make a case for this charge, the Commonwealth has to prove that, believing that an official proceeding was pending or would be instituted, the defendant
destroyed, mutilated, concealed, removed or altered physical evidence that he or she believed would be used in the
proceeding, with the intent to impair its verity or availability. The Commonwealth alleged that after the murder,
Josh discarded the murder weapon and bloody clothes and
this was the basis for the charge of tampering with physical evidence. If this was the only crime Josh was charged
with, he would not have been eligible for transfer and

the case would have been adjudicated in juvenile court. However, he was also charged with Trey's murder. Joshua was over fourteen years old and the charge of murder is a capital offense in Kentucky, so this case was eligible for transfer to adult court and the Commonwealth elected to seek transfer. The relevant statute for the murder charge is KRS 507.020 and it states:

(1) A person is guilty of murder when:
  (a) With intent to cause the death of another person, he causes the death of such person or of a third person; except that in any prosecution a person shall not be guilty under this subsection if he acted under the influence of extreme emotional disturbance for which there was a reasonable explanation or excuse, the reasonableness of which is to be determined from the viewpoint of a person in the defendant's situation under the circumstances as the defendant believed them to be. However, nothing contained in this section shall constitute a defense to a prosecution for or preclude a conviction of manslaughter in the first degree or any other crime; or
  (b) Including, but not limited to, the operation of a motor vehicle under circumstances manifesting extreme indifference to human life, he wantonly engages in conduct which creates a grave risk of death to another person and thereby causes the death of another person.
(2) Murder is a capital offense.[3]

Prosecutors appeared to operate under the theory that Josh had killed his stepbrother and that he did so deliberately and with the intention to kill Trey.

The Jefferson County Attorney's Office is the prosecutorial office that handles juvenile cases. After Josh was formally charged with Trey's murder, the Jefferson County Attorney's Office made the decision to seek transfer. However, prior to doing so, in Kentucky, the juvenile prosecutor is required to consult with the Commonwealth Attorney to determine whether the office is in agreement with the attempt to transfer. If that transfer is successful, it will be the Office of the Commonwealth Attorney who prosecutes the offense.

The transfer hearing in juvenile court is comparable to a probable cause hearing in adult court. Basically, the Commonwealth is given the opportunity to put up proof in the matter through witnesses. Generally, the main witness will be the officer or detective who made the charge. The defendant's attorney is then given the opportunity to cross-examine any witnesses called by the prosecutor.

After hearing the evidence, the judge makes a determination whether the case should remain in juvenile court or proceed in circuit court. In making his or her determination, the judge must consider several factors: the seriousness of the offense, whether the offense was against a person or property, the maturity of the child, the child's prior record, the best interest of the child and the community, the prospects of adequate protection of the public, the likelihood of reasonable rehabilitation of the child by the use of procedures, services and facilities currently available to the juvenile justice system and evidence of the child's participation in a gang.

At the completion of the hearing, the judge must consider whether the child meets these criteria. If two or more of the factors favor transfer based on the testimony heard during the hearing, the judge may transfer the case to circuit court at his or her discretion. If two or more of the criteria are not met, the case proceeds in juvenile court.

The judge heard the transfer hearing in Joshua's case in two parts, on August 9 and September 14, 2011, and she found that the case was appropriate for transfer. Although Josh had no serious charges on his record, the severity of the crime and that fact that it was committed against a person was enough to warrant transfer and his attorneys stipulated that those two criteria were met by the facts of the case. Joshua was remanded to the juvenile detention center pending his indictment.

After the transfer hearing, the case was presented to a grand jury and the prosecution secured an indictment. Josh then appeared for the first time in front of the new judge who would ultimately preside over the trial, Judge Barry Willett. As judge in the matter, he was responsible for setting bond for Josh. He set that bond in the amount of $100,000 cash only. Until someone was able to post that bond, Josh had to remain in the custody of the Jefferson County Youth Center pending trial.

While Little Josh was being held at Louisville's youth detention facility, his father was miles away in Alabama, also incarcerated. Gouker continued to be held on the kidnapping charges involving Erin Specth and that was not the only thing keeping him behind bars. Gouker was the subject of two other holds. He was in violation of his parole in Kentucky and a detainer was lodged for those cases. He was also the subject of a hold out of Indiana for prior theft charges.

Gouker, it appeared, was stuck. Even if he made bond on the Alabama case, both jurisdictions to the north wanted to extradite him back into their states to face the charges against him there. It seemed there was no way out this time. However, Gouker had a way of getting what he wanted. He wanted out of custody and back onto the streets of Louisville. It seemed that this was something that would never happen. However, luck was on Gouker's side. Someone in the corrections system made a costly mistake.

Alabama courts released their hold on Gouker in October of 2013 and for some reason did not recognize the holds from the other two states. It was a mistake that would give Gouker his freedom, at least for a while. He was released from Alabama and the Kentucky and Indiana authorities were not notified in time. When officials of those states did not come to Alabama to claim Gouker, he was released outright. Gouker wasted no time making his way back to Louisville and he immediately sought out Angelic.

It wasn't long until Alabama authorities, as well as officials in Kentucky and Indiana, realized the mistake. They issued warrants for the arrest of Gouker. By that point he was well hidden at Angelic's and spent quite some time hiding there from the police. It was months later when police burst into Angelic's home and discovered her paramour hiding there. They arrested him and transported him immediately to corrections.

Even after the prosecutors filed charges against Josh Young, they continued to investigate his father. In November of 2011, Gouker agreed to undergo a polygraph test as requested by Detective Russ. At the time, Gouker was being held in Hopkins County for criminal charges from Louisville. The judge issued an order that transported Gouker to Madison, Indiana, to undergo a polygraph test. He signed a consent form and underwent the polygraph at the Madison County Jail on November 28, 2011. The exam consisted of two questions: (1) Did you help plan the boy's attack and (2) Did you strike the boy with a weapon? Gouker submitted to the test and the results were recorded as "Inconclusive."

As Louisville detectives continued to investigate Trey's murder, it became clearer that Gouker was involved and they made the decision to seek an indictment against him. Detective Russ procured a Direct Indictment of Gouker, meaning that the case did not originate in district court as many cases do. Instead, it was presented directly to the grand jury. Gouker was impoverished, so attorneys were appointed to represent him. Mark Hall and Don Major were both experienced and competent attorneys and did their best to diligently protect the rights of their client.

Gouker could not have been an easy client. He liked to dominate and control. Again and again, he spoke with the media in direct contrast to the advice of his attorneys. He told the media that he killed Trey and that his son had no involvement in the crime.[4]

When he appeared before Judge Willett for arraignment, the court set Gouker's bond at one million dollars. He was also a state inmate on previous Louisville charges due to his parole being revoked. Gouker faced more charges than Little Josh did. In addition to the murder charge, he was charged with two counts of felony cruelty to animals for killing Trey's puppy and his sister's cat. At the arraignment, Gouker asked the judge to allow him to plead guilty to all charges and he admitted that he killed Trey.[5]

The judge disregarded this statement and set the case for court dates in conjunction with his son. The pretrial preparations in the matter were time consuming and the discovery received from the Commonwealth was voluminous. Gouker was incarcerated outside of the city, so his attorneys were forced to file motions that allowed them unfettered access to him. Prison visitation rules are notoriously strict, even for attorneys, so in order to adequately prepare the case for trial, they needed more access to Gouker than the usual client. This was a murder case and a convoluted one at that. Gouker's legal team spent hours painstakingly reviewing discovery in their offices and with Gouker at the prison.

After a significant amount of time with Gouker, they apparently assumed that some deep-seated mental issues existed with the man. His attorneys filed a motion to have Gouker evaluated for competency to stand trial. Any defendant must be able to aid in his own defense. In order to determine whether he is able to do so, an incarcerated defendant may be sent, on the motion of his attorney, to the Kentucky Correctional Psychiatric Center for evaluation by a psychiatrist. That psychiatrist will generate a report for the court and the attorneys indicating whether the defendant is competent to stand trial. The court then holds a hearing to determine whether he is competent.

Gouker was sent to the Kentucky Correctional Psychiatric Center. The competency report is a confidential document and is sealed in the court file. However, it is safe to say that, despite his mental health issues, the doctor's finding was that the defendant was competent to stand trial in the case involving Trey's death. Gouker did not have a competency hearing. Instead, his attorneys stipulated to the contents of the report on his behalf and, in accordance with that report, Judge Willett issued an order stating that Gouker was competent to stand trial and that the case against him could proceed.

His attorneys also arranged for an independent evaluation of their client. Gouker submitted to an evaluation with Dr. Michael Cecil, a respected neuropsychologist. Dr. Cecil also found that Gouker was competent to stand trial. However, he highlighted mitigating factors that could impact Gouker's criminal responsibility, including prior diagnoses of schizophrenia and schizoaffective disorder and several head injuries from Gouker's past. At the time Gouker entered his plea his counsel had not received Dr. Cecil's report but Gouker elected to go forward with the plea anyway.

Gouker indicated to counsel prior to a court appearance on May 10, 2013, that he wished to plead guilty to the charges against him. The Commonwealth refused to offer a plea bargain to Gouker, so any plea he made would be an "open plea" where the judge would choose the length of incarceration. If he entered an open plea, Gouker would have to plead guilty to all of the charges.

His attorneys strongly advised against the entry of a guilty plea. In a lengthy letter to his client, attorney Mark Hall urged Gouker to reconsider his decision, stating that he felt that there were viable defenses in the case and that it was a mistake to admit guilt prior to receiving and reviewing the report generated by Dr. Michael Cecil regarding competency.

Gouker did not listen and on May 10, 2013, he pled guilty to all of the charges in the indictment.[6] Judge Willett set July 26, 2013, as the date for final sentencing. At that time, he sentenced Gouker to the maximum penalty allowed for each of the charges which resulted in a life sentence. Gouker would not be parole eligible until he had served twenty years of the sentence, with his first parole eligibility date set in October of 2031. In his final sentencing order, the judge explicitly stated that despite parole eligibility in 2031, "it is the recommendation of the trial court that the parole board shall not grant parole to this defendant."[7]

With that pronouncement, Joshua Gouker was committed to the custody of the Department of Corrections to serve his sentence. However, the court had not seen the last of Gouker and, with his son's trial set to begin three days later, Gouker still had a trick or two up his sleeve.

Chapter 12

...And It Begins

T he Jefferson County Courthouse looms on the corner of Seventh and Jefferson Streets in downtown Louisville. The relatively new building is directly across the street from the Louisville Metro Detention Center on one side and the Hall of Justice, home of district court and traffic court, on the other. The courthouse is in the heart of the bustling downtown legal district. On any given day, one encounters crisp professionals in their courtroom best and stragglers who roam the downtown streets. It is a mix of people from all walks of life.

July 29, 2013, would have been like any other hot summer day in the legal district. Vendors manned the street corners peddling fresh sizzling chili dogs; an eclectic mix of vehicles were parked along the metered streets. A line formed at the security checkpoint metal detectors at the front of the courthouse structure and extended out the front door. Members of the media filed into the building.

Over two years after the heartbreaking murder of Trey Zwicker, Joshua Young sat poised at the defense counsel's table with his team of attorneys. After several continuances and postponements, the beginning of his jury trial had finally arrived. As he sat before the judge, Josh faced two charges: complicity to murder and tampering with physical evidence. Although he staunchly maintained his innocence, the prosecutors and many of Trey's relatives believed that he was involved in Trey's death.

Sitting at the defense table, Joshua looked terrified and anxious. After all this time, he would finally tell his side of the story and he could only pray that the truth would come out. He was confident in his legal team and was well aware that they were all personally invested in him and his case. They believed that he was innocent and he knew there was nothing they would not do to convince the jury.

Josh had remained incarcerated since his initial arrest in the matter, almost two years prior to the start of the trial. He spent both his fifteenth and sixteenth years behind bars with his bond set at $100,000 cash. There was no one able to post that amount of money on his behalf, so as the case progressed, the Louisville Metro Youth Detention Center became his "home." Prior to his charges in connection with Trey's death, Josh had never been in serious trouble with the law. His only brush with the criminal justice system was when, at eleven years old, he was apprehended with his mother's boyfriend as the boyfriend attempted to break into a vehicle.

The harsh confines of the Detention Center were a culture shock for Little Josh. This was his first time being locked up and, because of the nature of his charges, he was housed with children facing comparable allegations. Prior to being jailed, Josh was a freshman honor student. While incarcerated at the youth detention facility, he participated in educational services that were a far cry from the Advanced Placement courses he studied while in a traditional high school.

For the two years prior to the trial, however, he was consistent. He kept himself out of trouble, studied hard and waited for the day that his trial would begin. He just hoped that the jury would view the facts in the same manner as his attorneys and his loved ones.

As he awaited trial, Josh looked like any other seventeen-year-old boy. Only hours before, Josh had worn his detention center-issued jail garb, a one-piece, hunter green jumpsuit that he'd lived in for his two years of incarceration. It felt good to change into regular clothing. As he sat in his courtroom seat, Josh was taller and the chubby-cheeked boy was now a slender young man. The previous two years had been difficult and Josh had watched from afar as his friends went on with their lives and high school experiences. As they attended high school dances, Junior ring ceremonies and Friday night football games, he had observed them from prison, the fear always looming that he might never be free again.

With all this swirling in his head, Josh glanced at the crowd of spectators beginning to assemble for his trial. The electricity in the courtroom was palpable as everyone settled into their places. Two attorneys represented Joshua in the case. Both were appointed by the court due to the fact that Josh could not afford to hire a lawyer. Both attorneys appointed to represent Josh's interests were skilled and experienced in juvenile law. He felt blessed by their presence and genuinely liked them. They had been a constant in his life for the previous two years; he had come to depend on them and he trusted them implicitly.

Leslie Smith was a tall, slender and intelligent woman who exuded confidence in Josh. She was animated, compassionate and, once she believed in a cause, she was passionate and devoted. Josh was grateful that was how she felt about him and his case. As she sat next to Josh, she appeared the picture of poise, a close crop of platinum blonde hair adorning her features.

Pete Schuler stood at the other end of the table where Josh sat. Older than his co-counsel, Pete also showed belief in his client. When Pete glided across the courtroom, Josh could feel the confidence Pete had in his case. They had waited so long for this day and it was clear that soon Josh would either be returning to the grim walls of the Jefferson County Youth Detention Center or he would be returning "home," wherever that would be.

Josh remained a ward of the state and, because he was a juvenile, the public defender's office supplied a caseworker from the Department of Public Advocacy who attended the trial with Josh and sat at the defense table with him. Her constant presence at Josh's side reassured everyone that he was not alone, as did the presence of several members of Josh's extended family and his foster parents, the Walshes.

The two female prosecutors assigned to the case, Elizabeth Jones Brown and Erin White, were both experienced prosecutors with the Commonwealth Attorney's

Office in Jefferson County. The women worked well together and had spent countless days and nights preparing
the Commonwealth's case against Joshua Young.

To their right sat the lead detective in the case. By
the time the trial took place, Detective Scott Russ was
no longer with the Louisville Metro Police Department
Homicide Unit. With over twenty years on the job, he had
made the decision to forgo working in a department that
required around-the-clock availability in favor of working
as a patrol officer. He had a family and the set hours of a
routine patrol officer were more conducive to that lifestyle.
However, having been the lead detective in the investigation into Trey's murder, he would be called to testify and
would be permitted to sit at the prosecution table with
Jones Brown and White for the duration of the trial. He
would also aid in selecting the jury.

Commonwealth v. Joshua Young had received intense
publicity in the Louisville area and, as a result, Judge
Barry Willett made the decision to call in more potential
jurors than he usually would for jury selection in a similar
trial. By the time all the jurors eventually filed into the
courtroom, Judge Willett would remark that it was possibly the most packed courtroom over which he had ever
presided.

The court was prepared for the jury pool and had specific seating arrangements for each of the one hundred and
four jurors who appeared. Each was assigned a number
and it was by that designation that the court and attorneys would refer to him or her throughout the trial. Jury
selection can appear to be a very boring process to an outsider but it is an essential component of the trial process.

In fact, attorneys often remark that cases can be won or lost during jury selection alone.

It is the intention of the system that an accused face a jury of twelve impartial peers. Even prior to the selection process, jurors are asked to complete questionnaires that reveal tidbits of information about them including where they work, whether they have children and whether they possess any knowledge about certain cases. The parties may request these questionnaires prior to trial as a way to prepare for *voir dire*.

Much of what happens during this practice may not be available to the casual courtroom observer or even other jurors. During *voir dire*, the judge, the prosecutor and the defense attorney are given an opportunity to ask specific questions to the jury pool in the hopes of uncovering bias, prejudice or other issues that may affect a potential juror's ability to be fair and impartial. Each side is given the opportunity to strike a juror "for cause" if they believe that person has an inherent or specific bias that will preclude him or her from being impartial. Each side also has a set amount of preemptory strikes which can be used to eliminate a potential juror for no specific reason at all, except reasons like race and gender.

In gauging the potential bias of a juror, the court and attorneys must ask about sensitive topics and life experiences. In most cases, including *Commonwealth v. Joshua Young*, jurors may approach the bench and speak privately with attorneys and the judge outside the hearing of the courtroom. This practice affords privacy to the juror while still allowing the attorneys to discuss sensitive topics.

In *Commonwealth v. Joshua Young*, there was no short-age of potential jurors who were excused from duty due to the intense media coverage and the way that coverage had affected their beliefs or opinions regarding Josh's guilt. For instance, one juror was excused by the court because prior to the trial she stated that she believed prosecutors were right "98 percent" of the time. She had bought the "whole Sunday newspaper and read every word," and on a scale of one to ten she felt it was "close to ten that he is guilty," even though she had seen no evidence. The defense felt she was not a juror who could be fair and impartial as the Constitution required.[1]

On the flip side, one middle-aged woman was excused due to her sympathy for Josh. In a raspy voice, she informed the judge that she had recently lost her husband of fifty-one years. This had affected her greatly. She had grandchildren and, as she spoke with the judge and attor-neys privately at the judge's bench, she glanced to her left and her gaze rested on Josh. "After seeing this boy, I don't think I can convict. He's a kid. My heart goes out to him." This potential juror was excused as well.[2]

Voir dire in Josh's case lasted well into the afternoon of the first day of the trial and by the end of the process the parties had selected fifteen jurors, although the final jury which would deliberate the case would consist of only twelve people. Due to the nature of the alleged crime and the anticipated length of the trial, the court was clear that it would need alternates in the event of sickness or family emergencies. The alternates would be determined by ran-dom drawing at the close of testimony. As the trial began, any of the fifteen knew they could be called to deliberate Joshua's guilt or innocence.

By the summer of 2013, Judge Barry Willett had over thirteen years of experience on the bench. Originally elected in 2000, the judge had left behind a career specializing in complex tort and commercial litigation in favor of upholding justice as a Jefferson County Judge. An attractive man with dark hair, a salt-and-pepper goatee and a rosy complexion, he was both seasoned and fair. Throughout the trial he put deep thought into his decisions and listened contemplatively to the arguments of counsel and the testimony of the witnesses.

Erin White delivered the opening statement for the prosecution. She did a thorough job of setting the stage for the case the Commonwealth intended to present to the jurors.

Beginning by telling the jurors that Trey was afraid of the dark, she said that he would never have gone alone to the dim, secluded location where his body was found. She detailed the home where he lived with his mother, a home where Gouker ruled "with an iron fist," a house of horrors saturated in domestic violence and drug use.

As she stared into the eyes of the jurors, one by one, she drew them into the prosecution's case. She humanized Trey for the jurors:

> Trey Zwicker was afraid of the dark, yet his body was found in a dark ditch behind Liberty High School and behind [the street] where Trey lived with his mom— Amanda McFarland, with his sister...who was eight at the time, with his stepfather Josh Gouker and with the defendant, his stepbrother, Josh Young.

Trey's body was found in a dark ditch, a place where kids would go to hang out, some to smoke cigarettes or smoke pot. A dark place where Trey wouldn't go alone at night; a dark place where Trey was lured by the defendant, his stepbrother, and by his stepfather.

Trey Zwicker was afraid of the dark and it was in a dark ditch where he was brutally murdered by Josh Gouker and Josh Young. Where he was found face down, covered in blood. Where he was found with his face smashed in and teeth chipped. Where he was found with his skull bashed open, his head and back having been struck multiple times, maybe with a bat, maybe with a metal pipe.

We don't know what the instrument of Trey's death was because the defendant woke up his cousin in the middle of the night after he and his father committed the murder and asked her to help him get rid of a bloody bat and clothes and she did.[3]

For nearly twenty minutes, White detailed the gruesome nature of the crime, the horrific scene where Trey's body was found and the investigation that the prosecution contended ultimately led to Josh Gouker and Josh Young. She anticipated the testimony of the medical examiner, warning the jurors, "you are going to hear about the wounds Trey suffered—the damage that was done to his skull and to his face and his teeth. And because he was left outside, you are going to hear about the flies and the fly eggs."[4] Courtroom spectators could see the jurors were rapt with attention, soaking in every word. She implored the jurors to pay close attention to the witnesses and to do their best to gauge the credibility of each person who took the stand.

White likened the case to "one thousand pieces of a really complicated puzzle."[5] The basic strategy involved in assembling the pieces of the puzzle was building the framework and piecing together the exterior boundaries prior to filling in the interior. She promised that the prosecution team would do their best to build the framework for the jury, but she emphasized that it would be the duty of the jury to fill in the pieces.

Looking into the eyes of each individual juror, White revealed that there was no question that Josh Gouker was involved in the brutal and unfathomable murder of his stepson. She did not hide her disgust from the jury panel as she took a deep breath and switched gears to speaking directly about Gouker: "Ladies and gentlemen, make no mistake. There is one thing both sides agree on and that is that Josh Gouker is a monster and a murderer. But do not be distracted. This is not his trial. This is the trial of Josh Young."[6] She explained that she planned to call Gouker and did not know what to expect. She revealed that she had "no idea what he might say when he gets on the stand. We just want to give you the opportunity to hear from him, to hear his lies and get the full picture. We don't want to hide anything from you." Gouker was testifying of his own volition. There were no "...deals for testimony in this case. You are going to have to sort through a lot to get to the truth. That is what your job is."[7] She assigned the jurors the responsibility of deciding whether Gouker named Josh Young as the killer to save himself or whether he gave him a blueprint for murder.

After a short pause, she again made eye contact with the jury and eloquently wrapped up her opening statement:

> There is no question that Josh Gouker is guilty of the murder of Trey Zwicker. There is also no question that he involved his son, Josh Young, in that murder. He either threw him under the bus to deflect the attention from himself, or he took him under his wing and taught him how to commit murder. Ladies and gentlemen, we believe the evidence supports the latter.[8]

Once White had taken her seat behind the prosecution table, Pete Schuler rose slowly and made his way toward the podium that faced the jurors. He reminded the jury that the information they heard during opening statements was not evidence. He took a step further and informed the jury that the defense agreed with most of what the prosecutor said as she addressed the jury. He began by stating, "We agree with probably 80 percent of the stuff that the prosecutor said, but she is wrong about one thing. Josh Young was not involved in his stepbrother's murder."[9]

Schuler turned toward the projection screen on the wall of the courtroom and explained, "I have a presentation that I would like to present." He clicked to the first slide; the heading "A Tale of Two Victims" filled the screen. He continued, "So what is this case about? Every case has a theme. This is a tale of two innocent victims. The first victim is someone who will certainly not be forgotten in this case: Trey Zwicker. Trey Zwicker was fourteen when he was murdered by Gouker."[10] However, Schuler claimed that Josh Young was a victim as well.

Not only had Josh endured unspeakable horrors during the six weeks he lived with his father, but he also underwent a terrifying ordeal afterward. He contended that his client was a "patsy" and that "he was set up by his father to take the fall for his crime, for something that his father did. He is not guilty." His voice rising, he thundered, "The story you are going to hear is outrageous."[11]

Throughout his opening statement, Pete Schuler displayed an eye-catching slide show detailing the defense's position on many of the issues in the case and showcased what was to come. It included mug shots of Gouker and the scene where Liberty High School students discovered Trey's body. The slide show also highlighted the timeline in the case which was very beneficial to courtroom viewers. It gave a precise listing of specific events that were important to the case, like the date Gouker regained custody of Little Josh, the date the Department of Corrections released Gouker and the dates of various lies Gouker told.

Schuler continued by telling the jurors that they would meet a cast of characters in the trial who were not like them, who led lifestyles well outside what society considered normal. They were people who were motivated by things that the jurors probably could not understand. There would be witnesses who had never worked a day in their lives and who downed daily cocktails of drugs and booze. They would meet people who would say and do anything for a variety of reasons, none of which would be because their actions were the right thing to do.

Justice for Trey and justice for Josh Young meant holding the correct person accountable for Trey's brutal murder. Schuler emphasized the violent past of Gouker and the fact that everything he said should be suspect. He was a classic liar and a successful manipulator. Gouker was a true criminal mastermind, a puppet master with an innate ability to get other people to do exactly what he wanted. That's what he had done in this case. Schuler ended by telling the jurors that by the end of the trial, after hearing all of the evidence, he was confident that they would return a verdict of not guilty.

Both parties were eloquent and effective in laying out their respective cases and the jurors appeared primed for what was to come. Each side held a very different view of the upcoming evidence in the case. It would be up to the jurors to listen to all that evidence and ultimately render a verdict.

Chapter 13

The Prosecution

In the morning hours of July 31, 2013, the prosecution in the matter of *Commonwealth v. Joshua Young* began presenting its side of the case. Shortly before lunchtime, the Commonwealth called Molly Varner as its first witness. Ms. Varner, who was an Arts and Humanities teacher at Liberty High School, made her way to the stand. Dressed in a blue cardigan and black camisole, Ms. Varner appeared the quintessential schoolteacher with her strawberry blond hair pulled back and wispy fringes of bangs falling lightly across her forehead.

She described the afternoon of May 11, 2011, when she and her students took a respite from class to walk around the Liberty High School grounds, something she had done repeatedly on nice days during the six years she was employed there. She described a student's initial shout that he had discovered a body on the outskirts of the campus. Believing he was kidding, she had walked briskly toward the area where the student pointed. She told how she felt her heart sink when she realized that there was indeed a body there, face down on the muddy banks of the creek bed. The children were in a frenzy, yelling "Are you okay?" The body remained immobile. Quickly she ushered the children back inside the building and promptly notified administrators who got in touch with the police department. Her stark testimony set the tone for the trial and described graphically for the jurors the turmoil at the scene when Trey's body was discovered. Obviously, the situation still haunted the quiet schoolteacher.[1]

As Varner's testimony came to a close and she exited the courtroom, the Commonwealth next called Officer John Pittenger to the stand. Pittenger, a twenty-year veteran of the Louisville Metro Police Department, worked as a patrol officer in the sixth division where Liberty High School was located. He had been driving down Poplar Level Road when he heard a dispatch call that a body had been found at Liberty High School. Only a few minutes from the location, he headed there to assist.

As the officer pulled into the drive leading to the school, he was met by school security and then escorted to the back of the building. With their aid, he located Trey's body approximately fifty to seventy feet off of the bridge area behind the school. Pittenger knew he shouldn't touch the body but he observed it for signs of life. There were none. His training kicked into gear and he began to cordon off the area with yellow crime-scene tape to preserve the scene for the homicide detectives who were en route.

Although Pittenger was aware that the victim was male, he could not ascertain whether he was an adult or a teenager. There was obvious head trauma. He waited at the scene until the detectives arrived.

In his cross-examination of Officer Pittenger, Pete Schuler took the opportunity to emphasize what the defense perceived as the shortcomings of the investigation. In response to his questioning, the officer testified that although he did not touch Trey, he was close enough to touch him. He admitted that the area surrounding Trey's body was muddy and that anyone coming into the area would likely leave a footprint. Therefore, he was sure that he had as well. He did not notice if there were other footprints there. Despite the importance of this information due to the prosecutor's assertion that both Josh Young and his father killed Trey, no one from Homicide had asked Officer Pittenger whether he left footprints or the size shoe that he wore. It was also impossible for Pittenger to know whether any members of school security had approached Trey's body prior to his arrival. As Pittenger left the stand, the Commonwealth shifted gears by calling the most important person in Trey's life to testify.

In what was perhaps the most moving testimony of the entire trial, the next witness called to the stand by the Commonwealth was Trey's father, Terry Zwicker. It was immediately apparent to observers that Terry was completely devastated by the loss of his son. Terry settled into the witness box with a look of pain on his face that conveyed how desperately he was grieving and how much he had loved his son.

Turning his attention to the prosecutor, Terry clutched his white baseball cap in his hands, wringing it slightly. He had endured so much pain already and through his testimony he would be forced to relive the worst day of his life and its aftermath.

Terry began by detailing his relationship with Trey and the close bond that they had shared. He detailed his plans with Trey for the upcoming weekend when they were going to take a fishing trip together. His life was irreparably changed when his son was taken from him via the brutal murder. Every person in the courtroom could feel the anger and devastation that Terry exuded. It was clear that his ultimate goal was attaining justice for his son, whom he portrayed as a kind and thoughtful boy.

Terry described his hate for Josh Gouker and his belief that Josh Young was also involved in the death. He did not think that Trey would have ventured out to the creek bed late at night unless he was meeting someone. He thought that person was Josh Young. After his long and agonizing testimony, he was finally excused from the courtroom.

Next, the prosecution called another law enforcement witness to the stand. Detective Leigh Maroni strode purposefully to the witness box and promptly began to detail the scene of the crime in response to the Commonwealth's questioning. Perhaps the most important part of her testimony was her description of her interview with Little Josh at the school shortly after the discovery of Trey's body. The audio of the interview was played for the jury members. They sat upright and alert as the conversation came to life.

Little Josh sounded audibly distraught on the recording. He sounded shocked by the discovery. Trey's death seemed to have hit him hard. The Commonwealth emphasized one statement that Little Josh made during that interview as proof of his alleged guilt. Little Josh told the detective that he saw Trey after he showered for the evening and described the clothes he was wearing. This statement was in sharp contrast to the statements he gave in later interviews when he asserted that he left Amanda's house prior to Trey's shower and that he never saw him after that.

Skeptics wondered how he could know what Trey was wearing unless he met up with him later that night. They also wondered why he told two different stories. Terry Zwicker would say later that he believed Josh was lying, otherwise why would he have told the police two different things?

However, that discrepancy might also be explained by Gouker's lies to Child Protective Services the entire time he had custody of Little Josh. He knew that Child Protective Services would not approve of Cassi's home as an appropriate environment for Little Josh, so he told his caseworker that he and Little Josh lived in Amanda's house, two doors down. In his initial statement, Little Josh claimed to be at Amanda's later into the evening. Perhaps he was afraid that if he told the detective that he was not at Amanda's home, she would learn that he was not living there. He may have been worried that custody would be taken from his father and he would be placed back into foster care, perhaps not with his sister and the Walshes.

His grief and shock at the time may also have contributed to his statement. He had heard his father and Amanda speaking about Trey's attempts to sneak out of the house the evening before and heard them mention what he was wearing when he did so. This image in his mind may have contributed to the statement he made to Detective Maroni in the state of shock he was in immediately after learning that Trey was dead.

Detective Maroni's testimony lasted quite a while and was important due to the recorded statement she had taken from Little Josh. It was one of the main pieces of evidence that the prosecution felt implicated him. After she left the stand, the Commonwealth turned toward the forensic evidence it had compiled in the case.

Tracy Gutterman was the first witness called to the stand to address information about the crime scene. By the time of the trial, Gutterman had spent the previous six years employed as a crime scene technician for the Louisville Metro Police Department's Crime Scene Unit. Her regular duties included shooting photos and video of crime scenes along with taking fingerprints and collecting evidence. Any such evidence would be packaged and pre-served, then stored in the property room.

In the Trey Zwicker murder investigation, she had recorded a video of the scene which was played back for the jury. She also detailed the items that were collected from the scene of the murder: a pair of black sweatpants found in the grass, discarded cigarette packs and various other items. All items were collected and catalogued. She brought the sealed items to the attention of the jurors and the Judge instructed the jurors that they would be able to view and handle these items later in the jury room while wearing gloves.

Although the testimony regarding the police investi-gation and the evidence collected at the crime scene were an integral part of the Commonwealth's case, spectators and jurors alike seemed much more engaged when friends and family members of Trey took the stand as witnesses. One such witness was called to the stand shortly after Gutterman.

Amanda McFarland's brother strode confidently into the courtroom. He wore a simple white T-shirt layered underneath a blue button-down shirt. A handsome man in his thirties, he sported a shaved head and appeared to be all business as he settled into the witness box.

He stated that he was a former US Marine who had been discharged in 2004. Amanda's brother and thus Trey's uncle, he described his distaste for Josh Gouker and his disapproval of his sister's relationship with him. Because he felt that she was unsafe with Gouker, rather than start a fight with his sister, his visits to her home had become less frequent. In the months prior to Trey's death, he had less contact with Amanda and Trey than he was accustomed to.

For that reason, on the evening of May 10, 2011, he decided to let bygones be bygones and stop by the home for a cookout that his sister had planned. As he pulled into the driveway, he noticed Gouker in the front yard, his eyes trained on the vehicle as he adopted a menacing stance, bracing his body and staring down the vehicle. As Amanda's brother eased the car into park and opened the driver's door, a look of recognition sprung to Gouker's eyes as he realized the visitor was his brother-in-law.

Breaking into a smile, he escorted Amanda's brother into the home where Amanda was busily preparing food in the kitchen for the cookout. The majority of the attendees had congregated in the backyard where the grill was going and Amanda's brother spent much of the evening playing basketball with guys from the neighborhood and hanging out with Trey.

His sorrow and regret was obvious throughout his testimony. It was apparent that he had replayed the evening in his mind countless times. It was the last time Amanda's brother saw his nephew Trey and he revealed that when he left he had a fleeting thought of inviting Trey to come with him to the hospital as he had his hand stitched by the emergency room doctors. He had reconsidered before asking, realizing that Trey would probably not enjoy spending hours at the emergency room. It appeared to be a decision that he thought of and regretted often.

At one point Amanda's brother described a power imbalance between Big Josh and Little Josh. He claimed that while they were playing basketball as a group at the cookout, Little Josh had the chance to block his father's basketball shot. However, he hesitated and declined to do so. The Commonwealth seemed to think that those actions implied that Little Josh would do anything to help his father. In actuality, the testimony reinforced that Big Josh was a mean man who called the shots. Little Josh might have feared ramifications from his father if he made him look bad. After all, he was just a child and he could not risk Big Josh's wrath. Gouker had the power to do anything he wanted to Little Josh and this was likely frightening to his son. Amanda's brother's testimony was important because it highlighted Trey and the good and thoughtful boy he was. It helped to humanize him to the jury. It also showed how Big Josh ruled the home and his son with an iron fist.

It was obvious that Amanda's brother felt great sadness recounting his final day with his nephew and he clearly despised Gouker. As he left the witness box, he was understandably overcome with emotion.

Immediately after he exited the courtroom, his sister, Trey's mother, next took the stand. It was clear that Amanda grieved for her son. She also likely felt tremendous guilt that she had brought Gouker into her home, giving him access to Trey.

Although her hurt was evident, Amanda appeared to minimize the abuse Gouker rendered in her home and she also testified that he did not live in the house. This was in direct contrast to the emergency protective order that she sought after Trey's death. In her request for the order, she stated that Gouker had lived with her for the previous seven months. As she testified, she stated that Gouker never lived with her and only stayed the night occasionally. According to Amanda, he did not keep clothes or toiletries at her house and actually lived with Cassi and her family two doors down.

It is likely that Amanda's testimony was a coping mechanism. She did not want to admit to herself and the world that she had allowed a monster into her home. She did not want people to think that she had failed to protect her child. She struggled with believing that the person who claimed to love her could hurt her and her family in the way Gouker had.

Only a small portion of her testimony touched on her relationship with Josh Young. According to Amanda, she and Josh always got along fine and she thought that he got along well with her son. The judge allowed the attorneys to question Amanda by avowal and outside the presence of the jurors. During that questioning, she told the judge and attorneys that Little Josh was a jokester and liked to tease others in a mean-spirited way. However, Pete Schuler reminded her that in an interview with Detective Russ shortly after Trey's death, she had indicated that Josh, Trey and their friends in the neighborhood "loved each other." She did not mention any problems between Josh and Trey.

Amanda's testimony was heartwrenching. Losing one's child is the most difficult thing a mother can bear. However, when she minimized Gouker's role in her household and denied that he lived there, it invited skepticism about her statements since previously filed court documents clearly showed that he had.

As the trial crept along, Judge Willett allowed the defense to call their first witness out of order, interrupting the prosecution's case-in-chief. During the course of preparing Joshua's defense, his defense team had consulted with an expert regarding Trey's cause of death. That witness, Dr. George Nichols, ran a consulting firm and was only available on August 2 to present his testimony in the case. Courts will often allow a professional who is called as an expert witness to give his or her testimony out of order to accommodate the professional's schedule.

Gray-haired and distinguished, Dr. Nichols was a highly effective witness with impressive credentials as a pathologist that supported his expertise and testimony. Dr. Nichols approached the witness box in a gray suit.

He projected confidence indicative of his experience in the field of forensic pathology as he began by giving the jurors a short pathology lesson and detailed his education and career in the field. He had worked as a deputy coroner in Hamilton County, Ohio, for several years as well as a chief medical examiner for over twenty years. During the seventies, eighties and nineties, he served as a part-time faculty member at the University of Louisville and was president of an anatomical laboratory. By the time of the trial, he owned a consulting firm, through which he was routinely retained for forensic evaluation of legal issues.

Dr. Nichols revealed that he had previously testified in over one thousand trials, both for the defense and the prosecution. On June 6, 2013, he was asked to perform an independent investigation into Trey's death. In doing so, he examined photographs of the body and the scene where first responders found Trey's body. He also used the autopsy report and photos taken by Dr. Amy Burrows Beckham, the medical examiner who performed Trey's autopsy. Dr. Burrows Beckham had been a student and protégé of Dr. Nichols.

Dr. Nichols described the horrific details of Trey's injuries. Trey had a depressed nasal fracture and a deep black eye. He had suffered an internal skull fracture and a subdural hematoma. His back was covered in bruises. In considering all of the traumatic injuries present during the autopsy, Dr. Nichols told the jury that he was confident a rod-like object caused the injuries to Trey.

During the Commonwealth's case, the prosecution would continually argue that Trey was killed with a baseball bat. Specifically, Cassi would later testify that Joshua came to her in the middle of the night and asked her to help him dispose of bloody clothes and a bloody bat. Investigators believed wholeheartedly that a bat was the murder weapon. However, the defense's expert concluded that the murder weapon could not have been the size of a baseball bat. He was certain that it was a thin, rod-like object and, although there was no way for him to tell whether there were two people at the scene, he felt confident that all of the blows to Trey came from a person standing in the same position for the duration of the attack.

He felt that the attack began when Trey was knocked to the ground and rendered unconscious by the first blow of the rod-like object and that he was beaten repeatedly with at least four or five hits to his back and several that hit the back of his head, forcing the boy's face into the underlying stone and rock, causing the facial injuries that Trey endured.[2] The beating was a classic example of overkill. The traumatic brain injury that Trey sustained was the actual cause of his death. However, it appeared that the killer continued to pummel the teen's body even after he sustained that injury.

When the medical examiner, Dr. Amy Burrows Beckham, testified later in the trial, her opinion differed only slightly from Dr. Nichols's findings. She gave her opinion that the black eye sustained by Trey was likely caused by a direct blow or punch and she believed that this hit had initially knocked him to the ground. However, she felt that there was a possibility the injury was caused by his face hitting the ground.

She believed that Trey died within four hours of eating due to the contents she found in his stomach during the autopsy. Her findings initially reflected that the head injury was caused by a sharp object. However, after Detective Russ asked her whether a baseball bat could have been the murder weapon, she reexamined her findings to reflect that a bat could have caused the injuries.

Perhaps the most penetrating questions asked of the medical examiner were posed by the jurors. The bat that the prosecution believed was the murder weapon was an old bat, a collectible that belonged to Cassi's live-in boyfriend. It was a wooden bat. Jurors specifically asked Dr. Burrows Beckham whether a wooden bat would have left splintering or fragments of wood in the wounds. She believed that it likely would have, especially if it was an older bat. During the course of the autopsy, she had found no such wooden pieces. The forensic testimony seemed to indicate that a wooden bat did not cause Trey's death. This was the murder weapon implicated by Gouker's cast of characters, yet the forensic testimony did not support their assertions.[3]

When the prosecution resumed its case-in-chief following the testimony of Dr. Nichols, it called a parade of crime scene technicians and officers to the stand. After Trey's body was discovered and identified, the police had secured a warrant for Amanda's home and collected a variety of items, mostly ones that could have served as a murder weapon.

Three bats were collected from Trey's upstairs room and a sword and knife were taken from the garage. All items were fingerprinted and swabbed for DNA. After the investigation, analysts determined that none of these items were connected to the murder. The technicians also took photographs of the home and DNA swabs from Gouker and Amanda.

There had been other items collected from the scene of the murder which also were sent to the Kentucky State Police lab for testing, including swabs from concrete blocks and trees which confirmed that the blood found on those items belonged to Trey. None of the items at the scene bore DNA from anyone else.

At the conclusion of that portion of the testimony, it was clear that there was no forensic evidence that linked Josh Young to Trey's murder. In fact, there was no forensic evidence that linked *anyone* to the murder. The murder weapon was never recovered and it seemed from the forensic testimony that the murder weapon was not a wooden bat, as alleged by the prosecution, but a rod-like object as postulated by the defense.

The prosecution shifted gears and began calling to the stand the colorful cast of characters who had associated with Gouker when he was a free man. They began with Jahaira (or "Jennifer" as she was known to the woman whom Gouker kidnapped in Alabama). Jahaira had gotten married in the two years that had passed since the kidnapping and changed her last name to Friend to match that of her new husband.

Jahaira Friend and Angelic Burkhead were important witnesses for the prosecution. Both women claimed that while they were in Alabama, Josh Young confessed to them that he had killed Trey. If the witnesses had been credible, jurors may have believed that Josh made such statements. However, both women would instead damage the prosecution.

Jahaira claimed that Gouker drugged her for the entire trip and that she did not remember anything except that Little Josh had confessed to her in a motel room "with no feeling" that he had killed Trey. She claimed Gouker held a gun to her head and that when the group embarked on the trip to Alabama, she had no idea they were leaving the state. In the aftermath of Erin's kidnapping, Jahaira was arrested and criminally charged as well.

Leslie Smith used her cross-examination of Jahaira as an opportunity to confront her on her inability to recall even the most basic facts regarding her trip to Alabama with Gouker. Throughout the questioning, Jahaira continued to deny that she and Gouker engaged in a sexual relationship, despite evidence to the contrary.

"You were his sexual partner, though?" Smith pressed.

"No."

"You never had sex with Josh Gouker?"

"No."[4]

"He is not the reason that you and Angelic have issues between the two of you right now?" she asked, referring to the nearly lifelong relationship between Jahaira and Angelic that became irreparably broken after their trek south with Gouker.

"No," Jahaira stated, her series of one-word answers echoing through the courtroom.

Smith stared at her for a second and changed gears, "Let's just establish the timeline. You left Louisville on what day?"

"I have no clue," Jahaira shrugged.

Not missing a beat, Smith continued with her questioning, "At what time?"

"Don't know."

"On what day of the week?"

"I don't know."

"What day of the week did you return to Louisville, Kentucky?"

"I don't know."[5]

"You remember talking to anyone while in Alabama, anyone at all?" she questioned incredulously.

"No."

"Do you recall saying that Joshua Gouker choked you with a tube sock?"

"Before today, no."[6]

Her testimony appeared to weaken the prosecution's case against Little Josh.

The next in the trio of Gouker's women to take the stand was Cassiopeia Gouker, his cousin. She strode to the witness box in her University of Louisville sweatshirt. Gouker's ladies all resembled each other: they could be described as full-figured.

The Commonwealth used Cassi's testimony to show yet another person to whom Little Josh had confessed. All of the women seemed scared of and intimidated by Gouker. She testified that in the middle of the night on May 10, Little Josh had attempted to wake her up several times. After she ignored him twice, he returned to the room with his father, stating that he had killed Trey and needed her to aid him in disposing of a bloody bat and a garbage bag full of bloody clothes.

If Cassi's version of events was to be believed, she would have loaded the bloody bat into the back of her van, failing to leave any blood behind in the vehicle. Defense counsel Pete Schuler revealed that he had met with Cassi in his office prior to the trial. She arrived with her attorney and answered questions. Most notably, Schuler had drawn a sketch of a bat and asked Cassi to draw the way that the blood looked on the bat when she saw it. She drew one circle of blood. Both the medical examiner and the defense's medical witness had testified that based on the crime scene and Trey's injuries, blood would have splattered all over the bat and not pooled in one spot as Cassi claimed.

When Schuler finally had the opportunity to cross-examine Cassi, he immediately seized on her failure to alert police to her allegations regarding Josh Young. "You waited almost two years to tell somebody that Gouker was present," he said, alluding to her assertion that Little Josh visited her room with a bloody bat on the night of Trey's murder. As she testified, Cassi changed her previous story. Although she originally stated that Little Josh came into the room alone, she was now asserting that Gouker had come into the room as well and Schuler seized on that inconsistency, asking why her story had changed.

"Because they had told me that Amanda said Big Josh was with her the whole night," she replied matter-of-factly.[7]

"So you were basing what you told police on what other witnesses said?" he asked skeptically.

"I remembered at the time, after I thought of it," she said slowly.

Schuler continued to probe into whether Cassi had any indications prior to Trey's death that Gouker was plotting to kill him. "Did [Joshua Gouker] tell you he was thinking about killing Trey?"

"He didn't say he was thinking about killing Trey; he did say an eye for an eye because of the abortion," Cassi said, referencing the abortion Amanda underwent in the years prior to Gouker's initial incarceration.[8]

As the questioning continued, Cassi appeared to have trouble remembering some of the details of her previous police interviews. Pete Schuler approached the witness with a transcript of her prior conversations with police. He handed Cassi the transcript as she sat in the witness box. "See if you can refresh your memory with this."

Cassi took the next five minutes quietly flipping through the pages and once she completing reading the transcript, she looked up at Schuler. He continued with his questions, "So did Gouker talk about having Trey killed before that night?"

"No, he never talked about having Trey killed. He may have said 'an eye for an eye,' but that didn't lead me to believe that he was gonna kill Trey."

Judge Willett then gave the jurors an opportunity to pose questions to Cassi. After calling the attorneys to the bench and determining which questions were appropriate, the judge looked toward Cassi and read the questions to her.

"Did you ever witness any angry outbursts from Josh Young?"

"No."

"Did you think the blood from the bat would rub off or transfer to your house or car?"

"I didn't think about it."

"The bat was not in a bag when you saw it. Was it soaked in blood or just bloodstained?"

"Just bloodstained."

"In the three times Josh Young attempted to wake you, no one else woke up?"

"No"

"Was Josh Young at your house when you went to bed the night of the cookout?"

"Yes."

"Was Josh Young playing video games by himself?"

"Yes."

"Were you ever afraid of Josh Young or Josh Gouker?"

"No."

She also confessed that she had been drinking that night at the cookout.

Perhaps the most telling was the final question: "Were you controlled by Gouker?"

As she pondered the question, she looked to the side, "Maybe; I don't know if that's what you would call it." She admitted that she was in love with him at the time of the murder.[9]

This was news to her fiancé, who was the next witness in the *Commonwealth v. Joshua Young* trial. He testified to the events of the evening Trey was murdered and he also revealed that after Amanda fled her home, he had burglarized it with Gouker. Cassi's fiancé had since pled guilty to a felony in connection with those actions.[10]

Next Angelic walked to the witness box and settled in. She agreed that after the trip, she and Jahaira were no longer friends and that the trip was the reason for their falling out. Angelic was clearly terrified of Gouker.

She too claimed that Little Josh had confessed to her in a motel room in Tennessee. However, to some observers her claims appeared to be contrived and orchestrated by Gouker. Defense counsel played a tape of the telephone call between Angelic, the incarcerated Gouker and Detective Russ. After nearly ten minutes of prodding, Angelic had finally told the detective that Little Josh had admitted the killing to her.

As the tape was played, it appeared to some of those in the courtroom that Angelic was saying what she thought Gouker wanted her to say. During her cross-examination, it came out that in the past she was so loyal to Gouker that she hid him from authorities and had been charged with hindering prosecution.

"Did you all date that fall?" the prosecutor asked as she conducted her direct examination of Angelic.

"No."

"Did you date any time after he got out of prison?"

"No."

The prosecutor continued to touch on Angelic's relationships with Gouker, his family and the other residents of the neighborhood, "After Trey's murder, what caused Gouker to contact you?"

"He had said that Amanda was really emotional and that they were separated. They spent a few nights at our house because he said they didn't have anywhere else to go," she said, referring to Gouker and Josh Young.[11]

"At some point, did you go to Alabama with him?"

"Yes. We were in his mother's car, me, Joshua Gouker and Joshua Young."

"Did you know before you left that this would be a trip to Mississippi?"

"Yes."

"How long did you think this would take?"

"Long enough to get to Mississippi and home." Angelic then detailed how their plans changed when the car broke down in the middle of nowhere and left them stranded in Tennessee.

The prosecution concluded its questioning of Angelic and Pete Schuler took his turn. As the questioning wore on, he began to ask Angelic about the way Gouker was ultimately apprehended after he had appeared at her home following his stint in an Alabama jail.

"He showed up on your doorstep?"

"In my bedroom."

"Did US Marshalls pick him up?"

"The Marshall had come and given me their card," she began. "...It was a few days later I woke up to him in my bedroom."

"When he did show up, did you immediately call them?" Schuler asked.

"No, I contacted someone else and they called because he was standing right in my face," Angelic stated. She went on to assert her concern that Gouker would come after her or attempt to set her up in some way.[12]

To those who heard her testimony, Angelic was clearly scared of Gouker and had a legitimate fear that Gouker would do anything to protect himself even if he had to injure others in the process. She left many spectators in the courtroom shaking their heads as she sprinted up the courtroom aisle and out to the hallway after Judge Willett excused her from the witness box.

Many felt the witnesses connected to Gouker called to the stand by the prosecution rivaled a daytime talk show episode, but the witness who everyone was waiting to see take the stand was Josh Gouker himself.

Chapter 14

Mask on the Monster

Would the jury hear from Josh Gouker? Gouker had pled guilty to Trey's murder and contended that he had acted alone. However, that was just the most recent version of the many accounts of Trey's death that he told in the months following the murder. Many people felt he was a volatile, dishonest man at best and a sadistic psychopath at worst. Either side would likely be unable to control Gouker if he were called to testify; it was impossible to predict what he would say on any given day. His story of the murder had changed drastically throughout the investigation and, even after police charged Gouker as his son's co-defendant, he continued to alter his story. Those present in the courtroom wondered if he would have the opportunity to present yet another account from the witness stand.

Although it is not uncommon for a co-defendant to take the stand in a trial, the situation in this case was quite rare. Generally, a defendant has the constitutional right against self-incrimination under the Fifth Amendment of the United States Constitution. This precludes either side from calling that person as a witness and forcing him to testify if doing so would implicate that person in a crime. If a witness is in agreement, he may waive that right. If the co-defendants are tried together in a consolidated trial, they will often opt to remain silent. In cases where a co-defendant waives his or her Fifth Amendment right and testifies against the accused, there is almost always a plea bargain already in place with the prosecutor. Specifically, that person receives something in return for his testimony, usually a lighter sentence or probation.

The Joshua Young case was different. Josh Gouker had already pled guilty to the murder of Trey Zwicker and had received a life sentence. However, the guilty plea was not the result of a plea bargain with the prosecution. Gouker had entered an "open plea" and allowed the judge to select his sentence. He had repeatedly professed his desire to testify in his son's trial. However, it had been unclear whether either side would elect to take the gamble of actually calling him to the stand.

The prosecution took the chance and on day four of the trial, prosecutor Erin White stood and announced to the court that the Commonwealth's next witness was Josh Gouker. Nearly everyone in the courtroom sat upright; the tension was palpable. It took several minutes for Gouker to appear. A door on the left side of the courtroom led to the holding cell area, a place where prisoners were confined as they waited to appear before the Judge. This is where Gouker sat for hours during the trial, subpoenaed to testify and waiting to see if either side would call him to the stand. Gouker was now serving his life sentence for Trey's murder. He was also serving time for his previous crimes of robbery in the second degree, assault in the second degree and intimidating a witness in a legal proceeding. After he was charged with Trey's murder, the judge quickly revoked his parole on those charges and he had once again adjusted to prison life.

As his son's trial progressed, Josh Gouker was held at the Luther Luckett Correctional Complex. Located in Lagrange, Kentucky, "Luckett," as it is called by inmates, is a medium security prison that houses more than one thousand convicts. It was from that prison that Gouker was transported to testify and the fact that he was readjusting to prison life was apparent as he sauntered into the courtroom.

Gouker wore heavy shackles on both his hands and feet that forced him into a cumbersome-looking shuffle as he moved. At the same time, he attempted to maintain a relaxed, self-assured look, almost certainly the way he had strutted on the streets.

Gouker was a short man but what he lacked in height he made up for in mass. At approximately 230 pounds, Gouker was an imposing figure, even in shackles, and no one could doubt his ability to intimidate those around him. Gouker wore the orange prison garb indicative of his incarceration, a one-piece jumpsuit that snapped up the front, layered over a plain white t-shirt.

As he entered the witness box, Gouker never once looked in the direction of his son who sat nearby at the defense table.

Prosecutor Erin White began questioning Big Josh regarding his present living situation, asking where he was housed in the prison system. From the outset it was obvious that Big Josh would not be an easy or predictable witness. When the prosecutor asked him to speak up, he screamed into the microphone in an attempt to establish that he was in full control.

"What are you serving?" she asked and before the question was even completed, Big Josh blurted his answer.

"Life," he stated nonchalantly.

"Why?"

"For killing Trey," Gouker shrugged, an emotionless look on his face.[1]

Gouker's mannerisms and presence conveyed his message. He would talk and answer questions but he would do so on his terms. It was obvious that this man was accustomed to doing things his way and pressuring and intimidating those around him to comply. He was just warming up and as his testimony progressed, courtroom viewers and news commentators would question whether Gouker could really be so outrageous and narcissistic. Viewers wondered if his testimony was a well-rehearsed act to exert control on the justice system or a performance intended to free his son.

As the news hosts and talking heads expressed their impressions of the trial, many questioned whether the Commonwealth calling Josh Gouker to the stand was helpful or harmful. Surely the attorneys realized that as a career criminal he would probably do little to aid the prosecution in convicting his son. Gouker had spent his adult years manipulating the system. Regardless of the love he had or did not have for Little Josh, he seemed to thrive on controlling everything and everyone around him. If he could hurt the prosecution in any way, he would do it. Gouker held grudges and that very prosecution team had fought for his own incarceration. It appears most likely that the prosecution called Gouker as a preemptive strike. Gouker gave several media interviews and proclaimed that he alone was to blame for Trey's murder. In fact, in that very courtroom, he had entered a guilty plea and claimed on the record that he had acted alone. However, the prosecution knew if they did not call Gouker, the defense would, in order to show that someone else was convicted of the crime and had claimed that he acted alone. Perhaps the prosecution felt that by calling Gouker themselves it would defuse the situation.

White began to question Gouker regarding the murder and his statements when he entered his guilty plea. Even in response to her direct questions, Gouker said what he wanted to say. He took the opportunity to explain why he murdered Trey.

A look of resolve on his face, Gouker stated, "It just felt right at the time. It wasn't like I wanted Trey to die, or if I could do it over I would do it again. His mother killed a couple of mine and it just felt right. I know it sounds monstrous and all that shit, but it's not. If we were in the Old Testament it would be the same thing," he said, referring to the two previous abortions of his babies that Amanda underwent.[2]

A constant theme in the trial was "an eye for an eye," a mantra Gouker professed repeatedly. He continually alleged that one of the contributing factors to Trey's murder was the fact that Trey's mother, Amanda, had aborted Gouker's babies. Given the fact that Gouker missed the majority of his own son's life, worked only sporadically, was a violent ex-con and lacked stable housing, he was hardly father-of-the-year material. However, it was likely not fatherhood he craved so much as the ability to control situations. If Amanda gave birth to his child, he would have more control over her. It apparently enraged him that she made the decision to abort his children without his permission. Therefore, it was likely not the aborted fetuses which upset him as much as the fact that Amanda dared to make an important decision without him, that she stripped him of control. To Gouker, people were expendable pawns who were of no use to him if he could not control them. When Amanda took control and had an abortion, he had attempted to regain power by killing Trey: "an eye for an eye."

With the prosecutor's prompting, Gouker revealed his actions in killing Trey and his recollections of the night of Trey's death. He spoke about the family cookout at Amanda's and the fact that he and Amanda spent time at his cousin Cassi's home that evening. At some point, he contended, Amanda noticed that several of her things were at Cassi's home and she confronted Gouker about stealing her belongings. As was common in their relationship, the two fought. Gouker recounted that they later had sex several times and he alleged that was the way that they made up after fighting.

Gouker later went into detail regarding the sex acts. He testified that he and Amanda planned to have sex outside, but that plan was thwarted when Trey walked out onto the back porch. They eventually retired to the bedroom and had sex once, visited a local gas station to purchase cigarettes and then came home and had sex again, incorporating a banana into the act. He recorded the second session with Amanda's cell phone camera so that he could view it later. Per his testimony, he topped off the evening by playing a video game and smoking marijuana.

As White urged him to relate the details of the evening as testified to in his confession, Gouker became frustrated and lashed out, "I know what you're doing. You're trying to make microscopic little holes in the shit that I didn't even give a fuck about two years ago, so how can I tell you the exact thing now when I really didn't give a fuck then?"[3]

"If you're telling the truth it shouldn't be that hard."

"But I'm a fucking l...Yeah, but goddamn, I've lied this whole fucking time. Except for since arraignment, since arraignment I've told you I done it. I've admitted everything I've done. I've been sentenced for it, life in prison. Yet here I am, going over the same fucking story," he said, raising his voice and glancing back and forth between the jurors and the judge in the case. His frustration with the prosecutor's repeated questioning was evident.

The story Gouker told was that as he played video games, Trey came into the room and asked for a cigarette. Gouker noticed that Trey pulled a lighter out of his pocket, a lighter that belonged to Gouker. Although it annoyed Gouker that Trey was in possession of his lighter, he didn't say anything. However, Gouker became even more upset when he went to the kitchen to eat a plate of food Amanda had saved for him and discovered that Trey had eaten it. At that moment, he decided that he would teach Trey a lesson by scaring him. He offered to smoke with Trey and the two went out to the back porch.[4]

Before they could sit down, Gouker convinced Trey to walk with him to "The Spot," the area where Liberty High School students would ultimately find Trey's body. It is likely that Trey had no clue that he was in danger as he and his stepfather approached the creek bed near the culvert. It was an area where teenagers routinely met to sneak cigarettes and, occasionally, marijuana. The parents of neighborhood children had visited the same spot to do the same things when they were teens. Gouker described it as a place where Trey would have been comfortable.

As his testimony continued, Gouker set the stage for what transpired once he and Trey reached "The Spot" that evening. He stated that a discarded metal pipe lay on the creek bed and that Trey picked it up and started hitting a nearby tree. Gouker began to confront him about stealing from him, referring to the lighter he felt Trey had taken. According to Gouker, the man deemed a thief by almost everyone who knew him became upset because a fourteen-year-old boy was using his cheap lighter, a lighter Trey likely picked up in his own home. Puffing out his chest, Gouker warned Trey that the next time he stole from him, he would treat Trey like a man, insinuating that he would give him a beat down worthy of a grown adult. Gouker recalled Trey responding, "Then you and my dad will have a problem."[5]

Trey was likely referring to the fact that his father, already wary of the situation, would file custody papers to remove Trey from Amanda's home. Gouker testified he knew exactly what Trey meant and exactly what Trey's

father, Terry, would do if Trey told him Gouker had mistreated him.

"What he does is he calls [Child Protective Services]
and it gets me and Amanda in a bunch of shit," Gouker
testified and as that thought had crossed his mind, he "just
snapped" and punched Trey once in the face. The force of
the punch spun Trey around and he fell to the ground, still
clutching the metal pipe in his right hand. Gouker stepped
on his wrist, pulling the pipe from Trey's grasp and in a
haze began to beat Trey with the pipe.[6]

In the aftermath of the beating, Gouker rinsed the
pipe in the creek and traveled down the street to his
cousin Cassi's house where he took a shower. He stashed
his clothes and the bloody pipe in Cassi's backyard until
the following morning. The family had failed to pay the
garbage bill that month and he secreted the items in the
garbage which he loaded into the trunk of Amanda's car.
Amanda and Gouker drove to McNeely Lake that morning
and on the way Gouker disposed of the garbage bags con-
taining the murder weapon in a dumpster behind a restaurant at the end of the street. Amanda remained unaware
that the murder weapon used to kill her only son was in
her car trunk.

Only hours after Gouker disposed of the murder
weapon, police swarmed the scene of Trey's murder. Both
Gouker and Amanda arrived on the scene, Amanda anxious to learn what had happened and Gouker knowing
that Trey's body lay in that ditch and that he was the person who put him there. Despite the pressure of the situation, Gouker testified that he remained calm while he was
questioned by police. He even laughed on the stand as he

related how he told detectives that he would bet his life that the kids from the nearby apartments were to blame for the murder.

In the weeks that followed the crime, Gouker spoke with police several times. He testified that when he visited the police station to speak with Detective Russ, he did not think he would leave a free man; he felt it was just a matter of time until he was arrested. He could not believe that he was allowed to walk right out the front door after giving his statement.

As she continued to question Gouker, White pointed out the inconsistencies in his prior statements including the statement given to Detective Russ at the police station. She asked whether he remembered the various stories he told regarding his involvement in the murder and the events of the night of May 10, 2011, to which he repeatedly replied, "I don't remember," until he finally erupted, "I don't deny nothin' I've said. I'm a fucking liar. You know what I mean?"[7]

In addition to being a self-professed liar, Gouker was also an abuser. He began to address his other crimes at the prodding of the prosecutor and he admitted to several instances of animal cruelty that occurred in the months leading up to Trey's murder. When asked about the beating death of the black mixed-breed puppy that belonged to Trey, he flippantly responded, "It was just one whack. You all make it sound more sinister than it was. The thing shit on everything. It was broke. It was a broke dog." He also admitted to killing a cat and throwing it away. Others from the neighborhood had already notified police detectives that he removed the eye of that cat and affixed it to a stick, approaching people in the neighborhood and saying, "I've got my eye on you." Gouker detailed these sickening actions with no more emotion that a person describing his grocery list.[8]

As the testimony proceeded, the prosecutor questioned Gouker again regarding the various statements he gave to police during their investigation of Trey's death. Prosecutors were obviously skeptical that Gouker had killed Trey and acted alone. It was important for the jury to hear that prior to his confession and guilty plea, Gouker initially blamed his son for the murder. While being held in Alabama, Gouker had requested a meeting with Detective Russ. He admitted that he told the detective that Little Josh confessed to hating Trey and that he resented Trey for telling on him and getting him into trouble.

Gouker originally told the detective that Little Josh had confessed to him that he killed Trey on the night of May 14 and had brought the bat with him from Cassi's house. In this version, Gouker said that after luring Trey to "The Spot," Little Josh asked him the time. Trey pulled his cell phone out of his pants pocket and checked the time and when he placed the phone back in his pocket, Little Josh hit him with the antique bat he took from Cassi's. According to that Alabama statement, Little Josh couldn't stop hitting Trey. When he ran out of energy, he put the bat in a landfill. He walked up the road to return to Cassi's house. Little Josh didn't cut through the yards as he usually would because he knew Gouker and Amanda were outside. Gouker stated he heard Little Josh tell his grandmother that he hated Trey and Little Josh told him that he slept just fine despite the killing.

Gouker asserted that the statement implicating Little Josh was false, concocted to convince everyone of his son's guilt in the hopes of saving himself. As a juvenile, Little Josh would receive a much more lenient punishment. In a voice dripping with sarcasm, White called him a "mastermind."

Pointing to Detective Russ seated to the right of the prosecutor's table, Big Josh smirked, "All I had to do was convince that guy right there, which I did...It's not easy to be a mastermind when you're dealing with dumb people. That guy couldn't find tits in a strip club. I had to do what I had to do."[9]

The testimony was riveting. Jurors sat upright, tilted slightly forward, literally on the edge of their seats wondering what he would say next. As the prosecutor segued into Gouker's plans after his arrest for parole violations, he admitted after some hesitation that he wanted to get out of jail so that he could kill Amanda, Trey's mother. When asked about Trey's father, he testified that he had always hated him but would not go out of his way to kill him, "unless he just happened to be there and it was something convenient."

Perhaps the only men who were not afraid to contradict Gouker were convicts. Three inmates gave statements or testified against Gouker, claiming that he admitted encouraging his son to commit murder. Gouker wasted no time in discounting those stories.

Although the inmates, one of whom was characterized by Gouker as a friend of Trey's dad, were housed on the same prison wing as Gouker and often engaged in games of dominoes with him, Gouker maintained that he could not remember having any conversations with them regarding Trey's murder.

Gouker also discounted statements made by another convict. Big Josh was emphatic that he did not know the man and had never met him. He went so far as to state that he could not pick him out of a line-up. The only thing he did know was that the man was housed at Luther Luckett. Completely discounting the testimony of all three men, Gouker opined that many people, especially convicts with something to gain, often are hungry for fifteen minutes of fame. Everyone in the area was familiar with the Trey Zwicker murder and, by the time of the trial, the case had garnered national media attention. All of the inmates wanted freedom; he figured that they planned to capitalize on the situation by fabricating stories. Inmates falsely claiming to be on the receiving end of jailhouse confessions were nothing new. After Gouker's statements regarding the inmates who testified against him, the prosecution passed the witness.

At the close of the prosecution's case, Leslie Smith rose and made her way to the podium, positioning herself to the left of the jury box. Courtroom viewers were anxious to see how the defense would approach Gouker. His testimony could garner two drastically different reactions. Jurors would surely see Big Josh as the cold, sadistic monster he was and this could earn sympathy for Little Josh or the jurors could view the Joshes as two peas in a pod.

Smith immediately highlighted Gouker's controlling nature. She had to convince the jury that he had an unbelievable talent for controlling those around him. In order to help the jury view him as a puppet master pulling other people's strings, she needed to demonstrate that Gouker had convinced people to lie for him all the time. The defense theory was that Gouker manipulated the women who claimed Little Josh confessed to them, that they were following instructions from Gouker and were terrified to cross him. This fear was evident in the testimony of the witness who took the stand immediately prior to Gouker, Angelic Burkhead. As she was released from the witness box, she walked slowly toward the courtroom door. However, as she heard the prosecution call Gouker as the next witness, cameras caught her literally sprinting from the courtroom. Smith needed to make sure the jury recognized Gouker for what he was, a person who terrified the people he sought to control.

"Is 'tell the truth' code for tell a lie?" she inquired, gripping both sides of the podium and leaning forward.

Gouker agreed that it was, a smile curling the corners of his lips, "Sometimes you've got to say it over and over until they say the right fucking story, but yeah."[10]

Smith led Gouker through his admission that he had repeatedly asked to view Trey's body, the implication being that he wanted to see his handiwork in broad daylight. In fact, he was so taken with the facial imprint left in the ground by Trey's face that he had stopped by "The Spot" the day of Trey's wake to see it again.

Gouker seemed comfortable with killing and admitted that he had planned on killing someone for a while. He just never thought it would be Trey. Big Josh was forthcoming in disclosing that while in prison he had a lot of time to think and stew over those who had wronged him in the past. He had almost ten years to fantasize about the day of his release and the opportunity to hurt those whom he perceived as his enemies. He even wrote rap lyrics about the actions he would take. He had spent years planning whom he would kill when he was released from prison.

However, his plans were put on hold when Josh Young's mother passed away approximately nine months prior to his release. Gouker wanted custody of his son, who had been placed in foster care after the death of his mother. He had not had a meaningful relationship with Little Josh in nine years and Little Josh's mother, Angie, had ensured that Child Protective Services and the court system were well aware of Gouker's track record for violence. Gouker testified that Angie made it her mission to inform Child Protective Services that he was a "monster," which she likely did in an effort to protect her oldest child.

Gouker testified that he went to work gaining the trust of Child Protective Services and disproving Angie's previous claims; he jumped through hoops, attending classes mandated for reunification. He used his charisma to charm the Child Protective Services workers, banking on the fact that most people liked him right away, at least on a superficial level. He related that after the first meeting, the workers believed he was sincere, stating, "I cried and shit like that." He felt that listing Amanda's house as his address was extremely beneficial; it was a nice, stable four-bedroom home. Never mind that Little Josh stayed mainly at Cassi's house; he kept that from Child Protective Services. Gouker had only gained custody of Little Josh six weeks prior to Trey's death. As he conned Child Protective Services, Gouker also went to work at duping his probation officer.

As White continued to question Big Josh, she conveyed that Gouker was even able to trick his probation officer into believing he was in compliance with the terms of his parole. All the while, Gouker was residing at different addresses from what he had listed and was smoking marijuana on a daily basis. When asked about these examples of deceit, Gouker shrugged, stating that his probation officer was pretty much a rookie and that he had never supervised an ex-convict with a prison record as serious as Gouker's. Big Josh's attitude was evident; he did what he wanted when he wanted and even trained government workers could fall victim to his lies.

Gouker testified that he put that charm to use again as he and Amanda hurried to Liberty High School on the day officers recovered Trey's body. According to Gouker, when they arrived home from McNeely Lake, Amanda became worried because she noticed that Trey's backpack and school items were still at the house. Upon hearing that a body had been found at Liberty High School, they immediately went there.

Gouker knew he had to show his face at the crime scene. He needed to find out what the police knew. He needed to buy time. Shaking his head, Gouker told the jury that he "needed to put a mask on this monster—fast."[11]

Big Josh explained that as time elapsed, he made sure to keep the monster masked, even going so far as to implicate his own son when he felt the police were beginning to suspect him. Explaining that it is easier to tell a story with a little transference, Gouker implored police to investigate his son, expressing concern about whom he would hurt next and stating that he feared he would kill Amanda.

Killing Amanda was exactly what Gouker himself planned to do if given the opportunity. Through his testimony, Gouker related that while incarcerated in Alabama, he immediately went to work contacting people under his direct control. He was positive that his cousin Cassi would do anything for him. He convinced her to concoct a story that Little Josh confessed to her and that she helped him dispose of the murder weapon.

As she was bringing her questioning to a close, Leslie Smith pointed out Gouker's past convictions and his pattern of sneaking up on people, using the element of surprise to perpetrate his criminal acts. These acts kept him incarcerated from 2002 until his release in the fall of 2010.

Smith questioned whether Gouker had taken Trey by surprise, sneaking up behind him and punching him to the ground. In support of her argument, she noted his 2002 robbery and assault charges in which he was convicted of beating a seventy-one-year-old man in the face from behind while strangling him with his own belt. She revealed another criminal conviction where he admitted to sneaking up on his victim from behind, punching him, kicking him while he was down and holding him hostage. Admittedly, the element of surprise was very important to Gouker, but perhaps the biggest surprise to spectators in the courtroom was that after such horrendous acts, he was paroled in 2010 to roam the streets of Louisville.

Once Leslie Smith had concluded her cross-examination of Gouker, prosecutor Erin White rose to again question the witness. Convinced that Little Josh was the actual killer in the case, she repeatedly asked for details of the crime in an attempt to demonstrate to the jury that Gouker did not have knowledge of the crime scene because he was not the true killer. Gouker characterized that time as a blur.

At one point, looking straight at Gouker, White stated that had he committed the murder, it should not be so hard for him to relate the facts.

Tilting his head to the side, Gouker paused slightly, "You're sadistic, man. You want to hear that shit?"

"Tell us what you remember."

The courtroom quiet, he shook his head and said, "I mean just being covered in Trey, that's it."[12]

At least one juror later remarked that in that moment he firmly believed Josh Gouker was telling the truth.

At the close of the prosecution's redirect and the defense's brief re-cross of Gouker, the court inquired whether the jury had any questions for the witness. This is not a common practice in Kentucky and many judges do not allow the jurors to pose questions to witnesses in a trial. However, many benefits to this practice exist for both sides, especially relating to a controversial witness like Gouker.

The questions submitted by jurors allow each side to gauge issues that are prevalent in jurors' minds and also may give some indication as to how a juror feels on a particular topic or whether he or she finds the witness credible. This jury panel had no shortage of questions for Josh Gouker.

After taking a ten-minute restroom break to allow the judge and attorneys to discuss the jury questions, Judge Willett read those questions aloud to Gouker:

"Would you give your life for your son?"

"Did you want to see Trey's body so you could get facts to take the rap for Josh Young?"

"Was Josh Young with you when you killed Trey?"

"Did you have Josh Young help you in any way with Trey's murder?"

"Do you feel bad about anything you have done?"

"What time did you leave to kill Trey?"

"Did Josh Young meet you to help you kill Trey?"

"Did Trey ever go anywhere with you alone before the night he was killed?"[13]

Despite the time attorneys spent questioning Gouker, perhaps the most telling and poignant question came from one of the jurors:

"Do you love your son, Joshua Young?"

Taking a deep breath and glancing toward Judge Willett, Gouker responded, "This is gonna make me sound like a piece of shit. You've got to think though, I don't know him." Then after a slight pause he answered, "Much as I can love, yeah."[14]

Chapter 15

The Defense and the Media

B y the time the prosecutors concluded their case, the trial was in its ninth day. The defense was called upon by the court to present its evidence in the matter. Two of the defense witnesses had previously been allowed to testify out of order: Dr. Nichols, due to his work schedule and Erin Specth, the kidnapping victim from Gouker's Alabama fiasco, due to the long distance she had to travel.

Of all the witnesses, Erin Specth would likely be one of the most helpful for the defense. Although this woman was kidnapped by Josh Gouker, she felt compelled to testify on behalf of Little Josh. She had never visited Louisville before but she took a fifteen-hour bus ride just so she could testify for the defense. She was completely credible as she related the story of her abduction at the hands of Josh Gouker and Jahaira Friend. Interestingly, according to the woman, no one from the prosecutor's office or the police department had ever questioned her regarding her experience with Gouker in Alabama.[1]

She described how absolutely horrible she felt for all Little Josh had been through and that she did not feel he was a willing participant in his father's actions in any way. According to Specth, Little Josh said a handful of words the entire time she was with him. She found him to be a sweet and gentle boy who looked very uncomfortable with everything that was occurring.

The fact that a victim of Gouker who did not know Little Josh would travel such a long distance to testify for him was compelling. She had nothing to gain by doing so and this added exponentially to her credibility. Her testimony contrasted sharply with Jahaira's sworn statements. She garnered sympathy for Little Josh and her testimony portrayed him as a victim of his father and not an accomplice.

Having heard from Erin Specth and Dr. Nichols, the defense called three more individuals to the stand. Trey's dad was first. The defense recalled Terry Zwicker in order to ask him one question: "To your knowledge, was Trey afraid of Joshua Young?" Terry Zwicker's answer was a definitive "No."[2]

The next witness called by the defense was Bridget Fraley, an employee of the Cabinet for Health and Family Services Quality Assurance Department. At the time of Trey's murder, she worked for Child Protective Services in the Crimes Against Children Unit. Shortly after Trey's body was found, she was directed to interview his younger sister about the night of his death.

Trey's younger sister testified for the prosecution in the case of *Commonwealth v. Joshua Young* and she did a very good job staying calm and answering questions, especially considering her young age. It was apparent that she was telling the truth to the best of her ability. The defense hoped that by calling Fraley, it could contradict the girl's testimony. She was a young child at the time of Trey's death and defense attorneys believed she was influenced by the adults in her life and they also believed that she just did not remember some events of the night due to her age and the length of time that had passed between the crime and the trial.

Fraley testified that she had interviewed the child before at her grandmother's home only days after Trey's death. At that time, Trey's sister told her that she saw Trey that evening when she took her bath at seven o'clock. Trey took a shower later and they shared a bag of chips while sitting on the couch. She testified that the last time she saw him, Trey was going upstairs to go to bed.

This was important to the defense, because the child testified in the trial during the prosecution's case-in-chief that she saw Trey leave the home, which is not what she told Fraley. Whether or not she was sleeping on the couch that evening was important to the case, because Gouker claimed during his testimony that he and Trey stayed up late playing video games after Amanda fell asleep. Had Trey's younger sister been on the couch sleeping, she likely would have been awoken and seen them. If she was actually on the couch, Gouker was lying and Trey did not die the way that he testified.[3]

Fraley's testimony was short but it was helpful to the defense. The next witness would be the only family member of Little Josh called by the defense. Little Josh's aunt was an attractive woman in her forties with thick dark hair. She was very familiar with all of the players in the case. She had grown up in the same area and she was previously married to Josh's uncle.

Josh's aunt said she remembered Trey's funeral vividly. She had arrived with Big Josh, Little Josh and Amanda. Amanda was wearing dark glasses and moaning. Josh's aunt stayed next to Little Josh for most of the funeral when he wasn't performing his duties as a pallbearer.

She recalled that Little Josh was devastated and upset. He held his head low and could not bring himself to say much. Even as they left the funeral, he remained upset and agitated, crying as they rode home. Her testimony was important because at least one witness had testified that Little Josh was unemotional at the funeral, implying that he was not sad that Trey was dead. Josh's aunt contradicted that with her testimony. She was with him for the entire evening and she was positive that he was absolutely devastated about Trey's death. It was easy to see why Little Josh might hide his emotions in public but break down in private. He had been conditioned all his life to hide emotions and feelings and he was used to devastating change. He had experienced it time and again in his short life. Josh's aunt knew him well and she testified that she could easily tell by the way he acted at the funeral and during its aftermath that her nephew was very upset. At the conclusion of her testimony, the defense rested its case. They did not call Josh Young to the stand. Josh's attorneys advised him that he did not need to testify since they felt the prosecution had not proven its case and he had his Fifth Amendment right to remain silent. Josh had trusted his attorneys so far and opted to follow their advice.

By the time the trial began, the local and national media were captivated by the case. As the trial progressed, Gouker submitted to interviews with some news stations where he repeatedly stated that he was solely responsible for Trey's death and that his son was not involved. Viewers were fascinated as the media revealed the details of severe family dysfunction in the McFarland/Gouker household that resulted in a brutal and stomach-churning act. It was a story stranger than fiction: recently paroled ex-convict Josh Gouker wasted no time regaining custody of his fifteen year-old son, Josh Young, and within six weeks of that placement, Trey Zwicker was dead and Josh, a former honor student and high school wrestler, had descended on an unparalleled downward spiral, accused of murdering his own stepbrother at his father's behest.

The media tried its best to address the sociopathic tendencies of Gouker, whom it portrayed as a violent ex-con with the apparent ability to charm and puppeteer those around him. Among the TV programs featuring the case were the *Nancy Grace* show and Jane Velez Mitchell's nightly news program on CNN. They dubbed Gouker "Monster Dad" and asked if Little Josh was a "Baby Faced Killer."[4] As coverage of the trial progressed, viewers and reporters alike asked the same question: Was Josh Young a cold-blooded murderer like his demonic dad or just another victim of a sadistic psychopath?

The media could not get enough of the story and rel-atives from both sides of the family were quick to grant interviews to various media outlets. Even those closest to Gouker, like his mother Ruby, spoke out supporting Little Josh's innocence while blaming Big Josh for the crime. Sadly, shortly after speaking with the media on behalf of Josh Young, Ruby would succumb to her own demons. She died in 2013 of a prescription drug overdose.

With the amount of press coverage the case received, it was surprising that the parties were able to find jurors who had not seen reports about the case on various media outlets. The coverage on HLN focused on the fact that Josh Gouker appeared to be a psychopath and repeatedly replayed coverage of his media interviews.[5] It was hard to fathom how a person could seem so cold and calculating. Those reporting on the case in the national arena appeared to view Little Josh as a secondary victim of his biological father's crime spree.

It was shocking to the average viewer that Gouker, a virtual stranger to his son, was awarded custody of the boy so quickly after his release from prison, given his violent rap sheet and lack of connection to Little Josh over the preceding nine years. It was also surprising that although Gouker admittedly used drugs and alcohol daily, he was never given a drug test by Child Protective Services that showed a positive result or seemed to warrant removal from the household.

It appeared that the national media was sympathetic to Little Josh and his was the main story on many news outlets each evening as the trial progressed. In contrast, the local media in Louisville seemed to air more footage of the people who claimed that Josh *was* guilty of killing Trey. When he appeared, Trey's father was straightforward, passionate and unrelenting in his belief that Little Josh was involved in the crime. Local media did not show as much footage of Josh's supporters, in contrast to their national counterparts.

The social media firestorm that swirled around the story was even more damning than the news media. Josh's supporters created a webpage dedicated to freeing him from custody. Its members clearly believed that Little Josh was innocent. However, several pages also sprang up that sought justice for Trey and that justice, in their minds, included a murder conviction against Joshua Young.

The personal social media pages for several of the people involved in the matter, both integrally and peripherally, showcased commentary that threatened Little Josh's life. Some people commented that they hoped he would be killed if acquitted and that they would ensure he never had a normal life. Other people commented that they hoped he would be beaten to death or that someone would take the law into their own hands and kill the boy. Where some people were concerned, they felt there was no need for a trial. Little Josh was already guilty in their minds and they wanted him to suffer physically for what they believed he did to Trey.

As versions of the story proliferated, emotions raged out of control for friends and family members on both sides of the case which involved the savage murder of a child. Audiences across America turned to the media each night for updates on the story. Unfortunately, neither side appeared to feel that their entire side of the story was ever told. This was perhaps one of the most polarizing trials in recent history. To supporters on each side of the case, there was no gray area. The people who believed that Little Josh was a killer could not be swayed and the people who believed in his innocence did not waiver in their support.

It became evident as the trial moved forward that the jurors would have a difficult task deciding the guilt or innocence of Little Josh. Those twelve men and women would need to look at all the evidence from an analytical and objective perspective. It was daunting, given the fact that emotions ran so high on both sides of the case. Trial watchers everywhere collectively held their breath as they wondered what verdict the jury would return.

Chapter 16

Closing Arguments

After several long sessions of testimony, the time for closing arguments finally arrived. In the previous days of the trial, each side had presented its case through a parade of witnesses. Many of those witnesses appeared fiercely loyal to Josh Young and an equal number sought justice for Trey. Prosecutors had introduced countless pictures of the crime scene; jury members and viewers had endured cries of shock from Trey's broken-hearted family as they were forced to view the photos of his battered body. The jurors had asked many questions, often revealing doubts about the testimony of witnesses, especially Josh Gouker. On the afternoon that closing arguments began, no one seemed to know what the jury would decide.

Most experienced attorneys refrain from predicting verdicts. An attorney need only try one criminal case to learn the hard way that juries are unpredictable; submitting a case to a jury can be akin to playing the lottery or rolling dice. The jury in the Joshua Young case appeared competent and attentive throughout the trial. They obviously took their jobs seriously and were prepared to consider all the evidence and make a very difficult decision. They held the future of seventeen-year-old Josh Young in their hands.

News outlets streamed live coverage of the trial and the days of testimony exposed jurors and television viewers to violence and family dysfunction in an unfathomable form.

In the state of Kentucky, murder is a capital offense. Josh was a juvenile and, if convicted of murder, he faced a sentence of twenty years to life in prison. The jury could conceivably sentence Josh Young to spend the rest of his life behind bars if they believed him guilty of the most serious charge. He also faced a charge of tampering with physical evidence, a Class D felony. That charge held a penalty range of one to five years in prison. The defense team hoped for a complete acquittal in the case.

Josh Young's attorneys wanted jurors to retire to the jury room feeling sympathy for Little Josh. They needed to portray him as yet another unfortunate victim of Gouker, not a villain perpetrating Trey's death. Throughout the trial, attorney Leslie Smith appeared especially attentive to Young; she often leaned toward him whispering explanations and guiding him through the trial process. He was only a teenager, yet he found himself in a very adult situation and Smith remained exceedingly helpful in ensuring that he understood the proceedings. Little Josh appeared especially young and vulnerable as the time for closing arguments approached.

The courtroom was pin-drop quiet as the defense gave its closing statement first. Wearing a plum-colored suit, Leslie Smith rose and made her way slowly to the podium facing the jurors. Smith was the picture of professionalism as she began delivering her passionate pleas.

"An Amber Alert was issued on June 16, 2011, because people were scared that Joshua Young was dead. Because nobody could find him," Smith said, detailing the moment family members realized that both Big Josh and Little Josh were missing.[1] Terrified that Little Josh was his father's latest victim, they immediately notified police and a nationwide search for the pair began. She highlighted Jahaira Friend's testimony. Jahaira contended that she was kidnapped by Big Josh and forced to drive Big Josh and his son to Alabama. Later Erin Specth testified that after Big Josh kidnapped her and prior to her release, Big Josh forced her to look into Little Josh's terrified eyes and promise that she would not call police because his life literally depended on it.

Smith moved to Gouker and his testimony, urging the jurors to disregard everything he had said. Characterizing him as a master manipulator, she blamed him completely for Trey's murder. Her voice touched by strong emotion, Smith said that the only reason Little Josh was charged in the matter was due to statements made by his father. If police had not listened to Gouker, none of them would be in the courtroom. That was literally the only reason police even began to suspect Little Josh. She urged the jurors not to make the same mistake. They should not believe a word Gouker had uttered. After his chilling testimony, it was obvious that he enjoyed the attention and relished manipulating people. Her certainty was evident as she addressed each juror, "This guy is not a mastermind. He is a puppet master. He duped everybody...that's why you don't listen to him."[2]

Highlighting Gouker's manipulation and his lack of remorse, she exclaimed, "The crime was horrible and that's how you know who did it." Waving her hands in the air and staring deep into the eyes of each juror, she questioned, "Do you really think he didn't kill Trey?"

Smith emphasized Gouker's chilling testimony, his admission that as he sat in prison for years, he fantasized about killing someone upon his release. She characterized Gouker as a cold-hearted individual, a methodical planner who thrived on making others scared of him.

She opined that this was actually a classic, clear-cut case of domestic violence. When Trey's mother allowed Gouker into her home after his release from prison, the brutality and control started almost immediately. Gouker thrived on it and he was good at it. He was skilled in manipulating those around him. Within months of his arrival, he forced Amanda to quit the job she'd held for seventeen years. He terrorized her and her children and he fooled people outside of the family, because on the surface he appeared to be a jovial and friendly guy. Shaking her head, she continued, "This is not a difficult case at all. This is a really typical, horrible case of domestic violence and let me stop right there."

Pausing, Smith took a deep breath, "This is not about demonizing anybody. Amanda was being abused. Let's get past that. It's not about putting her down or anything like that. This was a house of domestic violence. This crazy guy who was home from prison...he walks right out and right to her," she said referring to Amanda, "And that's where he began manipulating everybody and duping them."[3]

Smith told the jurors not to feel badly if they had laughed during Gouker's testimony. The counselor commented that Gouker appeared at first as a likable guy, a funny guy. He could turn on the charm if he wanted something from someone. He was able to fool so many people, people who were trained to spot manipulators like him. He convinced Child Protective Services that he should receive custody of his son despite his violent past and spotty track record. He persuaded his parole officer to allow him more freedoms and to believe that he was in compliance with his supervision plan when he was violating its conditions daily. When Amanda finally realized the true nature of Gouker, she terminated her pregnancy because she clearly saw the relationship's direction and she did not like where it was going. He viewed that child, like he did all people, as his possession and anyone who took something from him should be punished. In the aftermath of the abortion, the situation in the home slowly began to escalate until it combusted in Trey's murder.

Leslie Smith next urged the jury to come to terms with the fact that they might never know exactly what happened to Trey the night of his death. She implored them, "Do not convict this boy because you don't know," as she gestured toward her young client. There were questions in this case that might never receive an answer.

She proceeded to tell the jurors that Gouker had planned an alibi by making a sex tape with Amanda. However, she emphasized that this video had never been substantiated. There was never any proof that it actually existed. Gouker knew exactly what had happened to Trey and yet he continued to go about his life the next day.

Once Trey's body was discovered, his grief-stricken father, Terry Zwicker, was given the grave task of identifying the body and within five minutes he told Detective Russ that he believed Gouker was capable of the crime. But no one had listened. Gouker repeatedly asked to see the body as if he wanted to view what he had done in the light of day. Gouker convinced Detective Maroni that Amanda should remain with him during his police interview, even though that was against police protocol. These actions, Smith argued, were indicative that Gouker was a successful manipulator, a natural-born liar.

Leslie Smith asserted that the case against Josh Young only existed because of his father's statements. Gouker implicated his son to several people and Smith argued that all of his statements were a matter of transference, that the actions he attributed to his son were actually his own. He made statements that he felt no guilt; he disposed of the bloody clothes and murder weapon; he beat Trey to death. He was a violent man who had been previously convicted of sneaking up behind a seventy-one-year-old man, punching him in the face and choking him with his own belt. Smith contended that he did the same sort of thing to Trey; he snuck up from behind and hit the boy.

Then she reviewed the forensic testimony. The expert had testified that an old wooden baseball bat did not cause Trey's injuries. This was especially important, because the witnesses who claimed Little Josh confessed said he told them he used an antique bat. Per the medical testimony, that was impossible. The expert also testified that he firmly believed that Trey's injuries were caused by a single perpetrator who inflicted all the injuries while standing in the same position.

Smith was quick to inform the jury that they could review any testimony and any prerecorded statements introduced during the trial. She urged them to review Little Josh's initial interview with Detective Maroni at the crime scene. In the tape, "He was crying in shock like people who *feel* things," she emphasized, unlike his father who doesn't "feel anything, ever."

She advised the jury that Josh Young was an impressionable boy living in a house of chaos and horrors. During the trial, the prosecutors emphasized that Josh Young wanted to live with his father, even despite his history and the dysfunction in the home. Smith claimed that that "jerk of a dad" was all Little Josh had in the world after his mother's death and that wanting to be with his father was a natural feeling. It did not make him evil like his father. He was a child who wanted a family and wanted to feel loved. She asked the jury, "Why aren't all the kids in this situation victims?" Clearly they were all controlled and mistreated by Gouker. The answer, she claimed, was simply "because Gouker said so."[4]

Throughout the trial, the prosecution had argued that Josh Gouker was trying to protect his son from prosecution. Smith went to work dispelling this belief, arguing that Gouker's testimony had "nothing to do with saving his son." There was something "not wired right" in Gouker and he was incapable of feeling anything. Smith opined that "he took great pleasure in killing that poor boy" and that any benefit to Little Josh given by his testimony was only collateral. Gouker loved no one but himself.

As her argument wound to a close, Smith reminded jurors of the presumption of innocence and urged them to free Little Josh. With great conviction, Smith clutched the podium and, with her voice raised, she ended her statement by pleading, "The abuse continues for Joshua Young, who has been in jail for over two years for this with false allegations...This is a kid who was sleeping or watching a movie or something by a location where a boy was brutally murdered by someone who really, really enjoyed himself and that is disgusting; it's wrong; it's heartbreaking." She glanced back at Josh sitting at the defense table and then promptly directed her attention back toward the jury. "There is a little bit of brainwashing stuff going on here." She argued that even Josh Young initially believed that his father "...didn't do it. The only person who told the truth throughout this whole thing has been [Josh Young]. Young is the only person who told the truth. Why are we here? Why are we here? Send this kid home, wherever that may be...It's not a 'not guilty' thing. He's innocent and you know it. I can't believe that we are here. Send him home."[5]

At the conclusion of Smith's passionate argument, the court called on the prosecution to present its closing. Elizabeth Jones Brown began by re-reading the jury instructions to the jurors.

Young was charged with murder by complicity and Jones Brown explained to the jury that to convict him, they did not necessarily need to believe that he physically killed Trey. It was enough if he helped his father plan the murder and then helped him after the killing. She then attempted to dispel statements made by Gouker. She doubted that Gouker would become so outraged that Trey had used his cheap lighter. She emphasized that Trey had no recent marijuana in his system. Gouker had maintained that he and Trey went to the creek and smoked marijuana together. Jones Brown doubted that Trey would go alone at night to a creek with his abusive stepfather and she argued that the blood tests confirmed that Trey did not smoke marijuana that evening. She clearly believed that it was Little Josh who lured him there. She addressed the jury: "Nothing in Gouker's demeanor in court or anything else you heard in this case gave credence to the fact that, in the middle of the night, Trey would leave the house and go down to the creek bed to hang out with his mother's abusive husband."[6]

Elizabeth Jones Brown made some valid points during her closing argument. She noted Gouker's perceived inability to testify about the details of the murder, stating that he could not fill in the blanks. She even pointed out that at one point during his testimony, he said "we" when referring to his actions on the night of the murder. One of her most persuasive points was that Gouker testified that he was covered in blood after the attack. However, the convenience store surveillance tape from earlier that night showed him in the same outfit he wore at the scene of the body's discovery the next day, a University of Louisville jersey with the number "34" emblazoned on the back.

Referring to this issue, she reemphasized its importance to the jurors and she continued, "We know that Gouker and Amanda went to the [convenience store] between 1:06 and 1:09. We also know that Gouker was wearing the same clothes the next day." She turned to point out the pictures of Gouker illuminated on the projection screen in the courtroom which showed him wearing the same jersey that evening at the convenience store and the next day at the scene of Trey's murder after his body was found. She continued, "There he is at the store, and there he is at the scene the next day—number 34 Louisville jersey."[7]

She detailed the evening of the murder and the dysfunction in the household. She agreed that the home was rife with domestic violence. However, she did not agree with the rendition of the facts as related by Gouker and Little Josh. Gouker claimed he had played video games with Trey late on the evening of May 10, 2011. However, Trey's eight-year-old sister claimed that she slept on the couch that evening, according to her testimony, in the exact spot where Gouker claims he sat. Also, in Little Josh's initial interview with Detective Maroni, he testified that he saw Trey after Trey had taken a shower and changed that night. He knew what Trey was wearing. However, his later statements and the statements of others were that Josh was no longer at the home when Trey took a shower, so Jones Brown argued that the only way he could have seen Trey's clothing was if he was present at the crime scene.

According to Jones Brown, Gouker convinced Josh to participate in the killing. She urged the jurors to believe that although Josh was a small boy, he had the capability to swing a bat with enough force to cause Trey's injuries. She reminded jurors that children younger than him can hit home runs. At the time the murder occurred, she remarked, Josh was "not in the courtroom wearing a sweater vest," referring to Little Josh's innocent appearance as he sat in the courtroom looking like the young, seventeen-year-old boy that he was at the time of his trial.

She urged jurors to not fall victim to sympathy just because Little Josh had a bad dad and a bad life. According to Jones Brown, jurors should not let their sympathy cloud reasonable doubt. She felt even if he was pressured by his father, Little Josh had the free will to say no. She told them Little Josh had talked about the crime repeatedly without his father and that he "bragged and laughed" about it. According to Jones Brown, Josh Gouker was a control freak and his son desperately wanted to impress him. Jones Brown reminded jurors that their job was to go through the facts and hold Josh Young accountable for Trey Zwicker's murder. As her argument came to a close, Jones Brown had a final statement for the jurors:

> Trey Zwicker was brutally murdered at age fourteen when he was finishing his freshman year in high school, because Josh Gouker was a control freak and Josh Young wanted to impress him. Trey will never finish high school, never get to grow up alongside his dad, never get to take care of his sister. This was an utterly senseless and heartbreaking murder. One of the participants is being held now for the rest of his life. Now it's the defendant's turn.[8]

And with that contention, she rested the case for the Commonwealth.

Chapter 17

The Verdict

After the attorneys on both sides of the case completed their closing arguments, Judge Willett tendered his instructions to the jury and explained that as they deliberated, they would be secluded from the outside world. His bailiff collected their cell phones.

At the start of the trial, the court had chosen fifteen jurors with the understanding that three would not actually deliberate but would be designated alternates. As the trial progressed, one juror was excused for illness and another was removed from the jury because she was seen dozing during testimony. Immediately prior to submitting the case to the jury, the judge removed the final alternate and the remaining twelve jurors prepared to deliberate.

It was a terrifying feeling for Josh Young. He and his defense team had done all they could. As the jury deliberated, Josh spent the next hours in agonizing limbo. When the jurors came back with a verdict, one of two things could happen. He could spend the rest of his life in prison or he could receive a second chance at life after two years of incarceration in a juvenile detention center.

It was 8:17 P.M. Friday when the jury notified Judge Willett that it had reached a verdict. By this time, the trial had stretched from July 29 until August 9.

The feeling in the pit of his stomach was indescribable when Josh was notified that the jury had reached a verdict. He legs wobbled as he made his way back into the courtroom. As he settled into his chair, he was flanked by the two women who had worked so hard to support him as well as the man who'd worked tirelessly on his case. Leslie Smith sat to his left and his social worker to his right. Pete Schuler was to the social worker's right, the same positions as during the trial.[1]

It was a helpless feeling, because the decision was entirely in the jurors' hands. The attorneys related the information and made their assertions, but in the end the jury controlled the outcome. Those twelve people came from a variety of backgrounds and experiences and it was hard to predict how their life experiences would affect their decision making.

Now the jurors filed silently back into the courtroom and took their seats in the jury box. The audience buzzed with anticipation. Trey's family had waited two long years for this moment and so had Josh and his supporters. The moment of truth had arrived and it was clear that, regardless of the verdict, one side of the gallery would be very unhappy and one would feel satisfied that justice had been served.

Judge Willett looked toward the jury box, his face serious, then spoke, breaking the tense silence that hung heavily in the air. "Has the jury reached a verdict?" he asked, making eye contact with each of the jurors. As the jurors nodded, he gestured toward his bailiff, "If you'll hand the jury form to the deputy he'll bring it over."[2]

The foreperson nodded silently and handed the jury verdict forms to the bailiff who walked them to the judge sitting resolutely behind the bench. As Judge Willett retrieved the verdict forms and read through them, Josh's life hung in the balance.

Judge Willett glanced upward and began to speak slowly and determinedly, "Verdict form number one—murder. We the jury find the defendant not guilty under instruction number one." He took a breath and continued, "Verdict form number two—tampering with physical evidence. We the jury find the defendant not guilty under instruction number two."[3]

Josh felt happiness and excitement surge through him. He was going home, wherever that might end up being. Hands balled into fists, he shook them slightly in the air with his eyes closed and then buried his head into his arms on the table top, overcome with emotion. Leslie Smith reached over, patting the boy gently on the back. This is what they had worked so hard for. Josh suppressed a smile. He was so happy that he had a second chance at life, but he could not forget that Trey did not, and that knowledge hung over him. It was not truly a victory, because Trey was dead. The acquittal was bittersweet. Josh lifted his head and looked sadly at his social worker, meekly mouthing "Thank you" two separate times to the jurors who still sat in the jury box.

"Madam foreperson, are those in fact the verdicts of the jury?" Judge Willett asked as he laid the forms down on his bench.

"Yes, your honor," she said softly.

Judge Willett called the attorneys to the bench and asked them for permission to discharge the jury. With everyone in agreement, he again addressed the jurors, "I will ask you to retire back to the jury room to give me five minutes of your personal time to answer any questions that you may have and thank you personally for your service." The courtroom watched as the jurors filed out of the courtroom and with that, the judge turned to the gallery.

"Members of the gallery, thank you very much for staying calm and well behaved. These are tough cases for everybody involved. The case is dismissed. The defendant will be released from custody."[4]

Trey's family stood, looking agonized, then fled the courtroom. They believed that Josh Young was involved in the murder of Trey and they felt as though they did not receive justice. As they raced from the courtroom, Terry Zwicker appeared devastated by the verdict. He made a beeline for the elevator. In his opinion, the system had failed his son. A female relative of Trey could be heard blurting out, "I hate Amanda." Clearly, many of the members of Terry's side of the family blamed Amanda for bringing Gouker into Trey's life. They blamed her for allowing the monster around her children even though they believed she was well aware of the violence of which he was capable.

As she left the courtroom, Prosecutor Elizabeth Jones Brown could be heard remarking to the media that her team "always knew this was a tough case" and that "they've got a long road ahead of them."[5] The acquittal appeared to hit her hard, but she maintained her composure and professionalism.

Defense attorney Pete Schuler told reporters that he was "thrilled" with the verdict and that he hoped Josh could put the entire ordeal behind him. As Schuler spoke with reporters, the rest of the legal team was busy preparing for Josh's release. After two long years in custody, he was still a minor and needed to be released to the custody of the Cabinet for Health and Family Services. Social workers made arrangements for Josh to return home with the Walshes where his little sister would be waiting happily to greet him.

He would get to see her immediately and he was ecstatic. It appeared that after all he had been through, he would finally get that second chance he'd dreamed of for two years. Joshua Young walked out of Jefferson County Youth Corrections Center that evening. It was an overwhelming feeling, but he was happy. He was free and he had great hopes for his future. He was thrilled that the system had worked on his behalf. The previous two years in custody had been trying. However, everything had worked out for the best and he hoped that he could finally put the past behind him and look toward his future.

Several jurors on the case quietly discussed their deliberations in *Commonwealth v. Joshua Young*. None of the jurors felt the prosecutors had presented proof of Little Josh's guilt beyond a reasonable doubt. It was clear to those jurors that Gouker was the person who had delivered the fatal blows that killed Trey. They did not believe Little Josh was involved in the murder in any knowing way, although some jurors pondered whether he might have been his father's unknowing pawn in the matter. They opined that it was possible Trey and Little Josh snuck out together and that Gouker seized the opportunity to kill Trey without Josh's prior knowledge.

The jurors clearly did not believe the state had proven its case against Little Josh for murder and tampering with physical evidence and they made the decision to acquit the boy and send him home.

Chapter 18

The Real Culprit?

Josh Young was placed into a very bad situation with a convicted felon who had been in jail for nearly ten years. Gouker had a history of abuse, yet his son was removed from a foster home where he thrived to "live" (since he rarely slept under the same roof as his father) with a man known to have a violent streak.

The issues in Child Protective Services are a national problem. From Kentucky and Arizona to New Jersey and Vermont, there are problems. In New Jersey, four adopted boys were found to be so malnourished that one, at age nineteen, was just four feet tall and weighed only forty-five pounds. The situation was discovered only because a neighbor saw the nineteen-year-old looking for food in a trash can in the early hours one morning.[1]

Amy Dye was adopted in Kentucky in 2006 by her great aunt and cousins when she was five. When Garrett Dye, then twelve years of age, was asked to write what he would tell his friends about his potential new sister, he wrote: "I will tell them that she is the best sister ever. I would like her to be funny and happy wherever she goes."[2]

A little less than five years later, Garrett Dye beat Amy to death in the driveway of their home. Amy was nine.

Was this a tragedy that could have been averted?

Complaints of overworked caseworkers, children being left in homes they should be removed from and children being pulled from loving homes for unspecified reasons litter the child welfare landscape. In Amy Dye's case, it was revealed that Garrett Dye had started to have "worrisome behavior problems," like bringing a gun to school. In the years preceding her death, a school nurse, teachers and others reported their concern that Amy was being mistreated or abused at her adoptive home, but their concerns were ignored or not properly investigated, the judge in the case ruled.[3]

It has been reported that overworked CPS caseworkers in Arizona ignored, on average, about 26 percent of the 3,200 phone calls they received on their abuse hotline during a typical week.[4] So about 832 calls received no response. Is it mathematically possible that all of those calls were false alarms? Or was a child abused and no one did anything to stop it?

In the case of the four malnourished boys, a caseworker for the New Jersey Division of Youth and Family Services had visited the house multiple times over the previous two years. According to *The New York Times*, "The case is the latest in a series of discoveries revealing the collapse of New Jersey's child welfare system, which left the youngsters it was charged with protecting vulnerable to abuse and neglect in troubled homes with little oversight."[5]

In Vermont, the death of two infants has prompted a government investigation into the Department of Children and Families, according to a *VPR News* report.[6] The article's headline reads "Social Workers Expose Flaws in Child Protective Services" and tells of how social workers informed the government about "staffing shortages, lack of communication between state agencies, and what they said are sometimes unrealistic evidentiary thresholds needed to remove kids from dangerous homes. They said these problems, and others, are leading to the types of situations that might have led to the deaths of [the] infants."[7] One issue that a social worker raised was the fact that hearsay cannot be admitted in family court hearings: "When children tell doctors, for instance, that their injuries were inflicted by a caregiver, that information can't be admitted in court. And...abusive parents can easily convince children to change their testimony before a judge."[8]

There are many problems that plague Child Protective Services, according to an essay on the WSIU Public Broadcasting website on Child Protection Reform. "Nationally there is a very negative public opinion of state CPS agencies," the essay says. It goes on to point out that "the single most important reform that has the most impact on children and families is the amount of training that child protection investigators receive. In many states training is at best minimal."[9]

It is hardly a new revelation that children sometimes fall through the cracks when they remain involved with the child protection system. One need only turn to the mainstream media to encounter stories of children lost in the shuffle. Though the majority of people involved in the system work diligently to protect our youngest and most defenseless citizens, rising caseloads and strained budgets negatively impact the services rendered to children languishing in state care.

Over the last two decades, several cases highlighting the failures of Child Protective Services workers horrified our nation. In 2001, Florida's Department of Children and Families met with public outcry when the State's Attorney's Office revealed that four-year-old Rilya Wilson was missing from her foster home placement. The media later reported that she had been missing for over a year from her foster home and that her caseworker had been unaware of her absence.

It was discovered that young Rilya's caseworker had falsified documents stating that she made routine visits to the home when, in fact, she had not set foot in the residence for over a year. It was further learned that the caseworker's own supervisor had not reviewed the files as required by department policy. During the child's torturous time in that foster home, it is believed the young girl was routinely starved, abused and kept in a dog crate. Her foster mother was eventually convicted and sentenced to prison.[10] The young girl was never found. Sadly, she is one of many missing foster children in the state of Florida.

Arizona's child protective system came under similar scrutiny after the death of Raziah Bates, a ten-month-old baby girl, in 2010. After several anonymous calls to the department, a caseworker visited the child and her single nineteen-year-old mother. The worker advised the mother that the baby needed medical attention. She told the mother she would visit again and that if she had not sought medical attention, she would remove Raziah from the home. The caseworker never returned and the child died two weeks later. The mother faced torture and murder charges stemming from the death.[11]

Following this shocking loss, the shortcomings of the San Joaquin County CPS office became a hot topic of conversation. Employees within the agency went on record stating that "what killed this baby is a social worker who had too many cases and not enough time." Nearly one quarter of that local office's staff told reporters that "they aren't spending enough time with families to recognize all potential threats."[12] The workers had impossible caseloads and not enough time to adequately manage them.

There must be a mechanism for preventing senseless deaths and disappearances of children involved in the foster care or child protective systems. There is no doubt that there are thousands of caring, compassionate and dedicated CPS workers in America and the majority of those workers strive to protect the children involved in the system. However, even the most informed and well-intentioned worker cannot possibly overcome strained budgets, colossal caseloads and an ever-growing number of children in care. The system is overloaded and, as a result, children fall through the cracks.[13]

Our foster care system is in a sad state, with over half a million children living in foster homes and not enough workers and foster parents to adequately supervise and protect them all.[14] The system continues to deteriorate even with the dedication of many people. As more children enter the system, there are just not enough resources to adequately care for them. Individual caseworkers are oftentimes carrying a load three times higher than is appropriate and even the most well-intentioned cannot possibly devote an adequate amount of attention to all the children the states charge them with supervising. The three determining factors in the system's failure are "an upsurge in the number of children in need of care; an overburdened system and agencies; an inadequate number of foster parents."[15]

The system needs help but budgetary constraints impede progress. When lack of funding is coupled with overworked and underpaid staff, eventually the situation will implode and the children are the ones who suffer. The system needs improvement but, "For child protective agencies to improve, they must be valued as more than a wasteland of children of the underclass."[16] Our society as a whole has to take responsibility for these children.

It is a systemic problem that needs nationwide cooperation in order to fix it. Unfortunately, "caseworkers have become easy targets for venting frustrations and often recognize the indefensible position in which their agencies have placed them."[17] The issues many families involved in the system experience are complex and difficult. They require the caseworker to work closely with the family for long periods of time. Many are unable to do this due to their burden of high caseloads.[18]

In order to change the system, the professionals charged with protecting it must step up. CPS workers and foster children are "caught in a chaotic system that has been abandoned by the professionals who are equipped to fix it."[19] The professionals involved must dedicate themselves to repairing the system's inadequacies. In order to make a change, it is important that the public is aware of the problem at hand. Children's advocates like the attorneys involved in the dependency, neglect and abuse system must raise public awareness of the plights of these children. This can occur by lobbying for more financial support, better training and education.[20]

The youngsters involved in the system are not throwaway kids. Sometimes, all it takes is for one person to take an interest in a child and when something doesn't feel right to say something. How can the system protect these children if it is fundamentally ill-equipped? There is no overnight or quick fix for the problem. However, we can begin by focusing on the instances in which the system broke down and did not work in the hopes that it inspires more people to action.

That is the reason why it is important to examine situations like the one surrounding Joshua Young and Trey Zwicker. Although CPS had involvement in the home, it remained unaware that Joshua was not living at the location reported by his father. There was rampant domestic violence in the house that was ongoing during CPS's involvement with Gouker. It appears that no one saw the signs or, if they did, nothing was done about it. Could a lower caseload or more resources have prevented Gouker's violence? It is impossible to know for sure but, now that the public is aware of the situation, we as a community must work toward preventing such tragedies from happening in the future.

Reform is the solution to "overworked, undertrained, underpaid and often underappreciated" social workers.[21] Advocacy groups like the National Coalition for Child Protection Reform (NCCPR) are working to change public policy on everything from child abuse to foster care, child placement and family preservation. Groups like CASA— Court Appointed Special Advocates for Children—have programs all over the country ready to fulfill the group's mission statement: "The mission of the National Court Appointed Special Advocate (CASA) Association, together with its state and local members, is to support and promote court-appointed volunteer advocacy so that every abused and neglected child can be safe, establish permanence and have the opportunity to thrive."[22]

If the public is educated, if groups like NCCPR and CASA keep up their advocacy efforts, if the social workers are better trained and better supported, then perhaps failures like the case of Amy Dye, the four malnourished boys in New Jersey, the dead infants in Vermont—and especially the case of Joshua Young—may never have to be reported again.

Epilogue

Once the jurors had returned their verdict, Josh Young returned to the Walshes' home that night. Stepping outside of the walls of the detention center and the courthouse for the first time in two years was exciting but overwhelming at the same time.

Little Josh did his best to settle back into the household with his beloved little sister, where he planned to live as he completed his senior year of high school. His younger sister was the person he loved most in the world and he was ecstatic that he would be able to spend time with her outside the confines of the detention center. Waking up under the same roof as his sister made him very happy.

The Walshes were supportive of Josh and helped him every way they could in the days following his trial and release from custody. At that point, Josh Young spoke to the media for the first time since detectives initially charged him in Trey's death. When he was five months shy of his eighteenth birthday, he sat down with a reporter from *The Courier Journal*, Louisville's largest newspaper, in Pete Schuler's office. Josh expressed hope that he could live a normal life and escape memories of the trial that he feared would follow him forever. A jury acquitted him, but he knew some people would always doubt his innocence no matter how he tried to prove them wrong. He expressed sadness about Trey's death and disclosed that he felt Josh Gouker was crazy and that, at that time, he had no desire for further contact with the man.[1] He was nervous about the future but assured the reporter that he would do his best to succeed in life. Little Josh appeared happy in the Walsh household and it appeared that it could become a permanent home for the young man.

The Walshes expressed interest in adopting Josh, as they had his younger sister. It seemed as though the torn pieces of his life were coming together now and he would finally have a permanent family unit. It should have been a happy ending.

The two years that he spent incarcerated took their toll on Little Josh. After those years of living in a completely regimented and controlled environment where strict rules and regulations dictated every action he took, the freedom of being a normal teenager was overwhelming to him. Like many teenagers, he fought against authority and wanted to be free to spend all of his time with his friends.

One Friday afternoon, he failed to return from school and his foster family did not know where he was. Joshua spent the next several days roaming the city with friends and speaking with the media via Facebook chat. He was intent on being with kids his own age, perhaps due to such a long period of time incarcerated without the ability to make his own choices.

Eventually, authorities located Josh and police alleged that he fled when they attempted to apprehend him. He was charged in juvenile court with fleeing and evading the police. Josh was placed in a group home where he remained until Christmas of 2013. Within weeks of that date, he turned eighteen. His attorneys filed a motion to expunge his criminal record in the hopes of wiping their client's slate clean. In Kentucky, a motion to expunge a person's record can be filed sixty days after a dismissal. If a judge expunges a case, it no longer appears on that individual's criminal history. After pondering the motion to expunge for over a month, Judge Barry Willett denied Josh's motion, meaning that the murder charge continues to appear on any records check regarding Josh, despite the fact that he was acquitted by a jury. It was a huge blow to Josh, as inquiries by schools and potential employers revealed the fact that he had been previously charged with serious offenses.

Little Josh remained notorious in Louisville and was recognized nearly everywhere he went after the trial. It was impossible for him to obtain employment, as a routine background check immediately showed charges that understandably made any potential employer worry. In the months after his eighteenth birthday, he turned to his twenty-nine-year-old cousin for help and support. It was difficult for Joshua to trust new people. During his entire life, there were few people that he could truly count on to help him. Most of the adults in his life had betrayed him in some way. He was comfortable with his cousin, because he'd lived in his household during his mother's prison stint. Unfortunately, his cousin, now an adult, did not have a regular place to stay, so the two lived in hotel rooms on his cousin's savings, which rapidly depleted.

During their stay at a modest motel in the Louisville area, Josh was confronted at least twice by police. During one such occasion, a police officer held a gun to the boy's head. It seemed that the authorities were still wary of Little Josh and believed he might be up to no good. However, after each encounter, the officers determined that Little Josh had done nothing wrong. He just wanted to be left alone and that was increasingly difficult to achieve while living in Louisville.

There were people who would help him, but Josh desperately wanted to make it on his own. In September of 2013, approximately one month after his release from custody, Josh reconnected with a young lady he'd known since childhood at a cookout at his uncle's home. They made a cute couple. A pretty and bubbly blonde, she became a big part of Josh's life who worried about him constantly and cared about him. She was a student at a nearby community college and worked at a daycare center, caring for children. She encouraged Josh to go to college and he planned to enroll the following fall after obtaining his general equivalency diploma.

As Josh attempted to rebuild his life, his father was serving a life sentence for Trey's murder. He is currently imprisoned at Kentucky State Penitentiary, or "KSP" as the inmates call it. KSP is Kentucky's maximum security prison where the "worst of the worst" are typically housed. This site is also home to Kentucky's death row inmates.

Prior to Trey's murder, Gouker had spent the majority of his adult life behind bars, so he must have become accustomed to prison life. Gouker soon filed a motion to set aside his guilty plea due to ineffective assistance of counsel. He alleged in that motion that his attorneys were ineffective in allowing him to plead guilty to Trey's murder and the host of other charges that he faced in connection with Trey's death and the house of horrors where Gouker terrorized his wife and her family. He stated that he was unfairly influenced by the fact that his son was facing life in prison as his co-defendant and that his attorneys should not have allowed him to enter the open plea in Trey's murder.

I believe that Gouker would like the world to think that his guilty plea was an act of protection for his son and that the only reason he confessed to Trey's murder was to keep Little Josh from going to prison for the rest of his life. However, he thrives on attention and his claim of ineffective assistance of counsel seems yet another way to thrust himself back into the media spotlight. Gouker has nothing but time and filed the motion when the media announced that his son was set to speak out about his experience on a national stage.

Shortly after the acquittal, the popular *Dr. Phil* show got in touch with Josh's foster mother, stating that they wanted to offer help to the young man. When Josh turned eighteen in January 2014, his cousin contacted the show on his behalf. The company offered to fly him, his cousin and his girlfriend to Los Angeles, California to film a two-part segment of a show that would be titled, "My Father Tried to Frame Me for Murder." At the time,

Joshua had barely reached the age of majority; he was still a kid. However, the trip must have sounded good to a boy who had nothing—no place to live, no real "home" and no stability. His cousin could accompany him on the trip and would appear on the show as well, and Josh felt safe with his cousin. He felt the experience would give him the opportunity to tell his side of the story and express his feelings of sorrow at Trey's death. The producers and their assistant appeared to truly want to help him. At that point, Joshua had not publicly addressed the allegations against him and had not offered his version of the events on the night of Trey's murder. He hoped that now he could clear the air and show the world that he was not involved in Trey's death.

I remember where I was when I heard the first news account that the body of a teenager was found at Liberty High School. My own child was the same age and it frightened me to the core. I think all parents watching the news that night clutched their children a little closer. I became captivated by the story and haunted by it as well, especially after police revealed that family members were suspected in the crime. As I watched the trial unfold, I repeatedly shook my head as additional facts came to light.

I was a teenage parent like the parents of both boys involved in this horrible tragedy. It was frightening that something like this could happen so close to home. The more I delved into the backstory, the more convinced I became that this tragedy warranted an examination of how Joshua Gouker came to be what he is and how children are often lost in the child protective system. Having worked as a *guardian ad litem* in family court, I am all too familiar with how often the person most dangerous to a child is under his own roof.

I attempted to speak with Terry Zwicker in connection with this book but I could not obtain his cooperation. Therefore, I attempted to draw my information regarding Trey respectfully from trial testimony, public records, Mr. Zwicker's interviews with police and his comments to the media. I am sensitive to the fact that this tragedy altered his life immeasurably in a traumatic and ongoing way. My hope with this book was to bring light to a broken system and prompt positive change in that system. In doing so, I believe we, as a community, can endeavor to ensure that tragedies like this one do not reoccur. I wish the best for all the parties negatively impacted by Joshua Gouker's evil actions and I hope they find some measure of peace.

In researching this book, I read every account I could find, watched hours of trial testimony, pored over thousands of documents and viewed numerous media accounts. Finally, I attempted to reach out to many of the parties involved in the case. When I contacted Joshua Young, he agreed to meet with me to discuss his case.

When I first met Josh, I felt he was a very sweet kid. He was cautious and wary of people, a quality that is to be expected of someone who has endured the traumas in life that he has. Having had a difficult life myself, being a young mother who tried to take good care of her child and get an education, I developed an almost immediate and overwhelming feeling of empathy for him. I wanted to ensure that he was not exploited.

Before I reached out to Josh, I had heard in media reports that he was an honor student and a high school wrestler prior to his father regaining custody of him in the Spring of 2011. I knew that he had lost his mother and had a past spent in various foster homes. Having experienced firsthand how difficult being the child of a teen mother can be, I wanted to know how this kid ended up embroiled in such a horrendous act.

I first met Joshua Young in person when he visited my office in early 2014. Little Josh had just turned eighteen. He arrived with his cousin and his girlfriend. I was very happy for the opportunity to hear about his ordeal from his point of view. He wanted to speak out about his experience and give his side of the story.

What struck me immediately was that although he was eighteen years old, a legal adult, Josh was just a kid. He was very quiet and polite as he answered my initial questions. We only spoke briefly during that first meeting but when he left I felt suddenly overcome with emotion. He was an adolescent with no parent to help him navigate life.

Josh and his girlfriend indicated to me that they were both in the process of applying for college. Because of my past and the fact that my son is the same age as Joshua, this struck me and stuck with me. I am aware there are questions that must be asked of each college and there are certain things that must be handled. A parent helps the child complete the application, accompanies the child on campus visits and helps to select the college.

Josh did not have that support. He was essentially alone in the world and I recognized how difficult that could be. Because he was in the custody of the Cabinet for Health and Family Services when he turned eighteen, Josh can attend any public college in the state of Kentucky tuition-free, which he said had helped immensely in mapping out his future.

However, even as time passed and he tried to move forward, there continued to be encounters that reminded Joshua of the trial and people's suspicions, especially in Louisville. On more than one occasion, Joshua related that he walked into a public place and all eyes were on him. He recalled a situation when a lady passed him twice in a restaurant, then turned around and walked up to the table. Regarding Josh with a puzzled look, she said, "I know you from somewhere. I just can't place it," and she continued to stand at the table, unmoving. What could he possibly say in that situation: "You might recognize me from the trial where I was acquitted of my stepbrother's murder"? There was no appropriate way to answer her.

Every time Josh leaves home, he receives near-constant stares and some people are even bold enough to approach him. I think he hoped to curb this attention with his appearance on the *Dr. Phil* Show. He seemed to believe that if he sat down and finally told his version of events that people would no longer believe he was involved in Trey's murder.

Josh did not realize that, after he had agreed to appear on the show, *Dr. Phil* producers also had contacted Trey's father and stepmother and invited them on the show. They also invited Cassi to appear on the program to tell her side of the story.

The episode of *Dr. Phil* featuring Joshua Young appeared in two parts on February 24 and 25, 2014, only a few weeks after it was taped. Josh appeared articulate and straightforward on the broadcast, adamant that he had no involvement whatsoever in Trey's death. When asked about his dad, he expressed that he did not understand how a person could be born, go through life and end up like his biological father, Joshua Gouker. He stated that based on his father's actions in the previous years, he knew that Gouker did not love him as a father should and that he did not expect Gouker to love anyone. Josh expressed a deep fear of the man and told the audience that he was scared of what his father could do. He believed that Gouker was capable of anything.[2]

Dr. Phil asked Cassi and Josh to submit to a lie detector test. Initially, both agreed to undergo the test. However, after pondering the opportunity off camera, Josh changed his mind. Lie detector tests can be unreliable and for that reason they are inadmissible in court. False positives can occur and the general public is not necessarily aware of their potential unreliability.

Joshua Young had spent two years incarcerated for a crime he maintains he did not commit. It is not surprising that he decided not to take the lie detector test, especially when his cooperation in the past had brought him nothing but trouble.

However, Cassi did submit to the test. She was asked whether Joshua woke her up on the night of Trey's death and whether she took him to dispose of bloody clothes and a murder weapon as she had testified during Josh's trial. She stated that she had but the results showed "deception."

Although Terry Zwicker did not receive the answers to his ultimate questions regarding his son's death, it appears that he did find some comfort. He later remarked that his main objective in participating in the show was to stand up for his son and speak for Trey. He certainly did that. It is obvious that Terry is an amazing father who would do anything for his children and it is heartbreaking that he has had to face such a tragedy. I admire his love for his son and I hope with all my heart that he is able to find peace.

There will always be people who believe that Josh had some type of involvement in the death of Trey. No matter what he does or how hard he tries to prove his innocence, some people's minds are never going to change. I think that he is finally coming to that realization and understands that all he can do is to try his best to live his life and give back to society. The best way to prove people wrong is by living your life the right way, day after day. Joshua has stated that he might want to become a social worker so that he can help other kids, former foster kids like himself, navigate the system. He wants to ensure that no other children fall through the cracks like he did, which is a valiant goal.

In the aftermath of the trial, Josh has attempted to distance himself from his father. Gouker does not know where to find him and Josh appears to want to keep it that way. He still struggles with the fact that his father would implicate him the way he did. He stole two years of Josh's life that the boy can never get back and Josh doesn't understand why his father would do that to him. Little Josh is still shocked at the way Gouker was able to manipulate witnesses in the trial against his own son.

As I drafted this book, I attempted to contact Joshua Gouker. I mailed a letter to him at the Kentucky State

Penitentiary and did not hear back for quite some time. Eventually I received a letter at my office, addressed to me from Gouker; enclosed with it was a sealed envelope addressed to Josh Young. In the letter, Gouker insisted, "Not only is there zero chance I could've killed Trey, but I've got an alibi that can't be counterfeited or manipulated. I've had it hidden this whole time so I could save my son. Why he's going along with this story—I don't know, but I believe it had to do with image/book deal/fame/ acceptance of others/and shit like that. Josh can't be punished again, so the truth is about to come out."

He went on to offer to take a polygraph test and to speak with me as long as I gave the enclosed letter to Josh.

Josh Gouker sent me the letter shortly after he had filed a motion to set aside his guilty plea in Trey Zwicker's murder case. In that motion, he claimed that his attorneys were ineffective as his counsel and that, as a result, his plea should not be honored. He asked Judge Barry Willett to set aside his guilty plea and release him from custody. When I received the letter, Judge Willett had recently given the Commonwealth an extension of time to file its response to the motion and the matter was set for a hearing on May 15, 2014. Gouker filed his motion pro se, meaning without an attorney. However, he also filed a motion asking the court to appoint an attorney from the Louisville Metro Public Defender's Office to represent him. The motion to set aside his guilty plea was denied by Judge Barry Willett but Gouker appealed that decision. The appeal is pending.

Gouker appears to believe that if his son would make the statement that he was involved in Trey's murder and that Gouker was not, that the motion will be granted. In that case Gouker would be released from prison and would not have to serve his life sentence.

Josh Young maintains his innocence. I believe Gouker is doing what he does best, attempting to manipulate his son into taking the blame for Gouker's own actions. After speaking with local media and the *Dr. Phil* show, Gouker then attempted to reach out to me, a total stranger, in an attempt to manipulate me into third-party contact with his son. His son will not speak to him, so he has tried to convince me to influence Josh into communicating with him by telling me that he will speak with me if and only if I ensure that certain things occur: "I will agree to talk to you but before you write me again I want you to give my son a letter for me and I want a response." The message was clear: Gouker would only cooperate with me if I gave him what he wanted first.

As I read that letter, I felt strongly that this was the way he had manipulated every person involved in the case. Things had to be done his way, with specific stipulations. Jahaira Friend, Angelic Burkhead and Cassi Gouker, the three women who testified against Little Josh, all did so at the behest of Big Josh. Even from behind bars, it continues. Gouker is used to convincing people to do his bidding and, more often than not, he preys on those weaker than him who fall victim to his exploitation all too easily.

Eventually I spoke with Josh Gouker via telephone. The conversation occurred just weeks after I received his letter. He called me from the Kentucky State Penitentiary. Gouker was jovial and friendly and I could see why an unsuspecting person would like him. His innate ability to read people was astounding and he was very adept at telling me exactly what he thought I wanted to hear. He told me that he believed I should delay the completion of my book, because things were going to change in the upcoming months. He claimed that forensics don't lie and that the prosecutors did not realize that they had the key piece of evidence that would set him free. He claimed that the cell phone SD card listed on page 1505 of his trial discovery held the amateur porn video he and Amanda made during the exact window of time that forensics determined Trey had died. He also claimed that he knew of evidence of the weapon that was used in the murder, namely the recovery of a lead pipe found at the scene. He felt this evidence could exonerate him and claims that he expressly forbade his original attorney from investigating the issue of the pipe further.

He further argued that he had received letters from his attorney in which the attorney acknowledged that Gouker told him that he would do whatever needed to be done to spare his son from prosecution. He revealed that he spent hours upon hours in his jail cell memorizing trial documents and preparing for his performance on the stand during his son's trial. He alleged that the entirety of his testimony was concocted to free his child and that he was not even present at Trey's murder.

Gouker claimed that he would do anything for his son. He spoke about Amanda and how she understandably hates him. He expressed that he wanted a relationship with his son and told me that his son is the master manipulator. As we spoke, Gouker mentioned the Walshes, stating they were "good people." However, he claimed that they were gullible and that Little Josh had them wrapped around his finger.

Debbie Walsh, Josh's foster mother, is a seasoned professional who deals with children every day. She lived with Little Josh for quite some time and she saw firsthand his day-to-day routine. I trust her assessment of Little Josh and his character much more readily than I trust Gouker's. Over his lifetime, Little Josh has probably spent more quality time with his foster family than with his own father. Presently, Gouker wants to get out of prison, so I feel he is making Little Josh his scapegoat once again. According to Gouker, the story is nowhere near complete and the "real" story is much more enthralling that anything revealed thus far.

Shortly after I received his letter and spoke with Gouker on the telephone, I visited Josh Young and his girlfriend at their apartment. I felt honored that they trusted me enough to invite me into their home, especially when they were hesitant to tell anyone where they were living for fear of harassment. As they took me on a tour, I could not help but notice how excited they both were. Finding that first home of one's own is an exciting event for anyone, but I was especially touched by their enthusiasm. Joshua showed me the food they purchased and the way they had stocked their refrigerator and cabinets with it. He showed me their well-organized closets and their decorations. They obviously put great thought and care into their home and I was excited for them.

For a period of a few weeks, Josh had performed some odd jobs at my office. Sadly, after this last interview and after my contact with Joshua ceased, he was rearrested on new charges. He was accused of a domestic incident with his girlfriend and he was also charged with striking Cassi's boyfriend. He is currently awaiting resolution of those issues.

It's not unusual for young men and women who have been abused in childhood to commit domestic abuse acts as adults and that is why it is so crucial that they get counseling help.

Acknowledgments

There are so many people who contributed to the creation of this book and I would like to thank them all. I would first like to thank Darren for being the best thing in my life. I am so proud of everything you do and I cannot imagine what my life would be like without you. I would do anything for you and you make me strive to be a better person every single day. You are the best thing that ever happened to me.

I would also like to thank John Cook for his amazing ability to bring out the best in me and for supporting me as I worked to draft this manuscript. Without your support, this book would not exist. Thank you for sticking by me and allowing me to research and write about this fascinating story.

My friends and family have helped me with countless critiques of this work. Thank you all so much for taking the time and effort to help me make this book better with each rewrite. Thank you to Janice Woods for helping with clerical matters relating to my initial draft of the book.

I would like to thank my agent, Dr. James Schiavone, and my publisher, Dr. Joan Dunphy and everyone at NHP. Thank you for understanding that this was a story that needed to be told and for helping to give me the voice to tell it. You have assisted me more than I could possibly describe.

I also want to thank all those who contributed to the book through interviews and insights.

This was a story that haunted me well before I decided to write about it. There are no winners in this story and I never want to lose sight of the real victim in this convoluted tale, Trey Zwicker. I can only imagine the pain felt every day by his parents, family members and friends. I pray for them all every day.

I am sickened to think that a child was placed in the custody of Josh Gouker and then left there with no one to turn to. There are so many children lost within the child welfare system every day, children who have a monster living under their very own roof. This book is dedicated to those children.

Endnotes

PROLOGUE

1. *Commonwealth v. Joshua Young,* Jefferson Circuit Court 12-CR-2258-002 (2013).

CHAPTER 1

1. Zwicker, Terrence, *Commonwealth of Kentucky v. Joshua Young,* 12-CR-2258-002, Trial Testimony, July 31, 2013.
2. Zwicker, Terrence, Interview with Detective Scott Russ. Police Investigation Interview. Louisville, KY, May 11, 2011.
3. Ibid.
4. Ibid.
5. Ibid.
6. Campbell-Gouker, Amanda. Interview with Detective Leigh Maroni. Police Investigation Interview. Louisville, KY, May 11, 2011.
7. Gouker, Joshua. Interview with Detective Leigh Maroni. Police Investigation Interview. Louisville, KY, May 11, 2011.
8. Young, Joshua. Interview with Detective Leigh Maroni. Police Investigation Interview. Louisville, KY, May 11, 2011.

CHAPTER 2

1. *Commonwealth v. Joshua Young*, Jefferson Circuit Court 12-CR-2258-002 (2013).
2. Zwicker, Terrence, Interview with Detective Scott Russ. Police Investigation Interview. Louisville, KY, May 11, 2011.
3. *Commonwealth v. Joshua Young*, Jefferson Circuit Court 12-CR-2258-002 (2013).
4. Ibid.
5. Victim impact statements from Trey's stepmother and maternal uncle.

CHAPTER 3

1. Gouker, Joshua. Psychiatric Interview with Dr. Michael Cecil. Louisville Neuropsychology, Louisville, KY May 31, 2013.
2. Scott, Shirley Lynn, "What Makes Serial Killers Tick," Crime Library: Criminal Minds and Methods, http://www.crimelibrary.com/serial_killers/notorious/tick/5b.html.
3. Gouker, Joshua. Psychiatric Interview with Dr. Michael Cecil. Louisville Neuropsychology, Louisville, KY May 31, 2013.
4. *Commonwealth v. Joshua Gouker*, Jefferson County District Court Case 01-M-018259, (2001).
5. *Commonwealth v. Joshua Gouker*, Jefferson County Circuit Court Case 02-CR-931, (2002).
6. Ibid.
7. KY. Rev. St. 508.025 (2005).
8. *Commonwealth v. Joshua Gouker*, Jefferson County District Court Case 02-F-011711, (2002).
9. Ibid.
10. Ibid.
11. *Commonwealth v. Joshua Gouker*, Jefferson County Circuit Court Case 03-CR-231, (2001).

12. Gouker, Joshua. Interview with Janelle McDonald. Wave 3 News, June 13, 2013.

13. Gouker, Joshua, original rap lyrics, (2002-2010), turned over to defense by Ruby Jessie.

14. *Commonwealth v. Ruby Jessie*, Muhlenburg County District Court Case 07-F-313, (2007).

15. Weis, Jaimie. "Inmates Come Forward with Possible Motive for Murder of Fourteen-Year Old," WAVE 3.com, http://www.wave3.com/story/19132947/inmates-come -forward-about-possible-motive-in-murder-of-14-year -old.

CHAPTER 4

1. Author interview with Joshua Young, January 12, 2014, January 30, 2014, March 11, 2014.

2. Ibid.

3. Ibid.

4. *Commonwealth v. Young, Angelina*, Jefferson County Circuit Court Case 03-CR-724, (2003).

5. *Commonwealth v. Young, Angelina*, Bullitt County District Court Case 05-F-423, (2005).

6. Author interview with Joshua Young, January 12, 2014, January 30, 2014, March 11, 2014.

7. Ibid.

8. Ibid.

9. Ibid.

CHAPTER 5

1. *Commonwealth v. Joshua Young*, Jefferson Circuit Court 12-CR-2258-002 (2013).

2. Ibid.

3. Author interview with Joshua Young, January 12, 2014, January 30, 2014, March 11, 2014.

4. Ibid.

5. *Commonwealth v. Joshua Young*, Jefferson Circuit Court 12-CR-2258-002 (2013).
6. Ibid.
7. Ibid.
8. Ibid.
9. Gouker-Campbell, Amanda. Interview with Detectives Scott Russ and Roy Stalvey. Police Investigation Interview. Louisville, KY, May 19, 2011.
10. Ibid.
11. *Commonwealth v. Joshua Young*, Jefferson Circuit Court 12-CR-2258-002 (2013).
12. Ibid.
13. Ibid.
14. Author interview with Joshua Young, January 12, 2014, January 30, 2014, March 11, 2014.
15. National Coalition for Child Protection Reform, http://nccpr.info/the-nccpr-quick-read/.
16. Author interview with Joshua Young, January 12, 2014, January 30, 2014, March 11, 2014.
17. *Commonwealth v. Joshua Young*, Jefferson Circuit Court 12-CR-2258-002 (2013).
18. Ibid.
19. Ibid.
20. Ibid.
21. Ibid.

CHAPTER 6

1. Gouker-Campbell, Amanda. Interview with Detectives Scott Russ and Roy Stalvey. Police Investigation Interview. Louisville, KY, May 19, 2011.
2. Ibid.
3. Ibid.
4. Ibid.
5. Ibid.
6. Ibid.

7. *Amanda Campbell v. Joshua Gouker*, Jefferson County District Court Case 11-D-501407-001, (2011).
8. *Commonwealth v. Joshua Gouker*, Bullitt County District Court Case 11-M-1559, (2011).

CHAPTER 7

1. Young, Joshua. Interview with Detective Scott Russ. Police Investigation Interview. Louisville, KY, June 11, 2011.
2. Ibid.
3. Ibid.
4. Ibid.
5. Ibid.

CHAPTER 8

1. *Commonwealth v. Joshua Young*, Jefferson Circuit Court 12-CR-2258-002 (2013).
2. Author interview with Joshua Young, January 12, 2014, January 30, 2014, March 11, 2014.
3. *Commonwealth v. Joshua Young*, Jefferson Circuit Court 12-CR-2258-002 (2013).
4. Ibid.
5. Ibid.
6. Ibid.
7. Ibid.
8. Ibid.
9. Ibid.
10. Ibid.
11. Ibid.
12. Ibid.
13. Ibid.
14. Ibid.

CHAPTER 9

1. Author interview with Joshua Young, January 12, 2014, January 30, 2014, March 11, 2014.

2. Young, Joshua. Interview with Detective Scott Russ. Police Investigation Interview. Louisville, KY, June 21, 2011.
3. Ibid.
4. Ibid.
5. Ibid.
6. Ibid.
7. Ibid.
8. Author interview with Joshua Young, January 12, 2014, January 30, 2014, March 11, 2014.
9. Gouker, Joshua. Interview with Detectives Scott Russ and Roy Stalvey. Police Investigation Phone Interview. Louisville, KY, June 21, 2011.
10. Ibid.

CHAPTER 10

1. Gouker, Joshua. Interview with Detectives Scott Russ and Roy Stalvey. Police Investigation Interview. Alabama, June 22, 2011.
2. Ibid.
3. Ibid.
4. Ibid.
5. Ibid.
6. Ibid.
7. Ibid.
8. Author interview with Joshua Young, January 12, 2014, January 30, 2014, March 11, 2014.

CHAPTER 11

1. KY. Rev. St. 600.010 (2002).
2. KY. Rev. St. 524.100 (1974).
3. (1) Ky. Rev. St. 507.020(1) (1984). (2) Ky. Rev. St. 507.020(2) (1984).
4. Gouker, Joshua. Interview with Janelle McDonald. Wave 3 News, June 13, 2013.

5. *Commonwealth v. Joshua Gouker*, Jefferson Circuit Court 12-CR-2258-001, August 20, 2012.
6. *Commonwealth v. Joshua Gouker*, Jefferson Circuit Court 12-CR-2258-001, May 10, 2013.
7. *Commonwealth v. Joshua Gouker*, Jefferson Circuit Court 12-CR-2258-001, Final Sentencing Order, July 26, 2013.

CHAPTER 12

1. *Commonwealth v. Joshua Young*, Jefferson Circuit Court 12-CR-2258-002 (2013).
2. Ibid.
3. Ibid.
4. Ibid.
5. Ibid.
6. Ibid.
7. Ibid.
8. Ibid.
9. Ibid.
10. Ibid.
11. Ibid.

CHAPTER 13

1. *Commonwealth v. Joshua Young*, Jefferson Circuit Court 12-CR-2258-002 (2013).
2. Ibid.
3. Ibid.
4. Ibid.
5. Ibid.
6. Ibid.
7. Ibid.
8. Ibid.
9. Ibid.
10. *Commonwealth v. John Robertson*, Jefferson Circuit Court 12-CR-95-002 (2012).

11. *Commonwealth v. Joshua Young*, Jefferson Circuit Court 12-CR-2258-002 (2013).

12. Ibid.

CHAPTER 14

1. *Commonwealth v. Joshua Young*, Jefferson Circuit Court 12-CR-2258-002 (2013).

2. Ibid.

3. Ibid.

4. Ibid.

5. Ibid.

6. Ibid.

7. Ibid.

8. Ibid.

9. Ibid.

10. Ibid.

11. Ibid.

12. Ibid.

13. *Commonwealth v. Joshua Young*, Jefferson Circuit Court 12-CR-2258-002, Jury Questions during testimony of Joshua Gouker (2013).

14. *Commonwealth v. Joshua Young*, Jefferson Circuit Court 12-CR-2258-002 (2013).

CHAPTER 15

1. *Commonwealth v. Joshua Young*, Jefferson Circuit Court 12-CR-2258-002 (2013).

2. Ibid.

3. Ibid.

4. Linda Latham, Interview with Nancy Grace, Nancy Grace Show, HLN, July 28, 2013.; Shelley Stewart, Interview with Nancy Grace, Nancy Grace Show, HLN, August 5, 2013.; Rodney Gunter, Interview with Jane Velez Mitchell, Issues with Jane Velez Mitchel, HLN, July 31, 2013.; Dr. Drew on Call, HLN, July 30, 2013.

5. Issues with Jane Velez Mitchell, HLN, August 5, 2013.; Issues with Jane Velez Mitchell, HLN, July 19, 2013.

CHAPTER 16

1. *Commonwealth v. Joshua Young*, Jefferson Circuit Court 12-CR-2258-002 (2013).
2. Ibid.
3. Ibid.
4. Ibid.
5. Ibid.
6. Ibid.
7. Ibid.
8. Ibid.

CHAPTER 17

1. Author interview with Joshua Young, January 12, 2014, January 30, 2014, March 11, 2014.
2. *Commonwealth v. Joshua Young*, Jefferson Circuit Court 12-CR-2258-002 (2013).
3. Ibid.
4. Ibid.
5. *WHAS 11 news*, August 9, 2013.

CHAPTER 18

1. Lydia Polgreen and Robert F. Worth, "New Jersey Couple Held in Abuse; One Son, 19, Weighed 45 Pounds," *The New York Times*, October 27, 2003, http://www.nytimes.com/2003/10/27/nyregion/new-jersey-couple-held-in-abuse-one-son-19-weighed-45-pounds.html.
2. Bill Estep and Beth Musgrave, "Kentucky's child protection system under scrutiny after girl's murder: state child-protection system did not act on record of family abuse," Kentucky.com, November 26, 2011, http://www.kentucky.com/2011/11/26/1972957/kentuckys-child-protection-system.html.

3. Ibid.

4. Catherine Calderon, "Official details CPS flaws leaving thousands of cases in limbo," *Cronkite News*, February 24, 2014, http://cronkitenewsonline.com/2014/02/official-details-cps-flaws-leaving-thousands-of-cases-in-limbo/.

5. Lydia Polgreen and Robert F. Worth, "New Jersey Couple Held in Abuse; One Son, 19, Weighed 45 Pounds," *The New York Times*, October 27, 2003, http://www.nytimes.com/2003/10/27/nyregion/new-jersey-couple-held-in-abuse-one-son-19-weighed-45-pounds.html.

6. Peter Hirschfeld, "Social Workers Expose Flaws in Child Protective Services," *VPR*, http://digital.vpr.net/post/social-workers-expose-flaws-child-protective-services.

7. Ibid.

8. Ibid.

9. WSIU Public Broadcasting, http://www2.wsiu.org/highlights03/030118protectingchildren2/childprotectionreform.pdf.

10. Mike Clary, "Trial Nears for Woman Charged with Killing Rilya Wilson." *Sun Sentinel*, September 11, 2011; Sarah Netter, "Finding Missing Foster Children: Kids Who Disappear From State Care Often at Disadvantage," *ABC News*, July 27, 2010, http://abcnews.go.com/US/missing-foster-children-state-privacy-laws-lack-family/story?id=11251835&singlePage=true; "Fla. Has Lost Hundreds of Foster Kids," *ABC News*, May 16, 2014, http://abcnews.go.com/GMA/print?id=126097.

11. Jennifer Torres, Christian Burkin, Zachary K. Johnson, and Daniel Thigpen, Did the System Rail Riziah, recordnet.com.

12. Ibid.

13. Sarah Netter, "Finding Missing Foster Children: Kids Who Disappear From State Care Often at a Disadvantage," *ABC News*, July 27, 2010 http://abcnews.go.com/US/missing-foster-children-state-privacy-laws-lack-family/story?id=11251835&singlePage=true.

14. Sharon Balmer, "From Poverty to Abuse and Back Again: the failure of the legal and social services communities to protect foster children," *Fordham Urban Law Journal* (Sept. 1, 2005).

15. Timothy L Arcaro, "Florida's Foster Care System Fails its Children." (2001) Faculty Scholarship. Paper 38. http://eshark.nsulaw.nove.edu/faculty_scholarship/38.

16. Ibid., 221.

17. Ibid., 661.

18. Ibid., 662.

19. Ibid., 222.

20. Ibid.

21. National Coalition for Child Protection Reform, http://nccpr.info/the-nccpr-quick-read/.

22. CASA Mission Statement, http://www.casaforchildren.org/site/c.mtJSJ7MPIsE/b.5301303/k.6FB1/About_Us__CASA_for_Children.htm.

EPILOGUE

1. Jason Riley, "Joshua Young on Killer Accusations 'That's Not Me,'" *The Courier Journal*, August 17, 2013.

2. "My Dad Tried to Frame Me for Murder," *The Dr. Phil Show*, February 24 and 25, 2014.